SOAS Studies on South Asia

Beyond Purdah?

SOAS Studies on South Asia

Beyond Purdah?

Women in Bengal 1890–1939

Dagmar Engels

DELHI
OXFORD UNIVERSITY PRESS
BOMBAY   CALCUTTA   MADRAS
1996

Oxford University Press, Walton Street, Oxford OX2 6DP

Oxford   New York
Athens   Auckland   Bangkok   Bombay
Calcutta   Cape Town   Dar es Salaam   Delhi
Florence   Hong Kong   Istanbul   Karachi
Kuala Lumpur   Madras   Madrid   Melbourne
Mexico City   Nairobi   Paris   Singapore
Taipei   Tokyo   Toronto

and associates in
Belin   Ibadan

ISBN 0 19 563720 8

Laserset by S.J.I. Services, New Delhi 110 024
Printed at Wadhwa International, New Delhi 110 020
and published by Manzar Khan, Oxford University Press,
Y.M.C.A. Library Building, Jai Singh Road, New Delhi 110 001

FOR
ROB AND JULIA

PREFACE

Born in a country where masculinity is venerated to the extent that you talk about your *Vaterland*, 'fatherland', I found research on women's history and gender ideology in Bengal a fascinating and rewarding experience. There femininity, not masculinity, was the central value in many political and social discourses. On a closer look, however, the impact of this value was limited, particularly when male power was seriously threatened. Nevertheless, without retreating into essentialism, my research brought me close to a culture which is very distinct from my own and I am grateful that I was accepted as a curious guest in India, especially in Bengal, and even more especially by many Bengali women. My research in Calcutta relied to a large extent on their co-operation.

In 1984–85 I interviewed more than thirty women and I am extremely grateful to them for sharing their time and memories with me. In particular, I would like to thank the women in 'Naba Nir', an elderly-ladies' home in Tollyganj, Calcutta; they provided invaluable information for my research through reminiscences about their lives in the 1910s and 1920s. Sabita Sarkar assisted during the interviews and their success was largely due to her. Numerous other women arranged contacts and located source material including rare books. In particular Sevati Mitra, my Calcutta hostess, supported my research in many ways and kept me going in the unusually hot spring of 1985. Padmini Sengupta was kind to let me consult the *Indian Ladies Magazine*—published by her mother—and the director and staff of the Saroj Nalini Dutt Memorial Association gave me access to their archival records. My long hours in the National Library, Calcutta, were shared by Nivedita Chatterjee who shouldered the arduous burden of improving my Bengali.

There are also Bengali men whom I would wish to thank (among them the traffic policemen in front of Writers' Building who helped me twice a day to cross the road on my bicycle during the Calcutta rush-hour). At all times in Calcutta I was made welcome by Professor N.R. Ray at the Institute of Historical Studies; I have benefited greatly from his vast knowledge of 'Old Calcutta'. For help in minor 'emergencies' in Delhi and Calcutta I would like to thank Dr D.N. Panigrahi, Mr S. Kitson and Mr Penn Anthony.

In India and England I have worked in numerous archives and libraries. I should like to thank in particular the directors and staff of the West Bengal State Archive and the National Library, both in Calcutta; the National Archives of India and the Nehru Memorial Museum and Library, both in Delhi; the India Office Library and Records, London, the Libraries of the School of Oriental and African Studies and the University of London and the British Library.

In 1987 an earlier version of this study was submitted as a PhD thesis at the School of Oriental and African Studies, University of London. I owe my deepest gratitude to my supervisor Professor K.A. Ballhatchet. He has been a source of great intellectual stimulation and support ever since I first came to SOAS in 1981–82. His understanding, and patient and encouraging supervision exceeded my expectations at all times. Coming from a large German university like Freiburg, the individual attention and personal atmosphere I found at SOAS was an unusual experience. I have also benefited immensely from the teaching, advice and additional supervision of Dr T. Mukherjee, Professor A. Mayer, Professor K.N. Chaudhuri, Dr Peter Robb and Mr John Harrison. At the same time the administrative staff always found time to cope with my problems. I would like to thank in particular Joyce Hutchinson, Anne Mackintosh, Kay Henderson, Nora Shane and Maryjayne Hillman.

Friends and scholars have discussed my work and commented on various aspects. Geraldine Forbes has been a friend and mentor ever since we first began to correspond. Tapan Raychaudhuri was a great help on Bengali sources. David Arnold advised me on the transformation of the thesis into a book. Shula Marks and Deborah Gaitskell broadened the horizon of my work by challenging some results from their Africanist perspectives. Two anonymous readers of the manuscript helped with very useful suggestions for revision. Michelle Maskiell was so kind as to give up her anonymity when she assessed an earlier draft of this book. I have profited no end from her comments and hope that she will find some, if not all, of her thoughtful suggestions in this rewritten version. In addition I have learnt from discussions with Veena Oldenburg, Gervase Clarence-Smith, Sergio Aiolfi, Indivar Kamtekar, Rosalind O'Hanlon·and Devadas Moodley. Earlier versions of some chapters were discussed at several seminars and conferences. I would like to thank in particular the London Feminist History Group, the South Asian History Seminar at SOAS, the Indian History Seminar, St. Antony's College, Oxford, the History of South Asia Seminar, South Asian Studies Centre, Cambridge, and a range of seminars at the Institute of Commonwealth Studies, ·University of London.

During the preparation of this work I received financial support from a number of sources. The German Academic Exchange Service enabled me to begin my studies at SOAS. My fieldwork in India was financed with a Travel Award from SOAS. For London-based research I received a generous grant from the German Historical Institute, London.

I owe much to my colleagues at the German Historical Institute. They provided a congenial working environment which made the task of writing and rewriting as pleasant as possible. Feminist and Indian social history was a new departure for some of them, but I always enjoyed their intellectual challenge. In particular, I would like to thank Susanne Bluhm for generous secretarial support, and my friend and colleague Peter Alter for his skilful editorial help and his growing interest in African and Indian history. He listened with admirable patience to monologues on Bengali women, as well as post-structuralist and feminist theory.

Finally, a word of thanks to my parents. They have supported my 'Indian ventures' since 1978 when I first travelled to India. In the book I mention the special position of Bengali daughters in families without sons. I am one of four daughters, and my parents encouraged my work in true Bengali style.

This book is dedicated to Rob Turrell and our daughter Julia. Without Rob's historical understanding, his scholarship and editorial skills, this book would not have been the same.

NOTE: In the footnotes to this work, citations to books and articles give full references on the first occasion, but thereafter only the author and date of publication. Full references are also available in the bibliography.

CONTENTS

ABBREVIATIONS

AOC Report	*Report of the Age of Consent Committee, 1928–1929* Calcutta 1929
COI	Census of India
Comm.	Commercial
Ests	Establishments
FA	*Annual Report on the Administration of the Indian Factories Act*
FCS	Financial and Commercial Statistics of British India
GOB	Government of Bengal
GOI	Government of India
IESHR	*Indian Economic and Social History Review*
ILR	Indian Law Reports
IOLR	India Office Library and Records, London
Judi	Judicial
Medi	Medical
n.a.	Author unknown
NAI	National Archives of India, Delhi
n.d.	No date
NLC	National Library, Calcutta
NMML	Nehru Memorial Museum and Library, Delhi
Poll	Political
RCLI	Royal Commission on Labour in India, 1931
RNNB	*Report on Native Newspapers in Bengal*
SBI	Statistics of British India
SNDMA Report	Annual Report of the Saroj Nalini Dutt Memorial Association from the years 1925 to 1931
TFF	Towards Freedom File
WBSA	West Bengal State Archives, Calcutta

INTRODUCTION

On Saturday, 24 May 1930, the inhabitants of Patuakhali, a small town in the East Bengali district of Bakarganj, declared a hartal. The hartal was a general strike which was aimed at paralysing the British authorities and local business, and was part of the Civil Disobedience Movement which Gandhi had declared in protest of British rule. Early in the morning the women of the town went out to stop colonial officials from reaching their offices. When the fourth Munsif (Indian judge) approached the court, women and girls barred his way. 'The talukdar [landholder] went to his rescue and his feet were seized by the women', the District Magistrate of Bakarganj later reported to his superior. But then the women were thwarted. A sailor from the talukdar's launch carried the Munsif through the women's lines. 'He narrowly escaped serious injury from the projecting corrugated-iron sheets of a roof.' The Magistrate continued, 'The "non-violent" males seized him and pulled him down from the khalasi's arms, his leg and arm being injured when he fell. He reached court...'[1]

This was by no means an isolated event. Less than a fortnight later, on 4 June, women in Noakhali, a district town south-east of Bakarganj, came out in force so that all the main roads leading to the courts were blocked. They stood in lines 'supported by men volunteers lying behind them several rows deep'.[2] Colonial officials only managed to get to the courts once police had found a lane which was blocked by men alone. Police cleared them off the road with brusqueness and brutality.

While women in East Bengal protested and picketed almost daily, women in the western part of the province in and around Calcutta were not idle either. On 22 June 1930, a demonstration of about 70 women in North Calcutta culminated when 'the ladies and these youths... encircled the police officers, fell down before them, clutched their legs and seized the reins of the Mounted Police horses'.[3] Such courage was paralleled by peasant women who confronted the colonial state during the no-tax movement which was started in July 1930. At Indas in Bankura hundreds of women lay down to stop the authorities from removing confiscated property.[4]

'Women', as the Chief Secretary to the Government of Bengal put it, 'who are taking an increasing part in public demonstrations on behalf of civil disobedience'[5] were an unknown new factor for the British in the province. The social fabric of Bengali society had seemingly been revolutionized by the emergence of the Swadeshi movement at the beginning of the century. Before then women only met privately to listen to adapted semi-religious stories which scolded Bengalis for having let the British into their country. By 1930 was the public appearance of women not proof enough of their breaking with traditional gender stereotypes?

The answer to this question is manifold. As we shall see purdah did not only mean secluding women behind veils or walls, but entailed an all-encompassing ideology and code of conduct based on female modesty which determined women's lives wherever they went. Accordingly women's political experience and participation[6]—even if we can establish its significance—needs to be deconstructed and contextualized by looking at a wider range of discourses. Women's political activities, their class-specific life-cycles as daughters, wives and mothers as well as their education and employment will be examined not only to trace developments and differences, but also to identify the underlying hierarchy of concepts which worked to keep women of all classes in a position of general inferiority to their male partners in private and public.

As such intentions indicate, from an epistemological point of view, this book attempts to combine post-structuralist and feminist theories.[7] Both sets of theories share the concern for 'the relationship between subjectivity and meaning, meaning and social value, the range of possible normal subject positions open to women, and the power and powerlessness invested in them'.[8] The political activities of women, for example, will not only be examined in relation to their importance for the women involved, but also in relation to their meaning in a wider discursive setting. Finally, I will suggest how far such activities were symptoms of modified power relations. Subjectivity and—to use a contentious term—female experience[9] will be qualified, but not denied, as have some post-structuralists, by deconstructing the liberal-humanist subject out of its epistemological existence.[10] Here I refer to Foucault who pioneered the 'contextualization of experience and an analysis of its constitution and ideological power'.[11] Compared to earlier feminist theories feminist post-structuralism follows a less dogmatic approach. While liberal, psychoanalytical and materialist feminists partly differ regarding the reason for female subordination, I will take up Joan Scott's suggestion and ask how gender differences conferred inequality on women.[12]

The aim of the study is, finally, political and emancipatory, namely to understand the changing power relations informed by gender, race and class—as shown for instance by the events in 1930—and to assist in the development of strategies for change. Within this approach language is central as the place where meanings are produced albeit 'socially and historically located in discourses'.[13] But material relations and practices, such as colonial concerns, the patriarchal Hindu family and economic interests, are recognized as elements in the domain of power which confronts the individual.[14] To summarize: Discourse, as understood in this study, refers to verbal and non-verbal constructions of meaning. Talking about discourses rather than debates or developments is based on two main assumptions: firstly that there is no meaning which exists outside or before the discursive context, for example, institutions or private and public power relations; and, closely related, secondly, that the individual has no prerogative as the bearer of truth, experience or innovation.[15]

Because of the diversity of discourses under examination a wide range of source material has been analysed. In the India Office Library and Records in London and the National Archives of India in Delhi, Home Office files, annual reports and official publications of the Indian government as well as private papers were the basis for the deconstruction of the official discourse on women in Bengal. Reports by a number of committees on labour and industrial development highlighted the role of women in economic development between 1890 and 1930. In the National Library in Calcutta, Bengali contemporary non-fictional literature and official publications by the Bengal government allowed a closer provincial perspective. Research there was complemented by an examination of the holdings of the West Bengal State Archive, in particular on provincial industrial developments and political unrest. The annual reports of the Saroj Nalini Dutt Memorial Association of Calcutta and the private collection of Padmini Sengupta, in particular, the Indian Ladies Magazine, documented contemporary discourses involving Bengali middle-class women. This angle of research was further pursued by interviewing about thirty septuagenerian and octogenarian women, whose recollections of the past added many valuable nuances to the findings from the written sources.

To date the history of women in Bengal has been written with a focus on female emancipation. The most comprehensive accounts have been provided by Geraldine Forbes and Meredith Borthwick. Forbes has analysed both the struggles of early women activists and the emergence of autonomous women's organizations in the 1920s. Although women saw themselves as complementary rather than as equal to men, their activities in the early twentieth century bore the marks of a 'First Wave' Feminism. Borthwick, in her study, The Changing Role of Women in Bengal 1849–1905, traces the impetus for female emancipation to the intellectual impact of European missionaries and administrators, as well as to western education, which first introduced Bengali men to the notions of individuality and equality. Such developments caused, in Borthwick's view, the redefinition of conjugal relations, of mother-hood, housewifery and of women's participation in social work and politics. Before 1905 these changes affected mainly women of the Brahmo Samaj, a reformist sect, but Borthwick argues that their achievements were soon emulated by Hindu middle-class women.[16]

Forbes and Borthwick's research dealt with the lives and activities of elite women who were, due to their social and intellectual background, strongly influenced by western thought and western-inspired ideas on social reform. Some scholars, like Ghulam Murshid, in his Reluctant Debutante, went even further in measuring the achievements of Bengali women by the yardstick of western concepts of individuality and independence.[17]

Other historians have dealt with the significance of woman-related issues in wider political discourses, in particular those concerned with social reform and nationalism. Nineteenth-century

Bengali reformers, like Rammohan Roy and Iswar Chandra Vidyasagar, agreed with their British utilitarian contemporaries that the status of women demonstrated the level of civilization which a specific society had reached. Thus, female emancipation from the traditional bonds of Hindu and Muslim society—such as purdah in the narrow sense of seclusion, *sati* (widow burning), child marriage and the prohibition of widow remarriage—became for them the *sine qua non* of political independence. The early reformers hoped to guide Indian society towards the ideal of enlightened western civilization as a pre-condition for participating in ruling India.[18] And the association of female emancipation with political independence was a powerful liberating influence for some elite women.

But western-style social reform could not filter through society on a larger scale.[19] Asok Sen, for instance, in his study of Vidyasagar, explains the reformer's failure to promote widow remarriage by reference to his lack of support—following Gramsci—from a hegemonic social class. Sen argues that the Bengali middle class was insufficiently developed to achieve cultural hegemony and to sponsor social reform in Bengali society. 'Lacking a role in economic advance and removal of general poverty, the middle-class ideas of social renewal found no route to reach the ordinary and routine life of the masses.'[20] Following a similar line of argument, Sumit Sarkar, in his analysis of Rammohan Roy, rejects the purely idealist tradition–modern dichotomy in the analysis of social reform. Such a differentiation, in his view, classified the ideologies of social reform, or conservative opposition, as intellectual constructs without linking them to material forces.[21] Lata Mani has taken this view as her starting point for deconstructing the early nineteenth century discourse on sati. She shows that social reform was not at the heart of the matter and that the alleged tradition–modern dichotomy was only superficial. Instead, the discourse was a product of 'colonial knowledge' on tradition, modernity and women in support of British colonial dominance.[22]

While redefinitions of gender ideology and gender roles which were based on western thought failed to reach the majority of women, intellectual developments informed by Indian culture had a larger impact. Tanika Sarkar has demonstrated how traditional images of female strength were activated by the movement for cultural revivalism which paralleled the early phase of nationalism.[23] In the present study we shall see how Hindu Revivalism gradually turned femininity from a passive object of adoration to a powerful agent for political mobilization. The development was extremely powerful and effective in the anti-colonial struggle, because the strategy was not to try and compete with western cultural achievements, but rather to claim superiority for Indian civilization which was diametrically opposed to western stereotypes. To some extent my attention to these developments was stimulated by Partha Chatterjee's analysis of nationalist discourses in India.[24] However, curiosity for women's history in Bengal cannot be satisfied solely by examining their place in dominant, but predominantly male, discourses, such as social reform and nationalism. Thus it is, I hope, possible to go further by widening the range of discourses under examination as well as the analytical perspective. Women's fate was not decided only by nationalist ideology, just as social reformist and feminist activities need to be seen in relation to wider social and economic developments.

Choosing to examine women's history in Bengal and not elsewhere may seem arbitrary. However, within the context of early twentieth-century India, Bengal was at the crossroads of far-reaching economic, social and political changes which were bound to have a considerable impact on the women of the province.

Between 1890 and 1930 the population of Bengal increased from almost 40 million to just over 50 million people. For the two decades from 1891 to 1911 there was a gradual decennial growth of about 7 per cent, which declined in the following decade to less than 3 per cent. During the 1920s, the rate of increase accelerated slightly to reach, once again, the 7 per cent mark.[25] The number of women grew from more than 19 million to just over 24 million, which was a decrease—from 49.3 to 48 per cent—in the proportion of women in the total population.[26] This decline in the proportion of women to men, which continues today, can be attributed to early and frequent childbearing, the pattern of migration and general malnutrition.[27]

As the Muslim gender system differed significantly from the Hindu, and as the Muslim response to British rule and the debate over gender relations was significantly different, I will concentrate on the Hindu population alone. It must be remembered, though, that Muslims formed the biggest religious community in the province during the whole period. In 1891 and 1931 they accounted for over 50 per cent of the total population:[28] 'The vast majority of Bengali Muslims were peasants, in origin probably low-caste Hindus, Buddhists or simply people who had never been fully assimilated into the structure of Aryan society.'[29]

The majority of Muslims lived in the eastern regions of the province, tilling land owned by Hindus. There was a small minority in the west, who were the descendants of the Nawab's ruling elite. Their sudden loss of power after the British conquest was a source of continuous communal tension in western Bengal.[30] As Muslims were, for the most part, reluctant to co-operate with the British once English had been made the official language, and were equally reluctant in their acceptance of western education, their political and social power was quickly eroded.[31] Yet Hindu dominance was threatened by the growing Muslim population and by the growing Muslim communal identity which paralleled developments in the Hindu community.[32]

While Bengal's total population grew only slowly, the number of inhabitants in towns and cities increased more sharply in our period. In 1891 only 4.8 per cent of the province's total population lived in towns or cities, but forty years later the urban population made up 7.3 per cent of the total. Of this, 7.3 per cent (almost half) lived in cities, that is, urban areas with over 100,000 inhabitants, namely Calcutta, Howrah and Dhaka. Between 1890 and 1930, Calcutta's population increased by 50 per cent from about 800,000 to over 1.2 million, while the population of Dhaka grew by 70 per cent to almost 140,000.[33]

The western and central parts of the province—the 'Hindu belt' with less than 30 per cent of the total population—were more strongly urbanized than the northern and eastern regions which underlined the focal power of the Hindu-dominated Calcutta area. Here, as a consequence, every fourth Hindu lived in an urban surrounding. On a provincial level, 12 per cent of all Hindus lived in towns and cities, which was three times the corresponding Muslim proportion.[34]

Women were under-represented in towns and cities and their proportion decreased continuously due to the pattern of migration. In Calcutta, where mills and the informal sector attracted a large number of long-distance migrants, the proportion of women was lowest, namely one woman to every two men in 1921. In industrial towns and more so in country towns, the proportion was more balanced. Bengali peasants, who had lost their land and took jobs as manual workers in nearby towns, frequently moved with their families. Calcutta was generally regarded by them as morally dangerous; accordingly men hesitated to take their wives when they migrated.[35]

Despite the rate of urban growth, Bengal was still, in 1930, a predominantly rural society.[36] Apart from jute mills in the Calcutta area and coal fields and steel factories in the Burdwan division, rural towns relied for survival on trading agricultural produce to Calcutta merchants. The production and distribution of the agrarian produce, most importantly paddy and jute, were, however, organized in a way which was highly disadvantageous to peasants, but increased the wealth of urban-based landowners, middlemen, merchants and jute-mill owners—the latter were, until the Depression, exclusively European and American. The increasingly indebted peasants had to sell their produce at low prices immediately after the harvest, but middlemen and merchants in the urban economy profited from fluctuating prices.[37] By 1900 'by far the largest sections of the peasantry...had been driven to, or even beyond, the margin of subsistence'.[38] In the wake of the First World War, prices of export goods declined, while prices of cloth, kerosene, salt and coarse foodgrains went up.[39] Declining export prices and inflation seriously undermined rural cultivators, and led to the dispossession of approximately 3 million peasants. While a major study remains to be undertaken on this social dislocation in the 1920s, most were forced, it appears, into the ranks of sharecroppers and agricultural labourers, but others became domestic servants, petty shopkeepers and small traders.[40] Peasant women, invisible to scholars and census collectors in this major transformation of rural society, joined the domestic labour forces in the households of wealthy landowners or the urban middle class.

The Bengali urban middle class has been the subject of a number of historical studies.[41] It excelled as a collaborator and later as the opponent of British rule in India. Until Gandhi's arrival in India, middle-class Bengalis dominated the Indian National Congress and from the days of the Swadeshi movement some were, together with Tilak in Maharashtra, at the forefront of supporting revolutionary strategies against the British. Due to the Permanent Settlement in 1793, the landed middle class was assured of a stable income throughout the next century. Shortly after 1800, earlier than any other group in India, Bengalis from landowning families took to western education and gained access to urban posts in the British Indian administration and the professions. But the industrial entrepreneurial sector in Bengal, namely jute mills, coal-mines and tea plantations, were British-owned and, in the higher echelons, British-staffed. This gave rise to frustrations among the growing number of educated Bengalis who, from the 1870s onwards, competed for a stagnant number of white-collar jobs in the administrative and professional sectors, in particular because it had become increasingly difficult to live off their landed income.

The middle class in Bengal included rich zamindars, who financed Calcutta mansions through income from their rural properties and their urban professional activities, as well as clerks in Writers' Building who barely managed to pay for their children's schooling. There were also regional differences in the middle class. In Nadia and Bankura, in the western districts, 'the smaller rent-receiving classes remained stay-at-home and preferred a lower standard of life at home to seeking employment and fortune' elsewhere.[42] The rent-receiving class in East Bengal, particularly in and around Bikrampur pargana in Dhaka district, responded to the stimulus of western education and the growing economic pressures that stemmed from difficulties with rent collections in a more innovative way than the gentry of West Bengal. In Bikrampur and its surrounding areas English schools flourished and

the highly educated, mobile and intelligent gentry of Bikrampur, belonging to the top-ranking section of the Brahmans, Vaidyas and Kayasthas, streamed out of their rural homes in the nineteenth century and secured a considerable portion of the jobs opened up by British administration.[43]

So far I have used the terms 'middle class', 'gentry' and 'rent-receiving classes' when I translated the Bengali word *bhadralok* (*bhadra* big, important; *lok* man, people). In fact, the Bengali term expresses the diversity of the group better than any of the translations, which imply a precision that did not exist. Bhadralok was used for the people who did not necessarily share the same economic background, but rather the concept of respectability as understood in 'the abstention from manual labour'.[44] Broomfield described the Bengal bhadralok at the beginning of the twentieth century as

a socially privileged and consciously superior group, economically dependent upon landed rents and professional and clerical employment; keeping its distance from the masses by its acceptance of high-caste prescriptions and its commands of education; sharing a pride in its language, its literate culture and its history.[45]

The position of women in bhadralok families was as heterogeneous as the social and economic background of their families. The regional differences had a strong impact on the lives of the respective women as well. Eastern districts were renowned for female education and less restrictive norms, for instance, with regard to the seclusion of women. Moreover, women led less restricted lives in reformist Brahmo and Hindu families than women in orthodox families. Bhadralok families of all social classes shared, however, the concern for respectability, although the definition of the term varied among the respective groups. But all bhadralok women were seen as the guardians of culture, a heavy burden on women in a situation in which bhadralok identity depended to a large extent on this very culture.

British colonization was more deeply rooted in Bengal than in any other Indian province. The cultural superiority associated with imperialism combined with a complex Bengali response to its impact, first positively to British education, and later negatively to British exploitation and exclusiveness, shaped a political atmosphere dominated by racial attitudes. British arrogance heightened the importance of issues relating to the cultural identity of the dominant and subjected people: gender issues were shaped by racism and cultural rivalry.

NOTES

[1] WBSA, GOB, Poll/Poll, 599/1930, Appendix G, 3.
[2] WBSA, GOB, Poll/Poll, 599/1930, Serial No 8, 9.
[3] Ibid., Serial No 12, 12.
[4] T. Sarkar, *Bengal 1928–1934. The Politics of Protest*, Delhi, 1987, p. 87.
[5] WBSA, GOB, Poll/Poll, 599/1930, Serial No 2, p.1.

[6] The best study in this field is T. Sarkar, 'Politics and Women in Bengal—the Conditions and Meaning of Participation', *Indian Economic and Social History Review*, 21, 1984, pp.91–101.

[7] The most useful theoretical studies are Ch. Weedon, *Feminist Practice and Post-structuralist Theory*, Oxford, 1987; Toril Moi, *Sexual/Textual Politics*, London, 1985; Mary Poovey, 'Feminism and Deconstruction'; and June Howard, 'Feminist Differings: Recent Surveys of Feminist Literary Theory and Criticism (a Review Essay)', *Feminist Studies*, 14, 1988, pp.51–65 and 167–90. For post-structuralist analyses in the Indian context, see G. Chakravorty Spivak, *In Other Worlds. Essays in Cultural Politics*, New York, 1987, Part Three: Entering the Third World.

[8] Ch. Weedon, *Feminist Practice*, pp.7, 19.

[9] For a rather polemical discussion of the term, see C.T. Mohanty, 'Under Western Eyes: Feminist Scholarship and Colonial Discourses', *Boundary*, 2, Spring/Fall, 1984, pp.333–58.

[10] J. Derrida, *Of Grammatology*, Baltimore, 1976; for a critical discussion of French post-structuralist feminist authors, see *Feminist Practice*, pp.63–73, 125.

[11] M. Foucault, *The Birth of the Clinic*, London, 1973; and *Discipline and Punishment*, Harmondsworth, 1979; and *The History of Sexuality*, vol.1: An Introduction, Harmondsworth, 1981.

[12] W. Scott, 'Gender: A Useful Category of Historical Analysis', *The American Historical Review*, 91, 1986, p.1065.

[13] Weedon, *Feminist Practice*, p.41.

[14] Weedon stresses this departure from pure deconstructivist approaches as does M. Poovey, 'Feminism and Deconstruction', *Feminist Studies*, 14, 1988, pp.51–65.

[15] D. Macdonell, *Theories of Discourse. An Introduction*, London, 1989, 1st ed., 1986.

[16] Geraldine Forbes has published a range of articles on women and the women's movement in Bengal. The present study is very much indebted to her work; for instance, G. Forbes, 'The Ideals of Indian Womanhood: Six Bengali Women during the Independence Movement', in J.R. Mclane (ed.), *Bengal in the 19th and 20th Centuries*, Michigan, 1975, pp.59–74; 'Women's Movement in India: Traditional Symbols and New Roles', in M.S.A. Rao (ed.), *Social Movements in India*, vol. 2, New Delhi, 1979, pp.149–65; 'Goddesses or Rebels? The Women Revolutionaries of Bengal', The Oracle, II, 2, 1980, pp.1–15; 'Caged Tigers: "First Wave" Feminists in India', *Women's Studies IF*, 5, 1982, pp.525–36. The history of the *bhadramahila* (middle-class women) was examined by Meredith Borthwick, *The Changing Role of Women in Bengal 1849–1905*, Princeton, 1984. This book was a valuable source of information and stimulation throughout my research; for the present argument, pp.26–59.

[17] G. Murshid, *Reluctant Debutante: Response of Bengali Women to Modernization, 1849–1905*, Rajshahi, 1983; another study measures the Indian women's movement with the movements in the West: J.M. Everett, *Women and Social Change in India*, New York, 1979. The connection between liberal political philosophy and female emancipation was first made in nineteenth-century England. In 1869, one of the first British male supporters of women's emancipation referred to the political progress achieved in nineteenth-century England to argue the case against female subjection: 'and that, so far as the whole course of human improvement up to this

time, the whole stream of modern tendencies, warrants any interference on the subject, it is, that this relict of the past is discordant with the future and must necessarily disappear.' J.S. Mill, 'The Subjection of Women', *Essays on Equality, Law, and Education*, Toronto, 1984, p.272. The relation between social and political progress was raised in Bengal during the Age of Consent Debate in 1890–91, see chapter 7. It gained particular prominence during the controversy between Tilak and Gokhale, see S.A. Wolpert, *Tilak and Gokhale: Revolution and Reform in the Making of Modern India*, Berkeley, 1962, pp.38ff. The connection has also been established by Indian post-Independence women historians: V. Mazumdar, 'The Social Reform Movement in India—From Ranade to Nehru'; B.R. Nanda (ed.), *Indian Women; From Purdah to Modernity*, Delhi, 1976, pp.41–66; R.K. Sharma, *Nationalism, Social Reform and Indian Women*, Delhi, 1981.

[18] James Mill, *The History of British India*, 4th ed., London, 1840, pp.445–7, quoted in Borthwick, 1984, p.27; S.N. Mukherjee, 'Raja Rammohun Roy and the Status of Women in Bengal in the Nineteenth Century'; M. Allen, S.N. Mukherjee (eds.), *Women in India and Nepal*, Canberra, 1982, pp.153–78, 161, 168ff; A. Sen, *Iswar Chandra Vidyasagar and his Elusive Milestones*, Calcutta, 1977.

[19] For the most perceptive study on the reception of western thought by Bengali intellectuals, see T. Raychaudhuri, *Europe Reconsidered. Perceptions of the West in Nineteenth Century Bengal*, Delhi, 1988; on Vivekananda in particular, see B. Southard, 'Vivekananda: The Search for Ethical Values and National Progress under Indigenous Leadership', J.P. Sharma (ed.), *Individuals and Ideas in Modern India*, Calcutta, 1982, pp.125–47.

[20] A. Sen, *Iswar Chandra Vidyasagar and his Elusive Milestones*, p.87.

[21] S. Sarkar, 'Rammohun Roy and the Break with the Past', V.C. Joshi (ed.), *Rammohun Roy and the Process of Modernization in India*, Delhi, 1975, pp.46–68, 66ff.

[22] L. Mani, 'The Production of an Official Discourse on Sati in Early Nineteenth Century Bengal', *Economic and Political Weekly*, 'Review of Women's Studies', 21, 17, 26 April 1986, pp.32–40; and 'Contentious Traditions: The Debate on Sati in Colonial India', K. Sangari, S. Vaid (eds.), *Recasting Women. Essays in Colonial History*, Delhi, 1989, pp.88–126.

[23] T. Sarkar, 'Nationalist Iconography: Image of Women in nineteenth-century Bengali Literature', *Economic and Political Weekly*, 22, 47, 21 November 1987, pp.2011–15.

[24] P. Chatterjee, *Nationalist Thought and the Colonial World—A Derivative Discourse*, London, 1986.

[25] *Census of India* (COI), 1931, v, 2, p.4.

[26] Ibid., p.5.

[27] The decreasing proportion of women in the total population was even more astonishing as infant mortality affected more (0.2 per cent) baby boys than baby girls. There is ample evidence that the frequency of births was the greatest killer of women. Between the ages of 20 and 45, the female death rate was higher than the death rate of men. COI, 1921, v, 1, p.209. For the ongoing trend, see P.B. Desai, *Size and Sex Composition of Population in India 1901–1961*, London, 1969, Appendix B,5.

[28] COI, 1931, v, 2, p.411.

[29] S. Sarkar, *The Swadeshi Movement in Bengal 1903–08*, New Delhi, 1973, p.408.

[30] Ibid., p.409; COI, 1931, v, 1, p.411.

[31] Sarkar, *The Swadeshi Movement*, pp.410–2.

[32] Ibid., p.415; R.K. Ray, *Social Conflict and Political Unrest in Bengal 1875–1927*, Delhi, 1984, pp.41–2.

[33] COI, v, 1, pp.74–5, 84.

[34] Ibid., p.411.

[35] COI, 1921, vi, 1, p.111.

[36] R.K. Ray, *Social Conflict and Political Unrest*, 6; COI, 1931, v, 1, p.74.

[37] During the last few years a number of excellent studies have been published analysing agrarian structures in Bengal. The most important are: A. Sen *et al.*, *Perspectives in Social Sciences 2, Three Studies on the Agrarian Structure in Bengal 1850–1947*, Calcutta, 1982; P. Chatterjee, *Bengal 1920–1947, The Land Question*, Calcutta, 1984; S. Bose, *Agrarian Bengal. Economy, Social Structure and Politics 1919–1947*, Cambridge, 1986. See also, R.K. Ray, 'The Crisis of Bengal Agriculture 1870–1927: The Dynamics of Immobility', *Indian Economic and Social History Review (IESHR)*, 10, 1973, pp.244–79; R.K. and R. Ray, 'The Dynamics of Continuity under the British Imperium: A Study of Quasi-stable Equilibrium in Underdeveloped Societies in a Changing World', *IESHR*, 10, 1973, pp.103–28.

[38] S. Mukherji, 'Some Aspects of Commercialization of Agriculture in Eastern India 1891–1938', A. Sen *et al.*, *Perspectives in Social Sciences*, p.233.

[39] S. Sarkar, *Modern India 1885–1947*, Delhi, 1983, pp.170–1.

[40] M.A. Huque, *The Man behind the Plough*, Calcutta, 1939, pp.139–44.

[41] For instance, J.H. Broomfield, *Elite Conflict in a Plural Society: Twentieth-Century Bengal*, Bombay 1968, 1st ed., University of California; R.K. Ray, *Social Conflict and Political Unrest*; N.S. Bose, *Racism, Struggle for Equality and Indian Nationalism*, Calcutta, 1981; S. Sarkar, *The Swadeshi Movement*; L.A. Gordon, *Bengal: the Nationalist Movement 1876–1940*, New York, 1974.

[42] Ray, *Social Conflict and Political Unrest*, p.66.

[43] Ibid.

[44] Broomfield, *Elite Conflict*, p.6.

[45] Ibid., pp.12–13.

1

PURDAH AND POLITICS

The view that 'the key to women's subordination is to be found in their identification with the domestic sphere' originally derives from Friedrich Engels' work on the origins of the family.[1] It is a view which today, despite the growth and divergence of feminist theoretical literature, commands widespread support.[2] But scholars have disagreed over both the causes and the structure of women's identification with the domestic sphere. Liberal and materialist feminists have singled out different aspects of domestic life, such as women's alleged affinity to biological nature or limited access to material resources, to account for female subordination. Scholars of psychology have stressed different ways of mothering and other aspects of socialization in the family. These approaches will not detain us. Instead it will be our concern to deconstruct a variety of discourses regarding women's identification with the domestic sphere in order to identify underlying assumptions which marked women as subordinate to men and in need of male control.

The most superficial comparison between the joint and nuclear family—the prevalent ideal types in Bengal and Europe respectively—shows that the family is a historical and cultural construct. But there is a similarity between Victorian and Bengali gender ideology in one important respect: in the conception of a separate sphere for women. Lynne Segal, in criticism of contemporary radical feminists, writes:

There is or course nothing new about the belief in women's moral superiority and unique sensibility, central as it was to the Victorian ideology of womanhood. Just as there is nothing new in my pointing out...how well this ideology of the 'good' woman serves to perpetuate male dominance. Women's sensibilities are seen as disqualifying them for the 'nasty' world of economic and political power, but equipping them for the socially ill-rewarded work of children and, of course, the general servicing of men.[3]

The veneration of women served to justify their restriction to and subordination in a separate world. The constitution of the family as a separate sphere from the outer world facilitated the control of women through their isolation and dependence on men.

Within this framework the complex of social practices known as purdah imposed an additional burden on Bengali women. Whereas sexual control is practised in many societies, purdah is an extreme form of sexual control. Apart from concealing women behind veils or keeping them within the walls of the *zenana* (female quarters in the house), purdah implied 'multitudes of complex social arrangements which maintained social...distance between the sexes'.[4] In poorer rural and urban families the domestic and work spheres were not clearly separated, but purdah-related values were nevertheless respected.

Yet purdah was more than a code of conduct for women in the family.[5] The control of women in the domestic sphere was reinforced through an ideological emphasis on the superiority of female values and feminine concepts. Bengali cultural revival in protest to British rule was based on the position of women in the family, embodied by the Mother. In order to portray this ideological development in the nationalist movement I shall concentrate on those—male—activists who set the trend.

Finally, I shall examine how far the cultural and political significance of purdah determined the ways in which women's presence outside the domestic sphere was negotiated by women and men. As this was most significant, I shall focus here on women's political rather than strictly intellectual activities. In contrast to the period of Hindu revivalism, this was the time when the nationalist movement had an impact on British authority mainly through mass protest rather than through intellectual innovation. The focus here first on men's writing and second on women's political activism does not suggest a gender-specific division of labour.[6] Rather it follows the development of women-related discourses within the nationalist movement and points to the delay with which Bengali women began to write on politics as compared with men. For at a time when Bankim Chandra was glorifying the political meaning of motherhood, educated bhadramahila expressed in novels and poems 'a wide range of private sentiments—undying faith in their husband; grief at separation from or on the death of the husband; affection for children; love for nature and...the need to educate their sisters who were still awaiting emancipation'.[7]

Bengali Hindu Families

The Bengali Hindu family was patrilineal and the household was patrilocal. Landed property was jointly held by the male members and was their strongest motivation for living together. Women owned no property apart from their *stridhan* which usually stemmed from wedding presents from their fathers and husbands; it included money and jewellery but rarely land. As wives, unmarried daughters and widowed daughters-in-law, women had only the right to maintenance. But even this was conditional. 'As to succession from males', it was argued in a Calcutta court case in 1903, 'not only does an unchaste wife become unable to inherit, but an unchaste daughter and an unchaste mother cannot inherit'.[8] Only in the absence of any patrilineal male relatives was a woman entitled to inherit land.

The average household consisted of three or four generations of the male line: father and mother, unmarried daughters and sons, married sons and their wives and grandchildren. As widows usually returned to their parental homes, the father's widowed sisters or widowed daughters joined the household. Often other relatives were present as well because they had either accepted work away from their homes or because personal conflicts had driven them from their families.[9] The total number of men and women in the family was not high. There were exceptions like the millionaire, Babu Ashutosh De, whose mansion resembled a 'small colony' or the Datta family in Nimtala where about 500 people lived together. The families depicted in contemporary Bengali novels were much smaller with one or two sons, their wives and one or two widowed female relatives. Moreover, it should be remembered that not more than two or three sons survived in most families due to the high infant mortality rate.[10] Even if all the sons survived, it was unlikely that they would continue to live in a joint-family household. The occurrence of such extended families amongst all classes was much less widespread than the popularity of the ideal seems to suggest.[11]

Urban middle-class migration due to the growth of the commercial and professional economic sector often meant the splitting-up of the family. During the nineteenth century a husband normally left his wife behind with the joint family, but by 1900 more educated couples migrated together.[12]

For the poorer classes joint families might also have been more fiction than fact. Famines and epidemics, apart from infant mortality, regularly diminished the size of families.[13] However, detailed data on family size and type only exist for the post-Independence period; by this time the Second World War, the Bengal famine in 1943-44 and Partition, had transformed the economy and society. In rural and urban West Bengal joint and nuclear families were almost evenly spread. Only middle-class peasants appeared to stick to the joint-family tradition, whereas wealthy families and urban or rural poor tended to live in nuclear units.[14] This takes us back to the significance of immovable property for the cohesion of a joint family. Either affluence acquired in the cities or the absence of property made a splitting up of a family more likely in the event of conflicts stemming from personal animosity or extreme economic scarcity.

In middle-class, joint-family households, where the male and female spheres were clearly distinct, there was a separate women's structure of authority. There were usually up to five or six women, including the mother and a widow, living in the zenana or working together in the household. The principle of seniority governed authority relations among women and either mitigated or aggravated the impact which patriarchal power had on women's lives.[15] Due to property relations, patrilocality and the religious significance of the male lineage, women were strangers in their husbands' houses until they had contributed to the continuity of the lineage with the birth of a son. It was here that the female rise to a limited power began; it culminated in the position of the *ginni*, the mature mistress of the house, mother of sons and superior to her daughters-in-law.

In many joint families the seniority-based hierarchy among women led to conflict as 'the power of the older women is great and is not always used without harshness to the younger'.[16] Also the relation between sisters-in-law and between the son's wife and his sisters was often disturbed by rivalry and 'an unaccountable coldness commonly springs up between them'.[17] The conflict may

have been 'unaccountable' to a male Bengali, but there were
causes for it which were inseparably linked with the patriarchal
structure of the family, such as the preference given by a mother
to her daughter as compared to the daughter-in-law and the
jealousy between the mother and daughter-in-law regarding the
son's/husband's love.

Much has been said and written about the propensity of Bengali
women to gossip and their preoccupation with sexual matters and
jewellery.[18] Indeed, women knew little about life outside their
homes or villages. Yet their position within the family and the
village depended to a certain extent on their familiarity with local
knowledge. They acquired information on subjects which their
husbands could not talk about or which was useful to their standing within the female household hierarchy. But indulging in gossip did not mean that women had little to do at home.

The rich women apart, the daily routine of most women was
extremely arduous. In the morning women of virtually all social
classes rose before sunrise to supervise or to clean the hut or house
and prepare the morning meal. They had a bath, celebrated a *puja*
(religious ritual) and decorated the court with *álpana* (ritual painting with rice paste). They supervised the children and spent long
hours on husking rice and sorting out grain. Moreover, plenty of
vegetables had to be cleaned and chopped. In middle-class
households a number of servants or older relatives would help,
but the larger and better-off a family was the more complex was
the woman's tasks. Apart from the routine of very wealthy
women, time for gossiping, visiting friends, playing cards or
resting was restricted to a few hours after lunch. The image of the
leisured woman was man-made and was only true of the lives of
elite women.[19]

Purdah was not just the veil with which women covered their
hair and their faces, but a complex of norms involving sexual
modesty and a generally demure behaviour towards men and
senior women. Strict purdah kept women hidden in separate
quarters, but the rules which regulated life within the household
were equally important. They limited a woman's communications
with male and female elders, restricted her access to food, and
allocated social space according to her ranking in the household.[20]
I will consider each of these elements in turn.

Avoidance rules were governed by the principle of male and female seniority. 'A wife...is forbidden', S. C. Bose wrote in the 1880s

to open her lips or lift her veil in order to speak to her husband in the presence of her mother-in-law, or of any other adult male or female member of the family. She may converse with the children without fear of being exposed to the charge of impropriety; this is the whole extent of her liberty, but she is imperatively commanded to hold her tongue and drop down her veil whenever she happens to see an elderly member in her way.[21]

Demure female behaviour served to keep the male and female hierarchies apart. It was 'an unpardonable sin' in a younger brother's wife 'even to come in contact with the very shadow' of the elder brother; the fear of sexual attraction between family members was at the root of this prohibition. 'Purdah was a form of social control by men over women's behaviour', writes Meredith Borthwick, 'which implied a view of women as simultaneously sexually vulnerable and in need of protection, and sexually aggressive and in need of control.'[22] Indeed, purdah in Hindu society focused on the separation of women from their male in-laws, while purdah in Indian Muslim culture kept sexually mature women, married or not, apart from society outside their families.[23]

In the late nineteenth century purdah, as the practice of female seclusion in the household, became less common first among reformist and, decades later, among orthodox Hindu women.[24] The associated value system, however, according to which a woman had to show respect to her elders and obey their orders, continued to be observed. Yet at the same time many high-caste women, who followed their husbands to the city for the first time, were subjected to stricter seclusion than before. Purdah was an expression of male honour and patriarchal control of female sexuality.[25] Thus, once a family left a village for Calcutta, real and imagined worries about female chastity and male honour grew, and male control increased accordingly.

In the cities or countryside most low-caste women who worked outside their houses and could not observe strict purdah, nevertheless appear to have accepted its associated value system. We know little about the behavioural code of these women, but there are hints in contemporary literature that, although they were not hidden in a zenana, they avoided contact with elder brothers-in-law and obeyed the orders of their mothers-in-law.[26] In addition, sexual modesty was essential and chastity was a female responsibility if a woman wanted to avoid being labelled a dangerous temptress. Bankim Chandra, in his novel, *Krishnakanta's Will*, first published in 1878, left his readers in no doubt about the question of guilt when a young widow, Rohini, aroused the passion of Govindalal who happened to be a married man.[27]

The rules surrounding meals reminded women of all classes and castes of their duty to worship their husbands (*pati devata*). Most importantly, they were never allowed to eat before or with their husbands. In joint families, it was the prerogative of the *grihini* (mistress) to sit with her grown-up sons over meals: 'not to eat, but to see that they are all properly served; she closely watches that each of them is duly satisfied; she would never feel happy should any of them find fault with a particular dish as being unsavoury...'[28]

In poor families, however, women were often undernourished because they ate only their husband's leftovers. Under favourable conditions the custom did not lead to malnourishment. Still, it certainly reminded women of their husbands' godlike status: a wife ate the left-overs of her husband as the devotees accepted the leftovers of the deity as *prasad*.

Moreover, women often had to wait till late to eat their evening meals, in case their husbands brought home guests or were out.[29] Couples who lived as nuclear families felt more at liberty to break with the custom because they were out of reach of their families' social control. Sudha Mazumdar, for instance, a middle-class woman from a Calcutta family, who ate with her husband once the door was closed and servants had been sent out, still feared that Pandey, the servant provided by her *sasur bari* (in-laws), would disclose her impropriety.[30]

Finally, the social segregation of men and women was usually built into the design of mansions and mud houses. But where the hut was too small to be divided, separate meals was the only visible norm which remained of traditional sexual segregation. 'On the floor of the hut' of a very poor woman, we are informed in a novel published in 1874

surrounded on all sides by mud walls and over-topped by a straw thatch, lay a coarse mat of palmyra leaves, which served as a bed for the mother and the daughter. In the four corners were some *handis* (earthen pots) which contained all their stores, consisting chiefly of rice, a few vegetables, and some culinary condiments like turmeric, salt, mustard oil and the like. There was no furniture.[31]

The houses of richer peasants, however, provided sufficient space for women to avoid the elder brothers-in-law. There was a courtyard encircled by a verandah and together they were the most important living and working areas of the home. From the verandah the family entered a number of mud huts which were used as store-rooms and sleeping-rooms, again without furniture but with mats on the floor. Such an arrangement provided some privacy. The courtyard was open at the main entrance and usually had an exit to the communal bathing pond. The latter had to be easily accessible because village women came here frequently for bathing and for cleaning their cooking utensils. Outside the court-yard was a special hut which the women of the family used for giving birth and during the subsequent period of confinement.[32]

The houses of wealthier families in Calcutta and in the *mufassal* were more architecturally marked by the concept of sexual segregation. The living space was divided into two sections which varied in size according to a family's income. But they always consisted of a relatively open entrance area where the male family members lived and received guests and the secluded female quarters, zenana, which were towards the back of the house. A typical mansion house in the Kidderpur area of Calcutta, for instance, had a front wing for the master with a dining-room, a Victorian drawing-room, a library and a marble staircase which led to the roof-terrace. In another wing were the female quarters, a suite for the master and a number of suites for the married sons. Slightly apart were the *amla* quarters for servants, managers and living-in relatives.[33]

The standard of living conditions in the zenana was much debated by British observers and Bengalis. European missionaries found the conditions appalling with women buried away at the back of the houses. One of them, Miss Mueller, recalled walking through, in her eyes, a very poor house:

A low narrow entrance in a most lowly attitude, led into a square court, through which we waded to a brick staircase about a foot and a half wide. The court was the receptacle of all thrown-away water from the kitchen. Only three pupils appeared, one by one, in the little prison-like bed-room, with its walls, which age and dirt had made of all shades from brown to black, and which some pictures and would-be decorations tried in vain to adorn.[34]

Missionaries repeatedly compared zenanas to prisons or cages. In a Calcutta house, inhabited by East Bengalis, Miss Mueller was struck by the 'very, very high dusty stairs, adorned with maimed warriors of unknown race' which she had to climb. At the top there was 'a steep, high ladder', and when at last she reached the summit she had to make her way 'over the high roof into the zenana, which certainly was secluded enough'.[35] No doubt life in a zenana was restricted and very unhealthy; often the morning and evening breeze, so important for ventilation in Calcutta houses, would not reach the secluded inner apartments.[36] But the level of comfort depended very much on the family's income.

Attitudes to the living conditions of women were culturally determined and a missionary's judgment was very different from a Bengali's view of his or her household. The Bengali author and Nobel prize-winner Rabindranath Tagore wrote that happiness and love came first in a Bengali home whereas material comfort was only secondary. In his opinion, Europeans were unable to understand this difference. 'When a lady doctor of the Dufferin Fund', he wrote in an article entitled 'Women's Lot in East and West'

enters our women's apartments, and sees there dirty small rooms, small windows, beds not at all milkwhite, earthenware lamps, mosquito-nets fastened with strings, few oleograph daubs of the Calcutta Art Studio, the walls blackened with the soot of lamps and the smudges of many fingers for countless years, she turns up her nose and thinks, 'Oh it is horrible! How miserable is their life! How very selfish are their men that they have kept the women like cattle!' Ah, she does not know that we all live thus. We read Mill, Spencer and Ruskin; we work in English offices, write to the papers, print books, but we light that earthen lamp, squat on that mattress, buy gold ornaments for our wives when we are in funds, and inside this string-knotted mosquito-net sleep we and our wives fanning ourselves with a palm-leaf fan, our baby between us.[37]

Later Tagore became more critical of Bengali domestic tradition and its celebration of male dominance without, however, accepting western values.[38] He and others criticised the worst aspects of purdah, but did not challenge its most basic assumptions regarding gender relations, such as the distinctiveness and complementarity of male and female roles.

Negotiating Purdah

Purdah and the associated code of conduct was more than a set of rules for female behaviour. Ideologically it elevated the domestic sphere into

a haven of cultural purity from which Bengali society was assumed to draw its strength. It was thus not astonishing that the—at first cultural and later political—movement, which fostered Bengali Hindu identity against British claims of cultural and political superiority, took purdah-related idioms as its point of departure.[39]

Encouraged by the discovery of 'the glories of ancient Aryans' by scholars like Max Muller, in the last decades of the nineteenth century Hindu revivalism reinterpreted the Hindu past as an ideological basis for future nation-building.[40] Within this approach an essentialist image of women focusing on motherhood became the incarnation of India's hope for an independent future. In Bankim Chandra's novel, *Anandamath* (1882), the long-standing tradition of Shaktism—the worship of female power in Bengal—was transformed into a political message. Bankim equated the incarnations of female power, the goddesses Durga und Kali, with India, the motherland. As every woman possessed *sakti*, every woman became the symbol of the motherland. Respect for women meant respect for India.

Bankim, by equating India with the Mother, created a strong emotional basis for the nationalist movement because he connected 'the most compelling and widespread religious idea among the Hindu people and ... the strongest and most profound emotional tie in their social relationships', as Van Meter (Baumer) put it in her thesis on Bankim Chandra.[41] In his novels, *Anandamath* and *Sitaram*, Bankim popularized the worship of the Mother as well as female duties and power, thus laying the foundation for women's active participation in the nationalist movement in years to come. But in his own novels he stopped well short of recommending female political activities. In fact he propagated the socially-conservative ideal of the Bengali Hindu girl who was to be, in Van Meter's words:

Basically educated, deeply religious, married at an early age, modest in behaviour, showing deep respect and devotion for her husband in the traditional Hindu ways, and ready to sacrifice her own life whenever the domestic situation demanded it.[42]

Accordingly, in his novels, a large number of women committed suicide.[43] Self-destruction, and not socially-constructive participation, was to be, in Bankim's view, the result of female heroism. Moreover, women not subjected to male control by fathers or husbands, that is widows, were morally too weak to comply with the high standards he set for female virtue. They were bound to succumb to the temptations of the flesh. Bankim saw their failure partly as a consequence of loosening morals and female emancipation from purdah traditions: in *Debi Chaudhurani* Bankim 'mourned the good old days' when women respected the rules of strict purdah and excelled in fulfilling their wifely duties without being distracted by other activities.[44]

In this context, the difference between the orthodox or revivalist protagonists of the 1880s and 1890s and the nationalists at the turn of the century can be clarified. Hindu orthodoxy in Bengal saw women in the private sphere as symbols of tradition which needed to be protected against reformist efforts. Bankim as a Hindu revivalist was, like his orthodox contemporaries, socially conservative with regard to female issues. But by identifying the Mother with India he invested female symbols with a political aura. For Bankim as well as for Sri Aurobindo, the Bengali revivalist and radical political activist, the glorification of motherhood was, despite its Hindu roots, less a cultural defence mechanism than the articulation of a new political programme.[45] Sri Aurobindo evoked the 'vision of the Mother' in order to inspire his fellow countrymen to struggle for India's independence:

Love has a place in politics, but it is the love of one's country, for one's countrymen, for the glory, greatness and happiness of the race, the divine *ananda* of self-immolation for one's fellows, the ecstasy of relieving their sufferings, the joy of seeing one's blood flow for country and freedom, the bliss of union in death with the fathers of the race. The feeling of almost physical delight in the touch of the mother-soil, of the winds that blow from Indian seas, of the rivers that stream from Indian hills, in the familiar sights, sounds, habits, dress, manners of our Indian life, this is the physical root of that love. The pride in our past, the pain in our present, the passion for the future are its trunk and branches. Self-sacrifice and self-forgetfulness, great service, high endurance for the country are its fruit. And the sap which keeps it alive is the realization of the Motherhood of God in the country, the vision of the Mother, the perpetual contemplation, adoration and service of the Mother.[46]

Aurobindo's invocation of the Mother was clearly action-oriented, not just defensive in the manner of former political campaigns. Love for the Mother was to inspire nationalist activities. Nevertheless the Mother stood for the great Goddess and for the mother country, not a living and active person. The essence of womanhood, that is, reproduction and nurture, which connected women with their biological nature rather than with achievement or performance, lay at the heart of the revivalist discourse.

Swami Vivekananda, the disciple of Ramakrishna (the worshipper of the Divine Mother and the founder of the 'mother cult' in nineteenth-century Bengal), was the first to connect female symbols with female activity and to outline the path the nationalist movement was to follow in the twentieth century. He spoke of a mother's love—not love for the mother—when he asked his Indian followers to work for India's future. 'Liberty is the first condition of growth', he said in his lecture on 'Vedanta and Indian life'. He continued:

It is wrong, a thousand times wrong, if any of you dares to say, 'I will work out the salvation of this woman or child'. I am asked again and again, what I think of the widow problem and what I think of the woman question. Let me answer once for all—am I a widow that you ask me that nonsense? Am I woman that you ask me that question again and again? Who are you to solve women's problems? Are you the Lord God that you should rule over every widow and every woman? Hands off. They will solve their own problems.[47]

Vivekananda questioned the reformers when they became obsessed with reorganizing the private sphere. But he did not support orthodoxy and its conservative approach towards gender relations. Instead he called on women to become actively involved in the country's social and political life. He had travelled to the West and it was obvious that the social position of women in the United States had deeply impressed him. Understandably, in his critique of the Bengali gender system, he went further than many of his contemporaries.[48]

After the turn of the century Rabindranath Tagore, whose literary and poetic comments on the events during the Swadeshi period were very influential in the development of the movement, was also representative of the prevailing attitudes towards women as well as to female social and political participation. During the partition years, like Aurobindo and Vivekananda, he perceived female nature as biologically determined. He shared the essentialist approach. But he gradually reconstructed his view, combining Bankim Chandra's and Sri Aurobindo's glorification of female symbolism with the action-oriented approach of Vivekananda.

As Sumit Sarkar has shown, shocked by the Hindu–Muslim riots in 1907, Tagore developed 'a basically anti-traditionalist and modernist approach'.[49] Writing about India's future he no longer referred to the glorious Hindu past, but called for mass mobilization through

patient, sustained, unostentatious constructive work in the villages—organizing associations, introducing co-operative techniques in agriculture and handicrafts, installing a sense of unity and self-reliance among the rayats, so that national consciousness really reaches out to the masses.[50]

Although he did not mention women, this programme indirectly depended on the involvement of women. It paved the way for a widening of the female sphere outside the family home, even before Gandhi had addressed Indian women in a similar way.

Before the First World War, Tagore did not explicitly associate female emancipation with the country's political progress. But in his novels he attacked the social conditions which subordinated women and in his educational efforts he supported female emancipation.[51] In 1908, for instance, he tried unsuccessfully to introduce co-education in his school in Santiniketan (see chapter 5). Still, in 1912, he wrote a passionate defence of traditional Bengali womanhood against western reformist ambitions, arguing that strength and equality were worshipped in the West only because people were denied the realization of their true selves. 'But our people', he continued, 'believe that woman's true happiness consists only in loving and being loved'.[52]

Thereafter, his writing changed. In Strir Patra he blamed the limitations of the Bengali gender ideology for driving women to suicide.[53] He did not champion western-type reform; instead his heroine chose to leave her husband for Puri, a generally respected refuge for Bengali single women. He stuck to the essentialist view of women, but for him, female otherness had become the reason for women to be involved in social life outside the narrow boundaries of their family homes. In 1924, he argued that women were the inspiration of everything men did and he regretted that their strength was wasted inside the household instead of being made use of in the wider society.[54] In Tagore's words, women should be encouraged to participate in public life without becoming like men. In this sense, he stuck to the idea, clearly expressed in 1912, of female otherness which was based on the values of purdah. Women who crossed the gender role boundary line created chaos, like Ela, who, in his short story, *Char Adhyay*, joined a revolutionary group. Even under moderate conditions, female emancipation and liberation implied social costs which men and women had to pay. In his novel, *Ghare Baire*, he sensitively showed the gains and losses—to men and women—of female emancipation.[55]

Women's involvement in the nationalist movement developed within the parameter of traditional gender ideology and colonial concepts of legality, both of which identified respectable women with privacy and domesticity.[56] By the 1920s, however, mass demonstrations, and shop and court picketing by women challenged Indian and colonial gender stereotypes. The British hoped that purdah-related values would inhibit women from breaking colonial law. However, when India became any Indian woman's home in the context of the nationalist struggle, purdah no longer prevented women from confronting British rule in public.

For the first time, during the period of the Swadeshi agitation following the partition of Bengal in 1905, women took part in politics on an organized basis. The issue, namely the division of the 'beloved motherland', was particularly suitable for politicizing women. Whereas political and economic rights were abstract values to many purdah women, the unity of the province was universally felt, not least because the migration of educated males to the cities of Calcutta and Dhaka spatially extended family networks and the notion of home.[57]

The activities in which women predominantly participated were ideologically and spatially linked to the private sphere of middle-class women. With few exceptions, women from the lower strata of society hardly participated: the Hindu middle-class bias in the Swadeshi movement excluded them just as much as their husbands. For middle-class women, however, traditional domestic activities were politically reinterpreted. Their mobilization for the Swadeshi cause was based on the essentialist notion of women as spiritual and fertile beings and as incarnations of the Mother, that is, India.

Religion was the ideal medium for drawing women into the movement—without in the least challenging traditional stereotypes regarding women's restriction to the private sphere. Women's domestic religious rituals, bratas, and customary rites within the family provided a pattern for their political involvement. Geraldine Forbes has illuminated this point by pulling together the various modes of female political participation during the period 1905 to 1911.[58]

The religious context was particularly clear in the case of the Banga Laksmir Brata Katha, the tale of the vow for the goddess Laksmi of Bengal. The story of Laksmi served to mobilize women against partition. On 16 October 1906, partition day, the katha was read in Jamokandir village, Murshidabad district, to a gathering of 1000 women. The brata recalled how the Bengalis lived happily with rich harvests once the Goddess had taken to Bengal. But soon 'people started forsaking the paths of virtue' and Laksmi considered leaving the country.[59] In fact, in the course of history, the story continued, Laksmi threatened to leave Bengal several times because the Bengalis disobeyed the teaching of the Vedas. Each time, however, the Bengalis returned to the path of virtue and Laksmi stayed on in Bengal.

In 1906 a new crisis faced Laksmi in Bengal. She was upset because the British, having exploited the weakness of the Mughal emperor in Delhi, appropriated:

The wealth, the products of Bengal (and) started to carry them away to their own country across the seven seas…making us fools by exporting to this country their cheap stuffs and selling them to us.[60]

When the Bengalis realized what was happening and started to resist, the English king's governor of the country, 'a petty clerk', suggested a division of Hindus and Muslims in Bengal in order to weaken the province. But it was impossible for Laksmi to live in a divided Bengal. However, the 'historical legend' provided a solution. The Bengalis begged:

Do not please leave Bengal...Mother be kind to us. From now on we will be real men and women. We will not exchange jewels and gold for glass beads, Mother stay with us.[61]

And Laksmi stayed, this time for good.

To remember the day of Laksmi's decision to remain, the women of Bengal took up the brata (vow) of Banga Laksmi.[62] On that day no oven was lit in any home. This ritual, called *arandhan*, was particularly effective in drawing women into the movement. Without leaving their houses they could show their concern for the country. Arandhan was a political gesture as well as a religious rite and thus particularly appealing. Moreover, the preparation of Bengali food was, even with the help of servants, extremely time-consuming so that women had an immediate benefit from their politically-motivated protest. Accordingly, arandhan was widely practised in middle- and lower middle-class homes.[63]

Rakhi bandhan was another protest activity started on partition day which involved women by transferring into a political context a popular custom that expressed the close relation between (married) women and their younger brothers. Once a girl moved into her in-laws' house her contact with her own family was limited. But on a particular day of the year her brothers were allowed to come and she would cook for them. Taking into account the difficulties many brides had in their new families, this day was the highlight of the annual calendar. After the meal the sister tied a yellow string to her brothers' wrists to remind them of her sisterly love once they had left. The poet Rabindranath Tagore suggested a transformation of the rite 'into a symbol of the brotherhood and unity of the people of Bengal'. On 16 October 1907 'Bengal, and particularly Calcutta, witnessed truly memorable scenes of fraternization...from which Muslim mullas, policemen and even whites were not excluded'.[64] One of the tightest bonds in Bengali families, the one between sisters and brothers, had been converted into a form of political expression.

Female activities were chosen to emphasize the comprehensive nature of Bengali dissatisfaction and to symbolize again and again the notion of India as the Mother. Thus, for instance, the preparations for the major religious festival in Bengal, Durga Puja, were linked with spinning and weaving, the most typical Swadeshi activities. Three Calcutta middle-class women, Lilavati Devi, Hemangini Das and Nirmala Sarkar:

Introduced spinning wheels and looms into the homes of their neighbour-hood [and] urged women to spin enough every day to make their Durga Puja saris. Other women were encouraged to take the vow of *Meyer kanta* to be observed by daily setting aside a handful of rice for the Motherland. Thus women would be reminded of their duty to the nation, children would learn patriotism first-hand, and a storehouse of rice would be created.[65]

Women participated only on a limited scale in the anti-partition agitation. The few examples of women's participation in the Swadeshi movement described here have been chosen because they highlight the essentialist view of women. They are by no means a comprehensive account. Such an account would include the innovative leadership activities of Sarala Devi Chaudhurani, the work of many—mostly unknown—women, such as Nanibala Devi, in support of anti-British revolutionaries, meetings of women in protest against particular events, for instance, the arrest of Bhupendranath Dutta, and spontaneous signs of anti-British feelings, such as the breaking of foreign-made glass bangles after theatre performances of Mukhunda Das' *jatra* group in support of Swadeshi.[66] Some of these activities were regarded as improper. Nanibala Devi, for instance, was not accepted at home when she was released from prison in 1919.[67] By politicizing the notion of motherhood, Aurobindo and Vivekananda politicized the female sphere. But the sphere of respectable women was still in the home; the 'extended sphere', much-analysed in feminist literature as a mass phenomenon had yet to be constructed.[68]

During Swadeshi and boycott agitations only a few women broke with gender stereotypes or colonial law. Some of them, like Sarala Debi Chaudhurani, were glorified as individual incarnations of the motherland. Her elite background, style and leadership qualities made her probably the most popular Bengali woman during the first decades of the twentieth century.[69]

But others were less fortunate. Those who neither conformed to the British image of a lady nor the Bengali ideal of a heroic woman, were singled out and harshly punished by both colonial authorities as well as Bengali society. Nanibala Devi, for instance, born in 1888 in Bali, Howrah district, supported the revolutionary movement in an unassuming way. Married at the age of eleven, Nanibala became a widow at sixteen and was then inspired by her brother to support the Swadeshi movement. But as a widow her family expected her to continue to obey the ritual restrictions connected with her status, to live and dress simply, to work in the house and to fast regularly. Instead she posed as the wife of revolutionaries in order to rent accommodation for them or, if they were arrested, smuggled messages in and out of prison. After her arrest Nanibala Devi spent several years in prison where she was treated harshly. Her revolutionary connections as well as her social background did not qualify her for the special considerations British officials reserved for respectable middle-class women freedom fighters. On her release in 1919 her family refused to take her back because her conduct was seen as dishonourable for herself and for her family. Being a widow, but having posed as a wife was an unpardonable sin for a Bengali woman.[70]

By then, however, Indian society was on the brink of a new era in women's political involvement. Non-cooperation in 1920–21 and civil disobedience in 1930 drew women out of the private sphere and into mass movements. Bengali gender ideology which marked women as incarnations of the motherland, now had to adapt to women being among the protagonists of the movement. To British officials the gradual and, later, widespread participation of Indian women in the struggle for freedom was a forceful reminder of the importance of gender issues and Indian woman-hood in nationalist ideology. Non-cooperation and civil dis-obedience apart, women protested alongside men in various satyagraha campaigns, in numerous rural protests and in revolu-tionary activities where they excelled in individual courage and will-power.[71]

Among the male leaders, Subash Chandra (Netaji) Bose, in particular, supported female activism, however, with an ideologi-cal twist which showed to what extent he still identified women with the domestic sphere. While Gandhi often restricted women to supportive tasks, Bose argued in favour of equal participation. For this purpose, he classified women into two groups, namely sisters and mothers, who were to fight and to support, respective-ly. Significantly, he chose classifications which did not carry sexual connotations. Netaji, then living in celibacy, was unable to accept sexually-active women—wives—as equals and fellow-fighters.[72]

British and Bengali officials of the Raj found it exceedingly difficult to cope with women *satyagrahis* because their activities ran contrary to what they regarded as fit for British or Bengali women. Changes in the image of Bengali women, which glorified them as saviours of the nation, could not be integrated into the *Weltbild* of police officers and district magistrates. Helpless, they tried to remind women activists of traditional female conduct. In 1922, P. Sen, a high-ranking Calcutta police officer, was still 'hoping to get them round and to create a feeling that these processions are not proper and should be abandoned altogether'.[73] When these hopes proved futile, P. Sen used his contacts with moderate politicians such as S.N. Banerjea and leaders of the Brahmo Samaj, a Hindu reform sect, in the hope of putting pressure on women to stay at home. The dominant impression among officials was that women activists had temporarily lost their reason or had been instigated into their unruly behaviour by men. The dogma of non-interference with the private sphere where women used to belong was challenged by women who came out.

Active women threatened male authority in a more complex way than male freedom fighters.[74] Political involvement and struggle was natural for men, but when women demonstrated, the ideological cosmos of British officials fell apart. In 1930, for instance, the District Magistrate of Noakhali feared the emergence of 'forces which I may be unable to cope with with barely a hundred constables' in case it came to violent scenes between 'unarmed peaceful women volunteers' and the police.[75] Large numbers of men could be *lathi*-charged and arrested. But what could be done with 'respectable' women while the urban public was watching? Against peasant women involved in the no-*chowkidari* tax movement in remote villages police did not hesitate to use lathis and even guns.[76]

The presence of women activists created disciplinary problems in the Calcutta police force. 'Any attempt made by them to assert authority has been questioned', wrote the commissioner of the Calcutta police in 1922, and he wondered when they would lose their tempers which 'has been stretched to breaking-point'.[77] A decade later, police in the mufassal faced the same problems. 'I believe our difficulties are unique', wrote the district magistrate of Tippera, and his colleague in Bakarganj informed the Bengal government, 'These encounters are apt to be demoralizing for the police.'[78]

The helplessness of the police stemmed from a strategy which aimed at avoiding women's arrests. In 1921–22, when only thirty to sixty women regularly participated in street demonstrations and shop picketing in Calcutta, the official policy was not to arrest any women 'unless in case of absolute necessity, e.g. if they are causing a hopeless obstruction'.[79] This policy did not express a special concern for women, but fear of the consequences of female arrests. In December 1921, the arrest of Basanti Devi, C.R. Das' wife, and two other women had had the clear effect of strengthening the movement. In addition, women jails in Bengal were in such a state that a respectable woman would have suffered a severe loss of status in such conditions and company.[80] This, however, would have led to a wave of nationalist protest which the government was anxious to avoid.

At the beginning of 1930 police violence against women in Contai had resulted in a Congress Enquiry Committee and much publicity in the press.[81] Consequently, the deputy superintendent of the Bengal police instructed 'all officers dealing with lady satyagrahis…to be very polite in their manners and to use the minimum of force if possible'.[82] After Gandhi's Salt March in April women participated in numerous civil disobedience campaigns in district towns in East and Central Bengal and created confusion among the local police forces. Women's activities were particularly successful when they interrupted local government by picketing law courts and other government buildings in many district towns.[83]

Police officers and district magistrates, barred in the early phase of the civil disobedience campaign from asserting their authority against women by force, recouped themselves by asserting their moral superiority over male satyagrahis. It was taken for granted that women had no independent political minds. They were either keen to escape male domination, 'jumping at the chance offered of coming out of purdah', or were victims of male 'mean tactics'.[84] In both cases, men were the active culprits, women the passive, innocent victims. Bengali men were described as culpable when putting 'their womenfolk on the streets' and deserving of little respect.[85] The Bakarganj District Magistrate wrote: '… they have literally thrown their wives and daughters into the streets with the cowardly satisfaction that they can thus cause annoyance and save their own skin.'[86] The commissioner of the Chittagong division drew his own conclusion from this and similar incidents. 'If they do not consider this a most unchivalrous act', he wrote to his government, 'I do not see how they can have any reason to resent any action taken against their women.'[87]

When it became impossible to deny that women were politically involved on their own initiative, their respectability and femininity were questioned. After an encounter with resolute women satyagrahis, the District Magistrate of Bakarganj consoled his men and himself with the thought 'that we were not the husbands of any of them. If they could perform like this in public they must be dreadful in their own homes'. Women who could not be controlled did not deserve his respect. 'They are not ashamed', he concluded, 'to prostitute themselves in this way to draw a crowd.'[88]

As long as police were confronted with women-only groups they could handle them with 'gentlemanly' tactics—carefully avoiding any physical contact—such as cutting off the water supply to their picket line in the hot sun or by cordoning them off for hours until they were bored and hungry.[89] During the Calcutta Civil Obedience campaign, however, Jyotirmoyi Ganguli and Urmila Devi, the organizers of women's demonstrations, co-ordinated their actions with male leaders to optimize the effect. To the surprise of the police, men mixed with on-going women's processions. The event was shocking to officials and the police commissioner gave an account: '...the ladies and these youths then grew violent, encircled the police officers, fell down before them, clutched their legs and seized the reins of the mounted police horses.'[90] Men and women in unity presented 'very difficult problems for the police'.[91] They could not violently break up the procession without injuring the women. More importantly their ideological stereotypes of cowardly men and manipulated women failed to explain the situation. The police needed more efficient means of control and the commissioner suggested 'applying for summons against Urmila Devi and Jyotirmoyi Ganguli and any other ladies whose identity can be established who took a prominent part in the procession'. Two months later, in September 1930, of all the provinces, Bengal had the highest number of women prisoners.[92]

For the average female satyagrahi, however, such drastic measures were not called for. Instead, the traditional institutions for the domestication of women were appealed to, namely religion and the family. A high-ranking police official suggested 'gentle persuasion' and 'most polite and courteous language' in order to convince members of the female sex of their true vocation:

They should also be told that it had been laid down in all religions that the women should be at their respective homes and look after the welfare of their family members and children and if they neglect to do it they would fail in their sacred duties and God would take revenge for their culpable negligence and their family would be ruined.[93]

Police were confident that such appeals would find support in many Bengali middle-class families who 'would really welcome action which would keep their womenfolk from participating in such public matters'.[94] Across political lines, patriarchal gender ideology, purdah, seemed to unite many Bengali families and the colonial authorities in their efforts to keep women in their subordinate positions—regardless of the essential contribution of Bengali women during India's struggle for freedom.

Conclusion

I have illustrated the power of purdah by examining how far purdah values determined women's activities, even under conditions which seemed in apparent contradiction to these values. Women's involvement in the nationalist movement was the most obvious step outside conventional norms of purdah. However, women's entrance into politics was but the tip of an iceberg, the massive base of which consisted of redefinitions of female roles in all spheres of life.

NOTES

[1] G. Rubin, 'The Traffic in Women: Notes on the "Political Economy" of Sex', in R.R. Reiter (ed.), *Towards an Anthropology of Women*, New York, 1975, p.159.

[2] J. Sayers *et al.* (eds.), *Engels Revisited. New Feminist Essays*, London, 1987.

[3] L. Segal, *Is the Future Female? Troubled Thoughts on Contemporary Feminism*, London, 1987, pp.146–7.

[4] P. Jeffery, *Frogs in a Well. Indian Women in Purdah*, London, 1986 (1st ed., 1979), pp.2–3.

[5] For more details on purdah, see H. Papanek and G. Minault (eds.), *Separate Worlds: Studies of Purdah in South Asia*, New Delhi, 1982; U. Sharma, 'Women and

their Affines: The Veil as a Symbol of Separation', *Man (N.S.)*, 13,2, 1978, pp.218–33; see also footnotes 17, 19 and 22 in this chapter.

[6] For an account of women's literary achievements, see Bharati Ray, 'Swadeshi Movement and Women's Awakening in Bengal, 1903–1910', *The Calcutta Historical Journal*, 9, 2, 1985, pp.84–6.

[7] S. Bannerjee, 'Marginalization of Women's Popular Culture in Nineteenth Century Bengal', in K. Sangari and S. Vaid (eds.), *Recasting Women. Essays in Colonial History*, Delhi, 1989, p.168.

[8] *Indian Law Report* (ILR), 30, 1903, Calcutta, p.523.

[9] G. Forbes (ed.), *Sudha Mazumdar, A Pattern of Life*, New Delhi, 1977, p.27.

[10] S.C. Bose, *The Hindoos as They Are*, Calcutta, 1883, p.2; Bankim Chandra Chatterjee, *Krishnakanta's Will*, New York, 1962, 1st ed., 1882. In early twentieth-century Bengal the rate of infant mortality was nearly three times as high as in England and increased when there were epidemics or economic crises. COI, 1921, v, 1, pp.209–10. One out of five children on an average died under the age of one. In Calcutta, the rate was even higher. COI, 1911, v, 1, p.269; vi, 1, p.30.

[11] In 1931, the average rural household consisted of five persons. M.A. Huque, *The Man behind the Plough*, Calcutta, 1939, p.92.

[12] In 1890, Ramananda Chatterjee, the editor of *Prabasi* and *Modern Review*, was upset because his family would not allow him to take his wife to Calcutta. However, Sudha Mazumdar, whose husband was posted to Faridpur twenty years later, could leave her husband's ancestral home in Murshidabad to accompany him to the district. Many women who were born during the first two decades of the twentieth century remembered their joint family home, but lived in basically nuclear units once they were married and old enough to run a household. R. Chatterjee, unpublished diary of his stay in Calcutta during the year 1890, held by Smt. Paramita Viswanathan, Calcutta; Forbes (Mazumdar), 1977, p.123; Interview with Phulrenu Chanda, Calcutta, 3 March 1985.

[13] Huque, 1939, pp.139–44.

[14] R. Mukherjee, *West Bengal Family Structures: 1946–1966*, Delhi, 1977, p.107.

[15] For comparison, U. Sharma, *Women, Work and Property in North-West India*, London, 1980, pp.134–76; U. Sharma, 'Dowry in North India: Its Consequences for Women', R. Hirschon (ed.), *Women and Property, Women as Property*, Beckenham, 1984, p. 63.

[16] A.R. Caton, 'Home and Marriage', A.R. Caton (ed.), *The Key of Progress*, London, 1930, p.102.

[17] Bose, 1883, p.4.

[18] Ibid., p.5; M. Borthwick, *The Changing Role of Women in Bengal 1849–1905*, Princeton, 1984, p.18; M.M. Urquhart, *Women of Bengal*, Calcutta, 1926, p.85; Lal Behari Day, *Bengal Peasant Life*, Calcutta, 1969, 1st ed., 1874, pp.119–24.

[19] U. Chakraborty, *Conditions of Bengali Women around the 2nd Half of the 19th Century*, Calcutta, 1963, p.5; Caton, 1950, p.104; Day, 1960, pp.48–9; Borthwick, 1984, pp.11–4.

[20] Jeffery, 1979, pp.2–6; H. Papanek, 'Purdah: Separate Worlds and Symbolic Shelter', H. Papanek and G. Minault (eds.), 1982, p.3; U. Sharma, 'Segregation and its Consequences in India', P. Caplan and J.M. Bujra (eds.), *Women United, Women Divided*, London, 1978, pp.259–82.

[21] S.C. Bose, 1883, p.18.

PURDAH AND POLITICS 37

22 Borthwick, 1984, p.228.

23 H. Papanek, 'Afterword—Caging the Lion: A Fable for our Time', R. Jahan (ed.), *Sultana's Dream and Selections from The Secluded Ones by Rokeya Sakhawat Hossain*, New York, 1988, pp.65–6; David G. Mandelbaum, *Women's Seclusion and Men's Honour. Sex Roles in North India, Bangladesh, and Pakistan*, Tucson, 1988, pp.76ff.

24 Borthwick, 1984, pp.228–70; Forbes (Mazumdar), 1977, pp.145–7; Saroj Nalini Dutt Memorial Association for Women's Work in Bengal, *Annual Report of the SNDMA from the years 1925 to 1931*, Calcutta, n.d. (*SNDMA* Report), 1926, p.22; ibid., 1931, p.17.

25 Mandelbaum, 1988; Borthwick, 1984, p.6.

26 Day, 1960, p.26.

27 Bankim Chandra Chatterjee, 1962. Elsewhere Bankim's portrait of women has focused on their representation of the liminal in the Hindu moral code and sexual desire. Bankim, it was argued, did not blame women, but showed them as victims of their nature. S. Kaviraj, 'A Taste for Transgression: Liminality in the Novels of Bankim Chandra Chattopadhyay', Nehru Memorial Museum and Library (ed.), *Occasional Papers on History and Society*, No 46, New Delhi, September 1987. Kaviraj's essay is a study which implicitly uses gender as a category to understand Bankim's artistic skills, but avoids problematizing Bankim's view of women. Kaviraj justifies this treatment of the subject by differentiating between the artist's and the real world and by choosing the former as the concern of his essay.

28 Bose, 1883, p.12.

29 Chakraborty, 1963, p.5; compare P. Caplan, *Class and Gender in India. Women and their Organizations in a South Indian City*, London, 1985, p.54.

30 Forbes (Mazumdar), 1977, pp.123–4.

31 Day, 1969, p.9.

32 Ibid., pp.23–4.

33 Forbes (Mazumdar), 1977, p.15.

34 N.a., *The Twenty-Third Annual Report of the Indian Female Normal School and Instruction Society* (issued April 1875), Birmingham, 1875, p.17.

35 Ibid., p.25; see also Mrs Weitbrecht, *The Women of India and Christian Work in the Zenana*, London, 1875, p.105, quoted in Borthwick, p.7.

36 Urquhart, 1926, pp.19–20; Correspondents, 'A Zenana', *Girl's Own Paper*, 6 August 1892, p.720.

37 R. Tagore, 'Women's Lot in East and West', *Modern Review*, 11, 1912, p.575; see also, S.C. Dutt, 'Home Life in Bengal', *India: Past and Present*, London, 1880, p.221, quoted in Borthwick, p.9.

38 R. Tagore, 'Strir Patra', R. Tagore, *Galpaguccha*, Calcutta, 1980, 1st ed. 1914, pp.669–80.

39 On the worship of the Mother Godesses, Kali and Durga, and the class-specific connotations of revivalist symbolism, see B. Southard, 'The Political Strategy of Aurobindo Ghosh: The Utilization of Hindu Religious Symbolism and the Problem of Political Mobilization in Bengal', *Modern Asian Studies*, 14, 1980, pp.353–76.

40 S. Sarkar, *Modern India 1885–1947*, Delhi, 1984, p.72.

38   BEYOND PURDAH?

[42] R.R. Van Meter, 'Bankimcandra Chatterji and the Bengali Renaissance', unpublished dissertation, University of Pennsylvania, 1964, pp.209–10.

[42] Ibid., p.74.

[43] Ibid.; on suicide as an act of female heroism, see chapter 2.

[44] Ibid., p.76.

[45] Compare Southard, 1980, pp.361 ff.

[46] H. Mukherjee and U. Mukherjee, Sri Aurobindho's Political Thought (1893–1908), Calcutta, 1958, p.25.

[47] B.B. Majumdar, Militant Nationalism in India and its Socio-Religious Background (1897–1917), Calcutta,1966, p.26.

[48] T. Raychaudhuri, Europe Reconsidered. Perceptions of the West in Nineteenth Century Bengal, Delhi, 1988, pp.300ff; Majumdar, pp.21–2.

[49] S. Sarkar, The Swadeshi Movement in Bengal 1903–08, New Delhi, 1973, pp.82–7, esp. p.83.

[50] Ibid., p.84.

[51] G. Murshid, Reluctant Debutante. Response of Bengali Women to Modernization, Rajshahi, 1983, p.220; S.N. Ray, 'Variations to the Theme of Individuality: Hinduism, The Bengal Renaissance and Rabindranath Tagore', Visvabharati Quarterly, 41, 1975–76, pp.200–9.

[52] R. Tagore, 'Women's Lot in East and West', Modern Review, June 1912, p.575.

[53] R. Tagore, Strir Patra, 1980, pp.669–80; Murshid, p.221.

[54] R. Tagore, 'Nari prasanga', Bharati, 1330, 1, p.459.

[55] T. Sarkar, 'Politics and Women in Bengal—the Conditions and Meaning of Participation', Indian Economic and Social History Review, 21, 1984, pp.99–100; R. Tagore, The Home and the World (Ghare Baire), English tr. S. Tagore, London, 1919; S.N. Ray, 1975–76, p.204.

[56] See T. Sarkar, 'Nationalist Iconography: Images of Women in 19th Century Bengali literature', Economic and Political Weekly, 22, 47, 21 November 1987, pp.2011–15, for Bengali gender ideology and nationalism.

[57] See 'Introduction', S. Sarkar, pp.22–3.

[58] G. Forbes, 'Political Mobilization of Women in India through Religion: Bengal 1905–1947', paper presented at 'Conversation in the Discipline: Women in Religious Traditions', SUNY College, Cortland, 14–15 October 1977; G. Forbes, 'The Politics of Respectability: Indian Women and the Indian National Congress', in D.A. Low (ed.), The Indian National Congress: Centenary Hindsights, Delhi, 1988, pp.57–60; Forbes (Mazumdar), 1977, p.58; S. Sarkar, 1973, pp.58–9, 287.

[59] Forbes, 1977, p.9; S. Sarkar, 1973, p.288.

[60] Forbes, 1977, p.9.

[61] Ibid., pp.10–11.

[62] Ibid., p.11.

[63] Forbes (Mazumdar), 1977, p.58; S. Sarkar, 1973, p.287.

[64] Ibid., p.287; Forbes (Mazumdar), 1977, pp.58–9.

[65] Forbes, G., 1988, p.57.

[66] S. Sarkar, 1973, pp.287–8; Kamala Das Gupta, Svadhinata-Sangrame Banglar Nari, Calcutta, 1370 (1963), pp.36–41; West Bengal State Archives (WBSA), Towards Freedom Files, No 47, pp.17, 21; Nos 51, 58, 63, pp. 7–8. For the most detailed description of women's swadeshi activities, see Bharati Ray, 1985.

[67] Das Gupta, 1963, pp.36–41.

PURDAH AND POLITICS 39

[68] G. Minault, *The Extended Family: Women and Political Participation in India and Pakistan*, Delhi, 1981; G. Pearson, 'The Female Intelligentsia in Segregated Society. Early Twentieth-century Bombay', M. Allen and S.N. Mukherjee (eds.), *Women in India and Nepal*, Canberra, 1982, pp.136–54.

[69] S. Sarkar, 1973, pp.287–8.

[70] Das Gupta, 1370 (1963), pp.36–41.

[71] T. Sarkar, 1984; G. Forbes, 'Goddesses or Rebels? The Women Revolutionaries of Bengal', *The Oracle*, 2, 1980, pp.1–15; B. Bhattacharyya, *Satyagrahas in Bengal 1921–39*, Calcutta, 1977, pp.63–5, 81ff, 95–6, 110, 193–4, 300–18; 'Report of the Contai Enquiry Committee', *Modern Review*, May 1930, pp.108–11; on women jute workers at the 1928 Congress interview with Santa Deb, Calcutta, 1 March 1985.

[72] M.K. Gandhi, *Women and Social Injustice*, Ahmedabad, 1942, p.3; M. Kishwar, 'Gandhi on Women', *Economic and Political Weekly*, 10, No 40, 5 Oct. 1985, pp.1691–702 and No 41, 12 Oct. 1985, pp.1753–8; G. Forbes, 'Mothers and Sisters: Feminism and Nationalism in the Thought of Subhas Chandra Bose', *Asian Studies*, 2, 1984, pp.29–30.

[73] WSBA, GOB, Political Department/Political Branch (Poll/Poll), 48/1022, Serial No 4 (Confidential Papers, Box II).

[74] K. Theweleit, *Männerphantasien, Band 1*, Frankfurt, 1977, pp.88–105.

[75] WBSA, GOB, Poll/Poll, 599/1930 and K.W., Notes, Appendix B.

[76] T. Sarkar, 1984, pp.96.

[77] WBSA, GOB, Poll/Poll, 48/1922, Notes, No 3.

[78] WBSA, GOB, Poll/Poll, 599/1930 and K.W., Serial No 3 and Notes, Appendix C.

[79] WBSA, GOB, 48/1922, Notes, No 1.

[80] Ibid., Notes, No 5.

[81] Dr Maitreyi Basu and Jyotirmoyi Ganguli were sent by Congress officials to inquire about the maltreatment of women. Interview with Dr M. Basu, Calcutta, 1 March 1985; 'Report of the Central Enquiry Committee', 1930, pp.108–11. The Midnapur District Magistrate rejected the Congress accusations as lies and described the women who had allegedly been stripped naked by policemen as victims of Congress propaganda and Congress volunteers, WBSA, GOB, Poll/Poll, 599/1930, Notes, Appendix A.

[82] WBSA, GOB, Poll/Poll, 599/1930, Notes, Appendix E.

[83] 'These women's hartals are all devoted to preventing people from going to court.' WBSA, GOB, Poll/Poll, 599/1930, Notes, Appendix G. Women were active in the civil disobedience campaign in many cities and towns, for instance, in Calcutta, Kalna (Burdwan division), Comilla, Manikganj (Dhaka division), Mymensingh, Noakhali, Nadia, Bankura, Barisal, Malda and Midnapur. Women produced and sold salt and picketed the law courts, in particular after arrests of nationalist leaders. These protest activities affected government more than the shop picketing in 1921–22; WBSA, GOB, Poll/Poll, confidential files, 1930–31.

[84] WBSA, GOB, Poll/Poll, 599/1930, Serial No 3.

[85] Ibid., Serial No 4; see also Poll/Poll, 48/1922, Notes, No 3.

[86] WBSA, GOB, Poll/Poll, 599/1930, Notes, Serial No 4.

[87] Ibid., Serial No 6.

[88] Ibid., Serial No 4.

[89] Ibid.

[90] Ibid., Serial No 12.

[91] Ibid.

[92] Ibid.; while the demonstration occured in June, by August both women and men had been arrested, 'Women Satyagrahis', *Modern Review*, August 1930, pp.226–7, September 1930, p.316.

[93] WBSA, GOB, Poll/Poll, 599/1930, Notes, Appendix E.

[94] Ibid., Appendix C.

2

BRIDES AND WIDOWS

Marriage and widowhood were the two most important phases in a woman's life-cycle. The first led almost inevitably to the second as a result of child marriage, hypergamy and the large age gap between husband and wife. In 1891 one in three Hindu women was a widow. The proportion of Hindu widows gradually declined over the next forty years as both child marriage became less common and the age difference between husband and wife narrowed. By 1931 the proportion of widows was down to one in four women. Still, the extent of widowhood among Hindu women was far greater than among Bengali Muslims who constituted over 50 per cent of the province's population. In this period only one in eight Muslim women was a widow because of the widespread practice of Muslim widow remarriage.[1]

Kanya day (the burden of the daughter) was largely the result of the financial costs of arranging a marriage and paying dowry. These costs occurred because of the rule of hypergamy which meant that a family improved its ritual status by giving a daughter in marriage to a husband from a higher ranking family, albeit of the same caste or sub-caste. Dowry payments were, however, not just ritual obligations, but economic transactions of often considerable size; goods or cash were an essential part of the 'gift of the virgin'.[2]

Marriage in Bengal has been widely analysed in anthropological literature. Members of the 'Chicago School' have concentrated on the symbols of marriage and related transactions for an understanding of Bengali Hindu society.[3] Most recently, L. Fruzzetti has examined the symbolic meaning of marriage and birth rituals. 'The analysis of rituals shows', she concluded

the separation and complementarity of women in relation to men in
Bengali society. Women are neither cut off from nor equal to men in the
society as a whole... In the very understanding of hierarchy as given by
the significance of marriage in Bengali society, women form one of the
culturally understood elements.[4]

This interpretation relies exclusively on the meaning of cultural
symbols and accepts the idealistic notion of complementarity. It
fails to analyse the way in which female subordination is built into
the structure of separate household spheres which determine
access to power and wealth within the family.

Whereas Fruzzetti's anthropological approach adopts a view
from inside Hindu ideology, in a contrasting approach, Borthwick,
an historian, concentrates on the impact of colonial ideology on
marriage among the bhadralok. Based on biographical data rather
than on cultural practices, she identifies the development in late
nineteenth-century Bengal of a new style of marriage incorporat-
ing qualities of romantic love and companionship. However, she
argues that the impact of these innovations was limited to 'an
individual level' without modifying the conjugal 'balance of
power'.[5] At the same time motherhood and household management were professionalized, creating a greater burden for the
bhadramahila.[6]

The bhadramahila's norms were derived from the Victorian
values of a group of reformist Bengalis. But the emulation of
colonial values only scratched the surface of Bengali traditions
without changing the power hierarchy in the family and, more
importantly, left the majority of women completely untouched.
Rather than taking a look at the symbolic structure of religious
ideals or at the changing values of a reformist minority, I focus on
aspects and consequences of marriage arrangements which highlight the impact of social and economic change on seniority and
gender relations in the family. But the extent to which seniority
and gender lent a greater or lesser disadvantage to women
depended on both the changing material conditions faced by a
family and the socio-political discourses in Bengali society.

Child Marriage and Hypergamy

Marriage was a virtually universal phenomenon for women in
Bengal. Only those girls who suffered from chronic diseases were

not given in marriage. This universality, combined with the early marital age of girls, resulted'in a much smaller proportion of the total population being unmarried than in Europe'.[7] Indeed, in 1911, only 3 per cent of all girls between the ages of 15 and 20 were unmarried. This proportion gradually rose to 4 per cent in 1921 and 5 per cent in 1931. Less than one per cent of all Hindu women over the age of 20 remained unmarried.[8]

While the universality of marriage for women remained unchanged between 1890 and 1930, child marriage—that is the marriage of girls below the age of 10—became less popular. Although statistics from before and after 1911 do not permit an accurate comparison, evidence suggests that the percentage of married Hindu girls below the age of 10 decreased continuously until at least 1921. Conversely, an increasing number of girls were married after the age of 15. In 1911 more than 70 per cent of all girls were married or widowed before their fifteenth birthday, but by 1931 the proportion had fallen to just over 50 per cent.[9]

Kanya dan (giving a daughter without expecting anything in return) was the burden fathers had to bear. The burden was aggravated by the ideal of hypergamy which made finding a suitable bridegroom difficult, particularly for girls from high-status families. Hypergamy also meant that the dowry paid for a daughter was higher than the dowry received from a daughter-in-law's family. Between daughters and sons getting married there was often a time gap, which made the'burden of the daughter' felt first.[10] Moreover, changes in the economic situations of bride-givers and bride-takers over this time unbalanced what was supposed to be an equilibrium of giving and receiving. It was in the wake of economic problems in the post-1910 period that marriage customs were challenged and sections of Bengali society started to rethink the tradition and implications of kanya dan.[11]

Religious injunctions underlay patriarchal relations in the family. Pre-puberty marriage was obligatory because only virgins were regarded as sufficiently pure to integrate into another family. This view was enforced by a Sastric injunction which indicted the father of an unmarried girl, who had begun to menstruate, for slaying an embryo and predicted that the ancestors of this girl were drinking her menstrual blood.[12] But those less versed in the Sastras practised child marriage as well, because they were concerned with the chastity of their daughters.[13] As female sexual desire was regarded to be too strong to be left unsatisfied, marriage was essential if a family's name was not to be besmirched by an unchaste daughter. Apart from the harm pre-puberty marriages wrought on the girls, little time was left to find suitable grooms and thus families were put under considerable pressure. As girls had their first menses any time between the ages of 11 and 13, by the time they were 8 or 9 years old, sometimes even earlier, their parents started to look for prospective bridegrooms.

Well into the twentieth century a large age gap between husband and wife was the outstanding feature of Bengali marriages. Almost 60 per cent of all Hindu men were still bachelors between the ages of 15 and 20 and the majority only married between the ages of 20 and 40. Ideally if the man was over 20 his wife would be a third of his age; 8-year-old girls were married to 24-year-old men. In other Indian regions the age difference between the bride and bridegroom decreased continuously from the turn of the century, but the gap remained significant in Bengal due, in no small measure, to the kulin heritage system which even allowed the marriage of 60-year-old men with pre-puberty girls.[14] The worst consequence of the age gap between husband and wife was child widowhood which rendered many girls unwanted guests in their husbands' and fathers' families without the option of remarrying or working elsewhere.

Over the years, class rather than ritual status influenced a family's decision for or against child marriage. The debate surrounding the passing of the Child Marriage Restraint Act of 1930 (Sarda Act) highlighted the fact that families from a lower class and caste background were more inclined to wed their daughters early than economically better-off families from a high-caste background. The Act fixed the minimum age of marriage at 14; pre-puberty marriage became illegal, but existing marriages, irrespective of the partners' ages, were not declared void.[15]

In the 1920s educated families began to abandon child marriages in favour of school education for their daughters and their healthy development into adulthood. The majority of witnesses to the Age of Consent Committee, 1928–29, all from a middle- or upper-class background, wanted an increase in the age of marriage. Early marriage, apart from ending in child-widowhood for many women, also meant the end of formal education in most cases. In Bengal, female education among middle-class families was comparatively widespread (see chapter 5). Because the women who lobbied, campaigned and gathered in meetings had been educated—mostly up to the graduation level—they .managed to convey the message that early marriage was unhealthy for Indian womanhood.

'It was in dealing with the Sarda Act', Geraldine Forbes has argued,'that Indian women first made their presence felt as a pressure group to be reckoned with in matters of social legislation.'[16] The Women's Indian Association (WIA) and the National Council of Women in India had both supported earlier legislative attempts to raise the age of consent and of marriage, and in 1927 the WIA collected signatures in support of Sarda's Bill in a house-to-house campaign. Subsequent National Social Conferences and All-India Women's Conferences (AIWC) passed resolutions in support of the Sarda Bill. Delegates from the AIWC went to see the Viceroy and lobbied in the Legislative Assembly while the Bill was under consideration. In Bengal, on 8 September 1928, a large number of women assembled in the Albert Hall to demand that the age of marriage be raised to 16 for women and 18 or 20 for men. The Saroj Nalini Memorial Association supported the Bill, and tried to implement the reform in villages where they had established women's groups.[17]

In contrast, many low-caste and poor families still married their daughters as children. There were usually three reasons for the continuation of the practice: to improve their ritual status, to relieve themselves of the burden of feeding their daughters or to cater for marriage expenses as soon as possible (especially in inflationary periods as in the 1920s), and to avoid having to save over a long period.[18] Reactions to the passage of the Child Marriage Restraint Act (Sarda Act) in autumn 1929 showed that low-caste and poor Bengalis felt strongly in favour of child marriage. In response to the strength of protest against the Bill the Indian government suspended the Act's implementation until April 1930. During the winter of 1929 and 1930 Bengal experienced a wave of Hindu child marriages, particularly of girls between the ages of 5 and 10; poor parents took the last chance to arrange pre-puberty marriages for their daughters. As a result, between 1921 and 1931, the percentage of wives in the age group of 5 to 10 increased by 200 per cent from 8.5 to 26 per cent.[19] Even 20 years later, early marriage was still a common feature among workers' families; in the jute mill areas of West Bengal, for instance, it was not unusual to find married girls between the ages of 6 and 10.[20]

Match-making

Traditionally, marriage was a religious rite that involved two families rather than two individuals. Marriage partners were not a matter of individual choice or of what was regarded as the arbitrariness of romantic love. Instead the decision was left to the experience of parents and *ghataks* (professional matchmakers) who approached the girl's parents on behalf of the bridegroom's family and carried on the actual negotiations. Such a proceeding saved families from the embarrassment of praising their children or virtually trading them for money; it enabled them to push their demands further than if they were personally present.[21]

Matchmaking became increasingly difficult towards the end of the nineteenth century. One reason for this was the growing choice of partners. The introduction of railways and steamers widened the radius of the circle in which parents looked for sons- and daughters-in-law. Another reason was the break-up of close-knit communities due to urbanization which made it more difficult to obtain information about suitable matches. However, at the root of the difficulties that the Bengalis faced was their changing expectations. Marriage still involved the whole family, but compatibility became a more pressing consideration. Accordingly, marriage negotiations became more complicated, eligible women were more closely scrutinized and the bridegrooms' families became more particular about the wives they selected.[22]

In orthodox families the bridal couple would not meet at all before the wedding. Radharani Basu, for example, from an orthodox north Calcutta family, who married at the age of 11 in 1904, was inspected only by her future father-in-law. Her husband was nine years older than she and, when she joined his family at the age of 12, she found it hard to live with him. By this time it was common for the bridegroom—accompanied by his father, brothers and friends—to see his future wife and to check if she had the features and abilities promised by the matchmaker. For both partners, but particularly for the bride, this was a humiliating experience. Some girls were seen by ten or more men before one agreed to matrimony. The bridegroom's relatives were aware of the power they wielded; they could afford to be choosy about girls who were not'charming' or whose family had, for some reason, a bad reputation.[23]

The examination of the bride focused on her physical appearance such as the colour of her skin and the quality and length of her hair. Pansy Ganguli, an English-educated Calcutta woman, married into an educated but conservative family at the age of 18 in 1916. She recalled with relief 70 years later that she had been accepted by the first man who came to see her. He had asked her name to discern if she was dumb, checked that she was not blind, and satisfied himself that she did not limp. In contrast, Abha Mukherjee, who went through the'visitation ceremony' in the late 1920s, was examined only on her intellectual abilities. She came from a reformist family and had studied at the Victoria Institution; her husband was a'double MA' and a disciple of Tagore. Thus he did not check her feet to see the colour of her skin, but instead had her sing and read one of her essays. In addition, he talked to her, impossible in an orthodox family.[24]

The decision about whom to marry was traditionally a patriarchal affair because the father's ritual status and the family's money were at stake. This did not imply that the senior woman was without influence regarding the choice of her son- or daughter-in-law, but the negotiations were held by the men of the family with the ghataks. Around the middle of the nineteenth century ghataks faced competition from *ghatakis*, their female counterparts, and by 1910 the ghatakis had taken over marriage negotiations.[25]

The emergence of ghatakis has been explained as a response to the lack of information urban purdah women had about the marriage market.[26] It seems, however, that ghatakis became more popular because women became increasingly involved with negotiations in middle-class families; ghataks had no access to the zenanas and female matchmakers were needed. While men continued to assess the bridegroom's schooling and academic qualifications, they no longer had time to conduct negotiations, most often due to their commitment to work outside the home.[27]

Sometimes, social changes, such as female education (see chapter 5) or the cultural westernization of men who worked in various professions, gave rise to family conflict when a daughter's marriage was to be arranged. Westernized men often opposed their

daughter's marriages before they had finished schooling, while
grandmothers, aunts and mothers were more keen to follow the
dictates of orthodox respectability. Abha Mukherjee's marriage
was arranged because her grandmother was anxious about her
becoming an old spinster. In Renuka Raychaudhuri's case, married in the early 1930s, an elderly aunt took the initiative after her
father had rejected numerous proposals.[28]

During the 1920s an increasing number of families found it
outdated to deal with traditional ghatakis and marriage arrangements depended on a number of new factors, including the will
of the wife-to-be. In her late twenties, Manilata Mazumdar
worked as headmistress at a girl's school in Serampur, but resisted
the increasingly desperate attempts of her family to arrange her
marriage. Finally, in 1940, she agreed to marry. Sucheta Kripalani,
the well-known Congress activist, was her main matchmaker.
Manilata accepted her suggestion as her husband-to-be was a
42-year-old science teacher at Presidency College. Other families
relied on newspaper advertisements, the family priest or family
friends for information about marriage partners.[29] In families
which did not ask for dowry the assessment of subjective qualities
like beauty and charm was not left to a ghataki, but was undertaken by the women themselves. Thus, the bridegroom's female
relatives inspected prospective brides for him and were extremely
particular about their choice.[30]

The services of an astrologer were essential to any marriage.
The astrologer's task was to determine the compatibility of the
couple and the predestined character of the union in the stars and
to decide on the auspicious day and hour for the marriage.[31] Once
the marriage date was fixed, cancellation destroyed a girl's hope
of a future marriage unless it was arranged within three days.
Pansy Ganguli's sister, for instance, whose marriage arrangements were broken off because of excessive dowry demands, was
married to another man within three days. He was a medical
doctor, but 'full of malaria' and she soon became a widow.[32]

The Father's Burden

The financial aspects of matchmaking were often more difficult to
arrange than those connected with horoscopes or individual
beauty and accomplishment. The issue of dowry was at the centre

of most marriage negotiations and at the heart of most problems linked with the Hindu marriage system in Bengal. Despite love and affection between fathers and daughters, the latter were seen, in general, as a burden rather than as an asset. This view was due, partly, to a daughter having to leave her father's home after marriage; in contrast a son stayed in his parental home. In sum, though, the social and financial obligations of raising a daughter and, in particular, giving her in marriage, were the most important part of the father's burden.[33]

Increasing competition for bridegrooms with the desirable ritual and economic background gradually changed the character of dowry. The voluntary character of the gift (in addition to the bride) was abandoned and dowry became essential in most marriages. Kulin Brahmans were notorious for their dowry demands. Due to their high rank they were much sought after as bridegrooms and could demand virtually any amount of money from their parents-in-law. In the 1880s, Ramchandra Mukherji, a Kulin Brahman from Hooghly, for instance, received a dowry of Rs 250 from the father of his thirty-third wife. The marriage was arranged by his son to secure the expenses of Ramchandra's *sradh* (funeral rites).[34] The amount of money paid in this case was not spectacular—about the annual income of a modest middle-class family. Yet the fact that any dowry at all was paid to a dying bridegroom showed the extent of dependency and pressure fathers faced. Traditionally hypergamy was based on the bride and bridegroom's status, but soon it came to include the economic standing of their families as well. Indian Civil Service officers or graduate bridegrooms were much desired; in 1911 a Kayastha matriculate or graduate could demand and receive up to Rs 10,000.[35]

Dowry demands gradually increased to such an extent that many fathers faced ruin 'to meet these expenses or (had) to wait reluctantly till they (had) saved enough to meet them without ruining themselves'.[36] In 1924 the British district officer in Malda testified to 'the devastating effect' of the dowry system

on the economic conditions of all classes, particularly the middle classes of Bengal... On many occasions I have had grey-haired officers weeping before me because they could not raise money to marry their daughters... In a Salaries Committee's report of, I think, 1887 I found a great deal of evidence to show that dowries had very greatly increased in the preceding twenty years. I fear there is little sign of the dowry disappearing for the oppressed of one generation become, not unnaturally, the oppressors of the next.[37]

In the 1920s, women's voluntary associations dealt with problems arising from dowry payments for girls from impoverished or fatherless families. A small dowry for, say, a widow's daughter, was two pairs of gold ornaments, seven cotton saris, one silk sari, five seers of rice, one set of articles (as a present to the bridegroom) and the cost of the wedding. In middle-class families dowries varied between Rs 1000 and Rs 4000, and were considerably more among the very rich.[38]

During the nineteenth century more and more castes abandoned the payment of bride-prices and started paying dowries. After 1900, 42 out of 51 census-registered castes were paying dowries. This development coincided with an increasing acceptance of the Brahmanical custom of hypergamy among low-ranking castes, such as the Sadgops, Pods and Chasa Dhobas.

The move from bride-price to dowry requires some explanation. Until recently, dowry was seen either as a form of pre-death inheritance or as an economic contribution by the daughter's parents to her future maintenance in her in-laws' house.[39] Both interpretations do not make sense in the Bengal context, where dowry was not paid to the daughter, but to the in-laws, and where dowry was increasingly paid for women who contributed actively to their in-laws' household budget. Instead the tendency for dowry to increase at the expense of bride-price is part of a general and widespread tendency to cultural convergence all over North India, favouring the form of marriage considered most prestigious and virtuous in the Sanskritic literature.[40]

Whereas the trend towards dowries was the outcome of elite emulation, increasing dowries have to be seen in the context of macro-economic developments. Significantly, a survey of public opinion in 1931 found that the dowry was a fairly recent development:'It was apparently not known 40 or 60 years ago'.[41] The indefinite explanation of its origination in'economic conditions' is neither clear nor does it account for its widespread occurrence.

Dowry emerged 'and increased in value in response to new social developments. Even where the bride-price system was still prevalent, as among the Sadgops in Bankura, dowries were paid for bridegrooms with university degrees. This was not because of 'any belief in education as an advantage *per se'*, but because of the better employment and higher income such a man would have.[42] As sons were sent to schools and colleges in order to supplement landed income with professional salaries, the relative exchange-value of women's contributions to the household budget decreased. Even those women who worked outside the home in the traditional sectors of the economy contributed relatively less, because men who worked in the modern sectors received higher wages. Moreover, because of the increasing commoditization of Bengal's economy and the additional income sources of middle-class families, the standard of living of these families rose as did the expectations of the majority of the people. Thus, the absolute or expected costs of supporting a daughter-in-law rose as well, and so did dowry. In the last instance, traditional concepts of femininity hampered women in participating on equal terms in an increasingly capitalist economy.[43]

Suicides

Immediately prior to the First World War the 'torture of daughters-in-law' became a much-discussed subject. The event which precipitated the debate was the suicide of a young Calcutta girl in her teens. In 1913 Snehalata committed suicide by setting herself on fire in order to save her family from the financial ruin which her dowry would have caused.[44] Whereas orthodox Hindus used the incident to argue in favour of child marriages, the majority of articles in the press saw in Snehalata's death an occasion to condemn the subordination of women and to demand the improvement of women's status, particularly through female education. Female education was the key to liberating women from their dependence on marriage. Others suggested inheritance rights for women to change their image as a burden in their in-laws' houses.[45]

Snehalata's self-immolation attracted widespread publicity, but it was not an isolated event. Many other girls committed suicide because of the financial problems created by their marriages and because of their unbearable position in their sasur bari. In 1919, in Suri, after her father had mortgaged the family property to pay for her dowry and she had been cursed by her grandmother, a girl set herself alight in a field.[46] In 1920, a 14-year-old girl drank kerosene mixed with opium because her mother had called her *dhari* (old maid), as due to the dowry problem she was still unmarried.[47]

Once the dowry was paid and the marriage ceremony completed, many young wives faced further problems. A woman's initial period with her in-laws was overshadowed by the same patriarchal ideology which justified the practice of dowry. Even without outspoken antagonism over a small dowry, girls found it difficult to adapt and girls of all social classes feared the first months in their sasur bari. Nagendrabala, for instance, from a Kayastha family and later an ally of Sister Nivedita, married and went to her sasur bari at the age of 13. She was not ill-treated, as appears to have been the case more often than not, but simply adapting to another family which happened to be in financial difficulties was traumatic.[48]

For many girls the *sasuri* (mother-in-law) was like a second mother and they became familiar with her ways and manners. But for others mothers-in-law were figures of terror who enforced the display of sexual modesty in a more far-reaching form than in their fathers' houses. In addition, in urban surroundings, families were not known to each other and could live in anonimity as compared to families in villages. Accordingly, traditional mechanisms of social control, which helped to protect daughters-in-law from being maltreated by their in-laws, could not be relied on in towns and cities.

Families were aware of their daughters' problems. Elaborate marriage rituals to protect the young bride and to secure conjugal happiness were performed with great attention to detail. The marriage ritual was the only one among the Brahmanical Hindu *samaskaras* (rites of passage to purify the male) which was performed by members of the Sudra *varna* and applied to men and women and not exclusively to men. The strictly religious rituals, *sastrachar* (based on the Sastras), invoked God's protection and guaranteed the purity of the future union. But families' anxieties regarding the social implications of marriage were expressed in so-called *lok achar* and *stri achar* (the customary rituals of men and women).[49] The wish for conjugal fidelity, for instance, was underlined by the bride placing one foot on a stone, the symbol of fidelity, and the wish for mutual love was invoked by garlanding and anointing each other. Finally biological symbols were used to arouse mutual passion and a number of stri achar expressed the hope for fertility and prosperity.[50]

In their *baper bari* (father's house), long before the extensive marriage preparations and celebrations began, girls learnt so many rules regarding their behaviour after marriage that they usually felt ill at ease in their new homes. Radharani Basu described her early years in her sasur bari as pure serfdom:

I used to obey to all the orders of my mother-in-law and my sister-in-law (husband's elder brother's wife). I always used to obey others. I had no personal opinion. I even had to obey one of our lady cooks... My mother-in-law was very proud. Being a rich man's daughter she could not understand me.[51]

Apart from sewing, cooking and household management the rules concerning a young wife's day-to-day life were numerous. Regular publications of advisory books testified to the attention society paid to the behaviour of daughters-in-law. Among the instructions for the young bride were veiling in front of superiors, keeping quiet, obeying all orders and being patient. After the first week or so a slightly more outgoing attitude was permitted as long as 'humbleness and good behaviour' were guaranteed. She had to move and speak slowly, but not too much, always bend her head, and not ask for help with her duties.[52]

Suicide was the last resort of some women who could not cope in their new homes or with their families' financial hardship caused by dowry payments. Female suicide cases were seen as heroines, as women prepared to give their lives to teach society a lesson regarding its social 'evils'. They chose death while obeying the maxims of Bengali self-effacing womanhood to the very end. Rather than ruin their fathers' fortune, their own honour or their father's family's status (by returning home) they killed themselves.

Suicide as a form of female protest was comparatively common in Bengal and had mythological backing through the goddess Sati's self-immolation. She had seen no other way out of a conflict between her father, Daksa, and her husband, Siva, without harming the honour of both. It was her death which set the example for sati (widow-burning).[53] Statistical evidence since the sixteenth century shows that in Europe the female suicide rate was about half that of the male suicide rate. In early twentieth-century Bengal, however, the female suicide rate was a third higher than the male. In 1916 Calcutta's official female suicide rate was four times as high as the male suicide rate; and the female suicide rate in Bengal was higher than in Bihar and Orissa.[54] While female suicide in nineteenth-century Europe was simultaneously medicalized and victimized, there is little evidence from Bengal for the'pathological approach' which suggested that there were gynaecological causes for women's suicide.[55] In Bengal suicide was ideologically accepted as it matched culturally specific stereotypes of femininity. Over centuries women had developed the technique of passive resistance instead of active self-realization. Gandhi who popularized the technique in India and in the west'admitted to having learnt the technique of non-violent passive resistance from women, especially from his wife and his mother'.[56] In fact, to him'woman (was) the embodiment of sacrifice and, therefore, non-violence'.[57] Accordingly, suicide was a woman's answer to many problems. Dowry demands or conditions in the sasur bari were important causes, but not the only ones.[58]

In early twentieth-century Bengal, suicide was, like satygraha, socially acceptable. But saving women from suicide by abolishing the practice of dowry became a nationalist issue during and after the war. In meetings all over Bengal young men signed petitions pledging not to accept a dowry on the occasion of their marriage.[59] Dowry refusal was seen as a sign of social enlightenment and of accepting responsibility for all members of society including women. During the 1920s this movement was supported by Gandhi. He thought it more honourable for women to remain unmarried than to have a dowry paid for them.'Marriage must cease to be', he wrote,'a matter of arrangement made by parents for money.'[60] He linked dowry payments with other alleged shortcomings of Indian society, such as the caste system and child marriages.

The publicity after Snehalata's suicide and Gandhi's opposition to dowry payments gave those families, who had managed to marry their daughters without a dowry, an image of respectability and even nationalist conviction. Young brides who until then had perceived of dowries as an essential asset to their future daughter-in-law status were now proud to be selected without any financial incentive. But many families continued to give voluntarily what had been demanded before. In other cases dowries were replaced by trousseaux, voluntary bridal outfits. Often, however, trousseaux were simply another form of dowry. The payment or non-payment of dowries continued to depend on individual families and their social and political outlook.[61]

Dowries were, to most, a heavy burden which prejudiced parents against their daughters. In this context, it is important to note that such prejudices did not lead to violence against daughters. Contemporary observers of Bengali society noted that the relatively high female suicide rate contrasted with the virtual absence of female infanticide, while female infanticide did occur in neighbouring regions.[62] While both kinds of violence stemmed from the same causes, they seem to have been mutually exclusive. Recently a link between female infanticide and cruelty to daughters-in-law has been observed in the case of Punjabi families. The Punjab was once the centre of female infanticide, but nowadays, middle-class Punjabis living in Delhi are involved in apparent dowry suicides, the killings of daughters-in-law. Such a sequence of events suggests that urbanization and profess-ionalization stressed altruistic moral values which go against the killing of helpless babies.[63]

Thus, what the British had criticized at length in Bengal—self-indulgence and the lack of martial attitudes which they admired among the people of the north-west—had its impact not just on the inter-cultural conflict between the British and Bengalis, but also on the domestic gender conflict. What might have been self-indulgence in British terms was, in Bengali culture, loyalty to the next of kin. The kin group was, however, narrowly defined and often excluded, in the case of mothers-in-law, their daughters-in-law and, in the case of husbands, their wives, especially if husbands had the slightest doubt as to their wives' sexual modesty or loyalty.

The perception of female suicide in Bengal took a woman's kin-specific pattern of loyalty into account. To parents, a daughter's suicide was a matter of immense pain, but not of shame. Following Sati's path the daughter had committed a heroic deed to save her family from financial ruin. Her courage was admired and her family was envied for the daughter's spirited decision, although pitied for the loss. The question whether the daughter had despaired over her parents' social conformity was not asked. Here Durkheim's model which explains suicide as a result of 'over-integration of social norms' seems to fit.[64] However, with regard to the impact a woman's suicide had on her in-laws Durkheim's explanation does not cover the whole ground. A family whose daughter-in-law committed suicide was at least indirectly found guilty for having driven the woman to suicide either through cruelty or greed. After her marriage the bride became a part of her husband's family with all the obligations this involved. By committing suicide she broke this loyalty. Such action was a matter of, however desperate, protest, not of 'over-integration of social norms'.[65]

Widows

In the early twentieth century some writers argued that sati, the immolation of a woman on her deceased husband's funeral pyre, was preferable to living the life of a widow.[66] Widow-burning had been legally abolished in 1829, but women still dreaded the prospect of widowhood.[67] The ideal widow renounced all worldly pleasures. She was only allowed to eat simple food and in small quantities. Once a fortnight, on the days of the full and new moon, she had to abstain from all food and drink for twenty-four hours. She was required to wear simple white saris and to sleep on a straw-mat on the bare floor; the wearing of jewellery and make-up was forbidden; and the sight of her by others was regarded as a bad omen. Most importantly, her position, unless she was old or belonged to a well-to-do family, was that of an unpaid maid servant in her father's or her in-laws' household. In poor families she had to leave the house and seek paid employment elsewhere. But at the same time many Bengalis paid great respect and attributed a high ritual status to the pure and chaste widows of their families. And elderly widows often had an important say in family matters or even replaced their deceased husbands as heads of joint families.

Apart from economic problems, which were severe in the case of poor women, an elderly widow's life was less difficult to bear than her younger counterpart's. She enjoyed the tremendous respect all older people were paid in Bengali society. More importantly, she had outgrown the age where her sexuality was regarded as dangerous. In contrast, a young widow was regarded as being full of sexual desires and this gave rise to rigid mechanisms of social control. The male fear of mature female sexuality, which was one reason among others for the custom of child marriage, was aroused by a widow between puberty and menopause. She was regarded as a source of immense attraction. The harsh regime prescribed for the widow was supposed to restrain her own sexuality and to reduce her desirability in the eyes of the remaining male family members.[68]

Many in-laws considered a widow, especially a young widow, responsible for their son's death. Her sins in former lives were assumed to have led to her husband's death.[69] Consequently, a childless widow preferred to return, if possible, to her father's or brother's house. In the last resort, however, their future—either in demure seclusion or in the labour market—depended on their class background. In a family which could afford orthodoxy and support her economically, a widow had to follow the strict rules which forbade all pleasures. Her husband's and his family's position in the cycle of rebirth depended on her conduct. Disregard for the rules had the immediate effect of dishonour and social ostracism for her paternal family, whereas a demure widow improved the status of her husband's and her father's family.

The rigidity with which the oppression of widows was practised, the number of women affected, and the actual daily routine of a Hindu widow depended on various regional, social and economic circumstances. (A table showing the regional and age distribution of Hindu widows is given as an appendix to this chapter). A higher percentage of Hindu widows lived in the western region (Burdwan and Presidency Divisions) than anywhere else in the province. There child marriage was practised more widely and female education, which delayed the age of marriage, was less appreciated. In addition, the purdah system, which confined upper-caste women to the female quarters of the house (antahpur), was more common in the west.[70]

There were fewer widows in the east—where Bengalis regarded themselves as being closer to Bengali culture than their fellow-countrymen—than in the west. The position of the Hindu middle class in East Bengal encouraged learning and self-development, values they were ready to share with the women in their families. Women were by no means regarded as equal to men, but they were allowed to move around more freely than in the west. When female education spread in the province after 1900 and girls' schools were opened, more girls went to school in East Bengal than in West Bengal.[71]

In the western part of the province, in Calcutta and its hinterland, the Muslim as well as the British influence was more entrenched than elsewhere in Bengal. While Muslim rule had been perceived as a threat to individual female chastity, British rule, in encouraging female education and women's social participation, was seen as a challenge to women's status, marriage and family, in short, the Bengali patriarchal gender system.[72] Apart from the few exceptions of reformers in the Young Bengal movement or the Brahmo Samaj, economic collaboration with colonialism was accompanied by a rigid cultural traditionalism, which reinforced the restricted role of widows.[73]

The need for security against western cultural alienation was felt more intensely in Calcutta than elsewhere, and consequently women in the capital and the surrounding area were forced to comply with more restrictions concerning education, purdah and other customs than women in other parts of the province.[74] Whereas men had to face the changing world, women were kept inside the walls of the zenana to preserve unspoiled Bengali values. Seclusion, child marriage and the rituals of widowhood were necessary to protect female honour and became status symbols. At the same time they allowed men to exercise strict control and domination over women. The home was defended as the last bastion of Bengali culture—and Bengali male dominance—in which men could and, in fact, did feel protected from British interference.[75]

The position of widows was not independent of the caste to which their families belonged. For middle-class widows the caste-specific pattern of female education was of particular importance. It delayed the age of marriage and reduced the age gap between the partners as well as the likelihood of becoming a child widow. At the beginning of the twentieth century, the daughters of an orthodox Brahman family were not as likely to receive formal education as were the daughters of the Dhaka-centred Vaidya caste. By 1930, 50 per cent of the latter were literate.[76]

Education provided some security in widowhood. Anupama Chatterjee, for example, was relatively independent of her husband's six brothers when she became a widow. She had been brought up in a Brahman joint family in Bogra in North Bengal and had attended high school until her marriage at the age of 14. After her husband's death, when she was 26, she took responsibility for the future of her three-month-old son and her daughters. She became a teacher in the Lower Primary section of Rangpur Girls' High School. She was able to breastfeed her baby at school in the tiffin hours. Her two elder daughters went to the same school, while the younger ones remained at home under the care of their grandmother and aunts. Her brothers-in-law respected her independence and strength, and each year when the harvest was divided she got more than her fair share.[77] But few women had Anaupama's choice. By 1931 only 4.9 per cent of all Hindu women in Bengal were literate—able to write at least their names—although in the past 50 years the female literacy rate had increased much faster than the male (see chapter 5).[78]

The restrictions widows faced had their origin in upper-caste ideology and were mainly observed among Bengali upper- and middle-class families. To a certain degree they filtered through to lower castes because they could be used to support the claim for a higher ritual status. Moreover, the negative connotation of widowhood could be used in situations of economic scarcity against women who were competing for their livelihood in the family or in the labour market. How far a widow was forced or allowed to follow the rules of widowhood, and how far her civil status was used to hinder her economic pursuits, depended not only on her caste and where she lived but, for the greater part, on the economic conditions of her family.

Independent of caste and class, most Bengali Hindu widows did not own land which would have provided an independent income. Only in the absence of sons, grandsons and great-grandsons or when a will in her favour existed, could she inherit her husband's property. In the case of the partition of property she was entitled to a share equal to that of her sons. But even then, according to the Dayabhaga school of law—regarded as authoritative in Bengal—a widow had minimal rights over the inherited estate. The basic concept in law was that of her maintenance. Accordingly, a widow was not allowed to sell land and, on her death, her husband's male heirs, and not her daughters, inherited the property.[79]

The actual position of a propertied widow in a joint family depended very much on her ability to defend her rights. The misuse of such women through their abduction into brothels by male kin while they were young and helpless was a common theme in contemporary Bengali fiction.[80] Mature widows were not so easy to get rid of. Male relatives tried to cheat widows of their share, particularly if the income stemmed from urban business which was more difficult to control than rural assets.[81] Others threatened to take widows to court when they insisted on their rights as documented in their late husbands' wills.[82]

Some families treated young widows so shabbily that they were forced to leave their matrimonial homes. The late husbands' families regarded this step as an implication of the forfeiture of any rights to property and maintenance. Under such circumstances widows had to go to court to secure their maintenance once they realized that they could no longer depend on their own families. In 1931, for example, the Calcutta High Court overturned a 1928 court order which had denied Sajani Sundari Debi, a widow, her rights of maintenance. She had been widowed in 1906. The family property was divided in 1910 and since then she had been treated badly. Finally, in 1925, she was unable to cope any longer. She left her in-laws' house, but found it impossible to rely on her father and brother who were both in debt. As she had married into a rich family, her gains through the court's ruling were considerable. Her in-laws were ordered to pay Rs 1326 for the jewellery she had left behind, and Rs 80 a month for her regular maintenance, backdated to the time she had left their house.[83]

If a child-widow was the sole heiress, her guardianship became a contentious point. In 1915, for instance, Atanu Nandan Tagore died, leaving 'considerable property...and an infant widow, Akhoy Kumar Debi'.[84] Akhoy Kumar's mother soon claimed the guardianship which was contested in court by Sarala Sundari Debi, a cousin of the deceased.

Yet most widows had no income of their own, and were dependent on other members of their families who had the legal duty to provide their maintenance. This did not create any problems in a big, middle-class joint family where at any time a couple of poor relatives, mostly distant unmarried uncles and cousins, found a place to eat and to sleep. Thus even a distantly-related old widowed aunt had no problem in finding a place, and even affection, if she was adept at chopping vegetables and nursing children.[85]

Young widows had no such position of influence within the family. If they were under ten, they often understood neither being married nor being widowed. It was unusual for a child-widow whose marriage had not been consummated to be left in her in-laws' home where she was of no further value to anybody. She could, however, become a useful and beloved member in her brother's family. Phulrenu Chanda, a woman born in 1906 in a village near Dhaka, recalled how her father's *pichima* (sister), who was a child-widow, always helped the daughters-in-law of the family whenever they had to communicate anything problematic to their husbands.[86]

A widow living in her husband's home often faced a difficult relationship with the female members of her own generation. A friendly relationship with her younger brothers-in-law could lead to conflicts with their wives, and living together was ideal for spreading false rumours and setting up intrigues. Throughout the period under discussion, additional rivalries would develop around newly-available consumer goods. A young widow was an unwelcome competitor for new luxuries and she was beaten, starved, poisoned, and in some cases driven to suicide.[87] The daughters-in-law, married or widowed, were all in a subordinate position in the joint family, but a widow was at the bottom of the hierarchy because she had no direct access to male protection.[88]

Rural widows of agricultural labourers and peasants and urban widows of artisans, traders and industrial workers suffered more from economic difficulties than from the ritual restrictions which were basic to the position of middle-class widows. Most of these widows, like the majority of women in Bengal, did not earn a wage. Their position in the family was not a happy one:'They never add to the income of the house, but rather form a drag to the healthful progress of the family as of the village.'[89]

Widow Remarriage and Reform

In the nineteenth century widow remarriage was common among the lower castes in the villages. At the beginning of the twentieth century, however, an increasing number of caste groups in Bengal started to restrict remarriage in order to prove their claims for a

higher ritual status. In 1906 widow remarriage was restricted to
such an extent that the marriage of a 21-year-old widow of the
Sadgop caste in Arail village, Nadia District, was advertised as a
special event of social reform.[90] A male companion was of
economic and social advantage to a widow; he provided protection and reduced the cost of living. Thus the answer to the restriction on widow remarriage was 'unmarried bliss'. In the 1920s it
was reported that the Poundria Kshatrias in the Rajshahi area,
such as washermen, barbers, potters and blacksmiths—all of them
'untouchables'—were regarded as outcastes if they accepted food
from a remarried widow, whereas no harm was done by sharing
one's hut permanently with a widow.[91]

In the middle of the nineteenth century, reformers tried to
improve the fate of middle-class and high-caste widows, ignoring
the economic hardships of poor and low-caste widows. The
reformers pursued two objectives: the arrangement of remarriages and the organization of education, vocational training and
co-operatives for widows. In 1856 widow remarriage was legal-
ized, following Iswar Chandra Vidyasagar's committed campaign. Vidyasagar spent a fortune organizing and financing the
marriages of virgin child-widows, but his campaign was not
generally supported in the Hindu community. In the 1880s his
campaign was taken up once again by the men of the Brahmo
Samaj. They helped young widows to flee from their homes and
then arranged their marriages. Yet, as the Brahmos were westernized and numbered only a couple of thousand members, their
reforms had only a limited impact on Hindu society, particularly
because many middle-class families regarded industrious
widows as an economic asset.[92]

After 1900 concerned middle-class Hindus started to organize
and finance the remarriage of child-widows. While reformist
newspapers and women's journals publicized the campaign, the
reformers were ostracized by their community. A special Bengali
term was framed to express their outcaste status, *ek ghare kara*,
which meant putting the family into one room and out of society.
For instance, Tarak Chandra Bannerjee, a Brahman timber mer-
chant from Barranagore in North Calcutta, arranged the marriage
of Tagar, a 16-year-old virgin child-widow from Baghbazar,
Central Calcutta. He had been approached to do so by a relative
of the widow. The girl's parents had been concerned about her

future as an unpaid maid-servant and, in particular, about the sexual harassment she would inevitably have to bear because of her outstanding beauty. They wanted to have her remarried, but needed a strong-minded matchmaker to make the arrangements. Tarak Chandra Bannerjee soon ran into familial problems. When Tarak's brother-in-law, a government employee in Writers' Building, heard about the plans, he strongly opposed them. Ever since he had married into Tarak's family he had feared that Tarak's social work would hamper his career, but arranging a child-widow remarriage meant that even his position within Hindu society would be at stake. He warned Tarak that it would be impossible to arrange marriages for his own daughters once the widow remarriage had taken place. Tarak refused to cancel the match he had made, but he took the warning seriously and went secretly to the wedding in Baghbazar with his family without arousing his neighbours' suspicions.[93]

The male pioneers of widow remarriage remained lone fighters. Bridegrooms were not even accompanied by their families to their weddings. Others were declared ek ghare for the sacrilege of, for example, having invited the supporters of widow remarriage to their mother's post-funeral ceremony. Such cases were not restricted to the Brahman community. A Kayastha girl, for instance, remained unmarried because a cousin of hers was a remarried widow.[94]

Widow remarriage did not become popular in Hindu middle-class society amongst widows and women. A married woman, who had lived with her husband, felt bound by her solemn wedding promises and believed in the uniqueness of their spiritual union. In addition, she internalized the ruling ideology of the loss of status attached to a widow remarriage. Anurupa Devi, a very popular author in the 1920s, criticised Bharati, which was edited by members of Rabindranath Tagore's family, for their ideas on widow remarriage. Widow marriage, she argued, was acceptable for virgin widows, but for all other widows she recommended education as a qualification for employment and/or deser kaj (service for the country).[95]

From the 1880s, shelter and employment for widows had been the prime areas of Brahmo Samaj social work. After 1886 two homes for widows were established, but middle-class families were reluctant to acknowledge their widows' needs for a meaningful life. They preferred to keep widows at home as status symbols and maid-servants. Sister Nivedita had a similar lack of success in her attempts to educate child-widows. While female education became important in the middle-class marriage market after 1900, education for widows was perceived to be a waste of time (see chapter 5).[96]

Non-twice-born caste groups started restricting widow remarriages to qualify for a higher ritual status. To them the restriction of widow marriage was a step in the process of sanskritization or elite emulation. Their terms of reference were strictly Hindu. Their improved economic conditions depended on their success in the colonial economy. Yet their socio-cultural framework was based on traditional values, namely high-caste symbols, such as the seclusion of women, which were popular in nineteenth-century Bengal. High-caste middle-class social reformers, on the contrary, were clearly influenced by western humanitarian concepts. However, apart from some Brahmo reformers, they did not argue in favour of female equality. Instead they supported widow remarriage by reference to old Hindu laws; low-caste and high-caste reformers' based their politics on Hindu religion. Reflecting the educational gap between the two camps, the former meant contemporary high-caste customs when they talked of Hindu religion; the latter profiting from their access to Sanskrit scriptures used these as points of reference for their reforms.[97]

In the 1920s nationalist innovations broke with the reformist ideologies of the past. Instead of reinterpreting religion, that is old values, new conceptions were introduced. The duties of middle-class widows in their families and in Bengali society started to change noticeably. There were three reasons for this: the stress Gandhi laid on female participation in the nationalist movement; the widened scope for middle-class social work; and deteriorating economic conditions.

Part of Gandhi's swadeshi strategy was the famous spinning-wheel campaign which transformed a traditional female occupation into a nationalist activity. Although he wanted both men and women to spin their own yarn, women, and in particular mature widows, responded in larger numbers. He carried the campaign from Congress meetings and public demonstrations into Indian homes and into female hands. Every woman was given a new duty to perform. Her work at home had suddenly taken on a new relevance in the outside world, and wearing *khadi* (homespun) saris and shirts became a political act.[98]

Gandhi's and Tagore's campaigns stressed the importance of women in India. Women were asked to apply their female skills for the sake of the nation. This meant the use of swadeshi goods in the house, and their involvement in teaching and social work as well as gradual political participation. No revolution of Bengali or Indian gender relations followed, but at the time it gave women, including widows, one of the first opportunities for wider social participation outside the family and home.[99]

The educational potential of widows, who were less restricted by claims of families and men than were married women, was discovered; the teachers' training school for widows in Calcutta gained acceptance.[100] In 1925 the Gandhian nationalist, Guru Saday Dutt, opened a central industrial training school in response to an increasing demand for such institutions from women in distressed circumstances, including widows. Moreover, widowhood became a feminist issue. In villages and towns, *mahila samitis*, women's groups, organized industrial training classes for widows and other working women. The same women's groups collected money to help needy widows finance their husbands' funerals or their daughters' weddings.[101]

The opportunities for female social and economic participation outside the home were enforced by economic changes. From the end of the First World War the cost of living had outstripped salary increases in the lower reaches of the middle class. Clerks and teachers, amongst others, found it increasingly difficult to keep up the standard of living to which the bhadralok were accustomed.[102] As a result, many of them allowed their widows to attend industrial training classes, to become involved in home industries for poorer women, and to train or work as primary school teachers.

Conclusion

Over the period under study, economic decline and the growth of the nationalist movement modified important aspects of marriage, dowry, widowhood and the Kulin legacy. However, the reform movements against dowry and the oppression of widows did nothing for women from low-caste or poor backgrounds. The

Hindu Widows Per 1000 Hindu Women

	1881	1891	1901	1911	1921	1931
ALL AGE GROUPS						
Bengal	-	-	-	257	254	226
West Bengal	-	305	-	270	282	248
Central Bengal	280	-	279	263	237-	-
North Bengal	-	288	-	229	228	207
Dhaka	-	-	-	243	244	218
Chittagong	-	-	-	-	200	175
AGED 0-5						
Bengal				1	1	2
West Bengal				1	2	1
Central Bengal				1	2	7
North Bengal				0.4	1	2
Dhaka				-	1	3
Chittagong				1	-	2
AGED 5-10						
Bengal				6	6	9
West Bengal				7	9	11
Central Bengal				6	10	-
North Bengal				6	5	9
Dhaka				-	5	9
Chittagong				5	2	4
AGED 10-15						
Bengal				34	38	22
West Bengal				40	52	25
Central Bengal				40	41	25
North Bengal				29	29	10
Dhaka				-	25	20
Chittagong				26	15	12
AGED 15-40						
Bengal	181*	172*	166*	224	232	210
West Bengal	289	263	229	229	259	224
Central Bengal	309	280	225	244	241	224
North Bengal	233	236	220	210	214	203
Dhaka	283	247	226	216	216	200
Chittagong	-	-	-	-	172	154

NOTE: East Bengal is comprised of the Chittagong and Dhaka divisions. Figures with* include Bihar and Orissa.
Source: Censuses of India, 1881–1931.

driving force of reform was not the liberation of women but the liberation of India. Accordingly, those who were not ritually but economically oppressed, like working-class widows, did not benefit from whatever improvements there were. On the contrary, while the struggle for survival became harder for the poorer classes, their leaders resorted to religious orthodoxy in order to stop the process of marginalization or to enforce the claim for ritual gains. But an improved ritual status implied the subordination of women, in this case the restriction of widow remarriage for low-caste women.

Child marriage, dowry, hypergamy and the restrictions attached to widowhood were all part of an interpretation of Hindu religion which was, in many aspects, borrowed from Kulin ideology. We turn next to discourses of sexuality in Bengali society through an examination of Kulin and other Bengali interpretations of Hinduism.

NOTES

[1] COI, 1891, III, p.183; 1931, VI, 1, pp.221, 416.

[2] L. Fruzzetti, *The Gift of the Virgin*, New Brunswick, 1982.

[3] R. Inden, *Marriage and Rank in Bengali Culture*, Berkeley, 1976; R. Inden and R. Nicholas, *Kinship in Bengali Culture*, Chicago, 1977; A. Ostor, L. Fruzzetti and S. Barnett (eds.), *Concepts of Person: Kinship, Caste and Marriage in India*, Cambridge, Mass., 1980; Fruzzetti, 1982.

[4] Fruzzetti, 1982, pp.133–4.

[5] M. Borthwick, *The Changing Role of Women in Bengal, 1849–1905*, Princeton, 1984, p.109.

[6] Ibid., p. 185.

[7] COI, 1921, V, 1, p.263.

[8] COI, 1931, V, 1, p.221.

[9] Ibid.; COI, 1901, VI, 1, p. 268.

[10] For a more detailed analysis, see U. Sharma, 'Dowry in North India: Its Consequences for Women', in R. Hirschon (ed.), *Women and Property, Women as Property*, Beckenham, 1984, pp.63–4.

[11] Probhat Kumar Mukherjee, 'Need of Hindu Inter-caste Marriage', *Modern Review*, March 1919, p.269.

[12] Yogindranath Mukhopadhyaya, *Jiban Raksa*, Calcutta, 1887, pp.15–7; B.N. Saraswati, *Brahmanic Ritual Traditions*, Shimla, 1977, pp.147–52.

[13] GOI, *Report of the Age of Consent Committee 1928-1929*, Calcutta, 1929, pp.66–7; Lal Behari Day, *Bengal Peasant Life*, Calcutta, 1969, 1st ed., 1874, p.57.

[14] COI, 1931, V, 1, pp.221; Yogindranath Mukhopadhyaya, *Jiban Raksa*, Calcutta, 1887, pp.15–17; B.N. Saraswati, 1977, pp.147–52.

68   BEYOND PURDAH?

[15] D. Engels, 'The Politics of Marriage Reform in the 1920s'.

[16] G. Forbes, 'Women and Modernity: The Issues of Child Marriage in India', *Women's Studies International Quarterly*, 2, 1979, p.413.

[17] GOI, *Report of the Age of Consent Committee, 1928–1929, Bengal Evidence*, Calcutta, 1929, pp.125ff.; Saroj Nalini Dutt Memorial Association for Women's Work in Bengal, *Annual Report for the SNDMA, From the Year 1925 to 1931*, Calcutta, n.d., Report 1927, p.32; Hemlata Devi, 'Meye samasyar kayekti dik', *Bangalaksmi*, 1334–5, pp.571–4; P.K. Sarkar, 'Banglar nari samajer prati nibedan', *Bangalaksmi*, 1335–6, pp.8–11.

[18] Day, 1969, p.57.

[19] COI, 1931, v, 1, p.221.

[20] Labour Bureau, Ministry of Labour, *Economic and Social Status of Women Workers in India*, Shimla, 1953, p.54.

[21] S.C. Bose, *The Hindoos as They are*, Calcutta, 1883, pp.41–5; Day, 1969, pp.56–60; Saraswati, 1977, pp.154–6; COI, 1911, v, 1, p.318; the last two references explain the procedure among Brahmans which deals with genealogies as well as horoscopes to make sure that the partners come from different groups of families.

[22] COI, 1911, v, 1, pp.316, 318.

[23] Interview with Radharani Basu, Calcutta, 7 March 1985; *Sudha Mazumdar, A Pattern of Life*, G. Forbes (ed.), New Delhi, 1977, pp.205–17.

[24] Interview with Pansy (Pankojini) Ganguli, Calcutta, 12 January 1985; interview with Abha Mukherjee, Calcutta, 7 February 1985.

[25] Borthwick, 1984, pp.46–7; Bose, 1883, pp.41–3.

[26] Borthwick, 1984, pp.46–7.

[27] Forbes (Mazumdar), 1977, pp.72–3: Sudha's father was said to be indifferent about the 'appropriate' timing of her marriage. Indira Debi, *Amar Katha*, Calcutta, 1912, p.43: her mother started to search while her father refused to co-operate. Amiya Sen's father was persuaded to give his daughter in marriage at the age of 14 on the promise that she could stay with him for another four years. But her in-laws claimed her before a year had passed: interview with Amiya Sen, 9 February 1985. Renuka Raychaudhuri's father delayed her marriage until she was 23 years old: interview with Renuka Raychaudhuri, 9 February 1985. Regarding the professionalization of motherhood, see Borthwick, 1984, pp.151–227.

[28] Interview with Abha Mukherjee; interview with Renuka Raychaudhuri.

[29] Interview with Manilata Majumdar, Calcutta, 2 February 1985; interview with Phulrenu Chanda, Calcutta, 3 March 1985; interview with Abha Mukherjee; Prabhat Kumar Mukhopadhyaya, 'Bibaher bignapan', *Prabasi*, 1312, pp.16–21.

[30] Forbes (Mazumdar), 1977, pp.205–17.

[31] Ibid., p.73; Day, 1969, p.61.

[32] Interview with Pansy Ganguli.

[33] Manilal Ganguli, 'Kanyaday', *Bharati*, 37, 1320, pp.1360–2.

[34] Bose, 1883, p.238.

[35] Manilal Ganguli, 'Kanyaday', pp.1360–62; COI, 1911, v, 1, 316.

[36] Probhat Kumar Mukherjee, 'Need of Hindu Inter-caste Marriage', *Modern Review*, March 1919, p.269.

[37] NAI, GOI, Home Department/Judicial Branch, 416/24 and K.W., 1924, 42.

[38] *SNDMA, Report 1926*, 28; Carucandra Bisvas, *Kanya-daya ba Hindu-bibaha-samaskara*, Calcutta, 1910, pp.8–9; Dhirendranath Caudhuri, 'Balabibaha o Darpan', *Prabasi*, 1320, 2, pp.616–25; Interview with Puspa Bose, 10 February 1985.

[39] S.J. Tambiah, 'Dowry and Bridewealth, and the Property Rights of Women in South Asia', in J. Goody and S.J. Tambiah, *Bridewealth and Dowry*, Cambridge, 1973, pp.59–169; J. Goody, 'Inheritance, Property and Women: Some Comparative Considerations', in J. Goody, J. Thirsk and E.P. Thompson (eds.), *Family and Inheritance. Rural Society in Western Europe 1200–1800*, Cambridge, 1976, pp.10–36.

[40] U. Sharma, *Women, Work and Property in North-West India*, London, 1980, p.140.

[41] COI, 1931, v, 1, p.399.

[42] COI, 1911, v, 1, p.316.

[43] This causality was first developed by U. Sharma, 1980, p.142.

[44] 'Notes: The Extortion of Dowries', *Modern Review*, March 1914, pp.366–8; Banganari, *Agami*, Calcutta, 1926, pp.20–30.

[45] Ibid.; Manilal Ganguli, 'Kanyaday', *Bharati*, 37, 1320, pp.366–8; Nagendranath Roy, 'Bibaha Samasya', *Bharati*, 38, 1321, pp.107–14; Dhirendranath Caudhuri, 'Balabibaha o Darpan', *Prabasi*, 1320, 2, pp.619–25; Muralidhar Bandhapadhyaya, 'Samaj Sanskar', *Prabasi*, 1327, 1, pp.242–9; Carucandra Bisvas, *Kanya-daya ba Hindu-bibaha-Samaskara*, Calcutta, 1910, pp.1–10.

[46] S. Mazumdar, 'A Pattern of Life in India', unpublished MSS, pp.309–10.

[47] Sundari Mohan Das, 'The Causation and Prevention of Suicide among Girls and Women', *Modern Review*, February 1920, p.143.

[48] Susanta Kumar Ghose (ed.), *Nari-ratna*, Calcutta, 1919, pp.18–24.

[49] Saraswati, 1977, pp.115–77.

[50] Ibid., pp.177–205.

[51] Interview with Radharani Basu.

[52] Saudamini Gupta, *Kanyar Prati Upades*, Dhaka, 1918, p.18.

[53] Betty Radice (ed.), *Hindu Myths*, Harmondsworth, 1975, pp.118–25.

[54] Ajit Kumar Cakravarty, 'Bange Atmahatya', *Bharati*, 40, 2, 1324, pp.691–4.

[55] M. Higonnet, 'Speaking Silences: Women's Suicides', S.R. Suleiman (ed.), *The Female Body in Western Culture*, Cambridge, Mass., 1986, pp.68–83, 70–1, 77. The only example of the 'pathological approach' I came across is Sundari Mohan Das, 'The Causation and Prevention of Suicide among Girls and Women', *Modern Review*, February 1920, pp.142–4.

[56] M. Kishwar, 'Gandhi on Women', *Economic and Political Weekly*, xx, 40, Oct. 5, 1986, p.1697.

[57] Ibid., p.1695.

[58] India Office Library and Records, V/24/3204/5, *Report on the Administration of the Police of the Lower Provinces. Bengal Presidency. For the Year 1911–1927*.

[59] Manilal Ganguli, 'Kanyaday', *Bharati*, 37, 1320, pp.366–8; 'Notes: The Extortion of Dowries', *Modern Review*, March 1914, pp.366–8; J.N. Gupta, *Rangpur Today. A Study in Local Problems of a Bengal District*, Calcutta, 1918, pp.122–4. The Rangpur Students' Association of Carmichael College, Rangpur, included the non-acceptance of dowry among its conditions for membership. Moreover, members committed themselves to not accept companions who were unsuitable in age and education and to help in every way to relax the difficulties of existing marriage laws.

[60] Kishwar, 1985, 1693.

[61] Jogesh Candra Roy, 'Darpan', *Prabasi*, 1323, 2, pp.42–7. S. Mazumdar's grandmother broke off a marriage arrangement for Sudha's elder sister because dowry had been demanded. 'A daughter of the Ghose family goes on her own merits to her father-in-law's home...' were her final words on the incident, S. Mazumdar, MSS, 309. Amiya Sen got married without dowry payments after her two elder sisters had been married with payments which continued during their first years in their sasur bari (interview). Renuka Raychaudhuri stressed 50 years after her wedding in 1935 that her father gave her wedding presents as voluntary gifts (interview). Pansy Ganguli got married in 1916 with a dowry of Rs 4000 to 5000. Her father refused, however, to pay the money in advance. He paid during the wedding ceremony (interview).

[62] 'Nari Prati Nisthubrata', *Prabasi*, 1329, 2, pp.470–1.

[63] Personal information on her fieldwork by Veena Oldenburg, August 1986; M. Kishwar, 'The Daughters of Aryavarta', *Indian Economic and Social History Review*, 23, 1986, pp.155–6.

[64] Fatima Meer, in her study *Race and Suicide in South Africa*, has shown that Indians, in particular, are pre-disposed to solve extreme conflicts in an auto-aggressive way. Although the Indian population in Durban is of mainly Gujarati descent, and although she may over-emphasize the Durkheimian stress on social rather than individual causes for suicides, her explanatory model is nevertheless of some significance for our evidence of early twentieth-century Bengal: 'It is the regulative force of the superego, constraining antisocial behaviour and developing strong guilt complexes so that aggression is more likely to be self-directed than other-directed. It suggests Durkheim's "altruism", or overintegration of social norms: Indians compared to Africans and Coloureds are more introverted, more restrained; thus perhaps their higher suicide rate. Their technique of aggression has most usually been satyagraha, which Gandhi defined as "soul force", in effect the use of self-aggression, or self-imposed suffering to shame the enemy into realizing his humanity and changing his aggression into positive feelings of sympathy. Satyagraha, shorn of its idealism, is a self-directed technique of aggression for purposes of revenge through the exposure of the inhumanity of the oppressor. Suicidal attacks often indicated desire for revenge, punishment and blame. If one cannot attack the direct cause of one's affliction, one may attack a substitute, and the substitute may be oneself.' F. Meer, *Race and Suicide in South Africa*, London, 1976, pp.51–2.

[65] In Taiwan, as M. Wolf has shown, female suicides were also more numerous than male suicides and the major causes were also connected with the problems of young daughters-in-law. Wolf suggests that women restricted to the domestic sphere had no chance of compensating elsewhere for family conflicts. Interestingly, these suicides understood their actions as a punishment inflicted on their in-laws. In fact, in-laws faced a loss of status and were blamed by fellow villagers and the wives' relations for the suicides. Thus female suicide was the ultimate form of protest and, as it sharply conflicted with social values, cannot be explained by Durkheim's 'overintegration of social norms'; M Wolf, 'Women and Suicide in China', M. Wolf and R Witke (eds.), *Women in Chinese Society*, Stanford, California, 1975, pp.111–41.

[66] See, for example, Srimati Hacel, 'Balyabibaha', *Bharat Mahila*, 4, 1909, pp.251–2; Banganari, *Agamani*, Calcutta, 1926, pp.181–93.

[67] B. Chatterjee, 'A Century of Social Reform for Women's Status', *The Indian Journal of Social Work*, XLI, 3, Oct. 1980, pp.241–54. Child widowhood was a constant concern (A. Sen, *Iswar Chandra Vidyasagar and his Elusive Milestones*, Calcutta, 1977).

[68] D.C. Sen, 'Hindu Ramanir Samajik Abastha', *Prabasi*, 3, 1905, pp.40–5.

[69] This ideology did not work the other way round. A husband was not responsible for his wife's death. On the contrary, a wife was regarded as fortunate if she succumbed before her husband and avoided widowhood (Banganari, *Agami*, Calcutta, 1926, pp.112–18; P. Vasu, *Grihadharma*, Calcutta, 1934, pp.39–48).

[70] See footnote 2; COI, 1891, VII, 183; Partho Shome, 'Tribute from a Grandson', *Telegraph Colour Magazine* (Calcutta), 3 March 1985; COI, 1931, VI, 1, p.338.

[71] Partho Shome, 'Tribute'; COI, 1931, VI, 1, p.338; Sri Cakraborti, 'Purbba Banga Assame Strisiksa', *Bharat Mahila*, 7, 1912, pp.124–6. The western-educated families in Calcutta were an exception as regards the hostility towards female education in the west. They sent their daughters to schools.

[72] See Rajkumari Das, 'Abrodh Pratha', *Bharat Mahila*, 3, 1908, pp.25–30. In the 1920s the argument was revived in a communalist context. See West Bengal State Archives (hereafter WBSA), Police Dep./Police Br. 535/29, 1–2, 1930.

[73] Interview with Malati Basak, 3 February 1985, Calcutta. In 1927–8 Brahmakumari Roy, a voluntary teacher at the Victoria Institution (girls' school) in Calcutta, went to each Subarnabanik family known to be extremely conservative and orthodox to convince it of the necessity of female education (interview with Renuka Chakraborti, 16 March 1985, Calcutta).

[74] Interview with Pankojini Ganguli.

[75] See chapter 3 and D. Engels, 'The Age of Consent Act of 1891: Colonial Ideology in Bengal', *South Asia Research*, 3, 2, 1983, pp.122–4.

[76] COI, 1931, VI, 1, pp.327–8.

[77] Interview with Anupama Chatterjee, 2 February 1985, Calcutta.

[76] COI, 1931, VI, 1, pp.326–7.

[79] Z. Ahmed, 'The Entitlement of Females under Section 14 of the Hindu Succession Act, 1956', unpublished PhD. thesis, University of London, 1985, pp.218–38. A widow who inherited her husband's share in a joint property had to administer the property with due care, otherwise she could be brought to court for 'waste', Durga Nath Pramanik *v.* Chintamoni Dassi, I.L.R., 1904, 31, Calcutta, p.214.

[80] P. Mitra, *Premendra Granthabali*, Calcutta, n.d., pp.1–48.

[81] Mathura Sundari Dasi *v.* Haran Chandra Saha, I.L.R., 1916, 43, Calcutta, p.857.

[82] Poorendra Nath Sen *v.* Hemangini Dasi, I.L.R., 1909, 36, Calcutta, p.75.

[83] Sajanisundari Dasi *v.* Jogendrachandra Sen, I.L.R., 1931, 58, Calcutta, p.745.

[84] Sarala Sundari Debi *v.* Hazari Dasi Debi and Gossain Dasi Debi *v.* Hazari Dasi Debi, I.L.R., 1915, 42, p.953.

[85] Forbes (Mazumdar), 1977.

[86] Interview with Phulrenu Chanda, Calcutta, 3 February 1985.

[87] See, for example, R. Tagore, *Ghare Baire*, Calcutta, 1916; Debiprasanna Rayachaudhuri, *Murala*, Calcutta, 1892.

[88] Interview with Aroti Ganguli, 3 March 1985; Rayacaudhuri, *Murala*; Sudhir Candra Bhandhapadhyay, 'Kalikatar Natik Abastha', *Prabasi*, 6, 1908, pp.427–35.

[89] N.C. Bhattarcharyya, L.A. Natesan (eds.), *Some Bengal Villages*, Calcutta, 1932, p.73; see also Introduction and chapter 5 and R. Mukherjee, *Six Villages of Bengal*, Bombay, 1971 (written in 1946), p.71.

[90] COI, 1931, VI, 1, 416–17; *Indian Ladies Magazine*, 4, 1906 (November), p.175.

[91] B. Seth, *Labour in the Indian Coal Industry*, Bombay, 1929, p.135; WBSA, Commerce Dep./Commerce Br., F 2R/26, B 1923, Proc. 77, *Report of Dr D.F. Curjel on the Conditions of Employment of Women Before and After Childbirth*; Government of India, *Report of the Age of Consent Committee, 1928–1929, Evidence Volume Bengal*, Calcutta, 1929, pp.229–30.

[92] S. Sastri, 'Autobiography', unpublished English translation, Calcutta; M. Borthwick, 1984, pp.49–50, 365.

[93] Interview with Monica Chatterjee, 7 February 1985, Calcutta.

[94] Ibid.; Phulkumari Debi, 'Bidhaba Bibaha', *Prabasi*, 3, 1905, pp.100–3; 'Bidhababibaha o Hindupatrika', *Bharati*, 33, 1909, pp.252–6.

[95] Anurupa Devi, 'Narir Sthan', *Bharati*, 46, 1923, 1, pp.517–26.

[96] N.C. Ray, 'Bharater Strisiksar Phal', *Bharati*, 14, 1890, pp.336–40; S.K. Caudhurani, 'Narisiksa o Mahila Silpasram', *Bharati*, 37, 1913, pp.1190–3; Borthwick, 1984, p. 285; J.C. Dasgupta, 'Bagani Nivedita', *Banga Mahila*, 7, 1912, pp.142–4; S.P. Basu, *Amader Nivedita*, Calcutta, n.d., pp.68–9.

[97] Just as opponents and supporters of widow remarriage backed their arguments with references to Hindu law so did British opponents and supporters of anti-sati legislation in the 1820s. Within the orientalist view of India, Hindu religion provided the most authoritative backing, L. Mani, 'The Production of an Official Discourse on Sati in Early Nineteenth-century Bengal', in F. Barker *et al.* (eds.), *Europe and Its Others*, Vol.1, Colchester, 1985, pp.107–27.

[98] Interview with Renuka Ray, 1 February 85, Calcutta; M. K. Gandhi, *Women and Social Injustice*, Ahmedabad, 1942, pp.163–8.

[99] Ibid.; Uma Das Gupta, *Santiniketan and Sriniketan*, Calcutta, 1983, pp.21–4.

[100] Government of Bengal, *Progress of Education in Bengal 1912–13 to 1916–17*, Calcutta, 1918, p.70.

[101] SNDMA, *Report 1925*, 9; SNDMA, *Report 1926*, 16, 22–5, 28; *Banga Laksmi* 1928–9, p.69.

[102] S. Sarkar, *Modern India, 1885–1947*, Delhi, 1983, pp.168–78.

3

SEXUALITY

Sexuality was central to a number of different discourses in Bengali society. Here we shall look at the construction of sexuality in Bengali Hinduism, in contemporary marriage manuals and in the regulation of marital and extra-marital affection. Although discursive strategies apparently aimed at social harmony, in most cases male sexual satisfaction was the underlying purpose. Finally, the discursive presentation of prostitution and marital consummation in Bengali society and in the colonial context will be traced to highlight assumptions regarding female nature and male dominance/authority on the one hand and Bengali licentiousness versus English civilization on the other.

Bengali Hinduism and Sexuality

'Women draw sacred attention', two feminist anthropologists have argued, 'primarily in connection with their reproductive statuses.'[1] Their point is that religious discourses deal with women only in relation to their biological sexuality. Moreover, in many religions female sexuality is seen as contaminating and polluting, and as a potential bringer of evil.[2] In Hinduism, in addition, female sexuality is associated with a particular power. In Bengal this power is reflected in the cult of the Mother Goddess in her two different incarnations: destructive Kali and benign Durga.

The contradiction between pollution and power, vital to the understanding of purdah, requires an explanation, especially because the respect in which the Mother Goddess is held is unique to Hinduism. The most common explanation of the hierarchical structure of Hinduism—a view most comprehensively expounded by the anthropologist Louis Dumont—focuses on the dichotomy between purity and impurity. This interpretation is based on the concept of *dharma* according to which the religious man 'seeks...by means of purity maintenance...social harmony (dharma) and good rebirth'.[3] Purity as 'the principal idiom of status differentiation' implies a 'major pre-occupation with the maintenance of female chastity';[4] sexuality is regarded as a dangerous source of pollution which needs to be strictly controlled. The status of a caste, a family and Hindu males in general depends to a large extent on female purity: 'primarily on that of their sisters and daughters whom they give in marriage, and secondarily on that of the women they take in as wives.'[5]

This view, however, is based on a monolithic interpretation of Hinduism. It does not explain the high status and domestic power which senior women held and exercised in the household. It does not address those ideological strands which made purdah acceptable to women—apart from the rewards which came with seniority in the female household hierarchy.

In a more sophisticated explanatory model, Michael Allen has qualified the 'purity–impurity' dichotomy. He argues that it reduces 'the complex ideology that focuses on women to a simple opposition between the pure and the impure', represented by 'such extremes as the pure virgin and the menstruating widow'.[6] Such a view perceives a woman as either in danger and in need of male protection as in the case of a virgin, or as dangerous, polluting and in need of male control as in the case of a menstruating widow.

Women's apparently destructive power can become potentially both creative and positive. Women are regarded as aggressive, malevolent and destructive if their *sakti* (power) is not under male control. Both men and women have sakti, but men are regarded as cultured and superior. Whereas *prakriti* (nature) is the second facet of femaleness, *purusa* (spirit) is the second aspect of maleness. Although prakriti and purusa are contained in every human being, the former is dominant in women and the latter in men. Therefore, only if the male purusa (spirit, culture) reigns over the female prakriti/sakti combination can femaleness imply fertility and benevolence.[7] Within this context women have no ritual identity independent of their fathers or husbands. But the extent to which they were subordinated or honoured depended on the spiritual goals of their husbands.

While purity is the 'encompassing' goal in Hindu ideology, there are other—although ritually inferior—ideological goals such as *artha* and *kama*.[8] They are achieved through worldly success and sensuous gratification, and are based on 'life affirmation as against life renunciation'.[9] Hindus who follow these paths to salvation value women, according to Allen,'on three counts; as providers of labour useful for property acquisitions, as producers of children, especially sons, and as source of a divine energy that can be trapped and utilised in the pursuit of worldly goals'.[10]

The attitude to women expressed here is far more positive than the one underlying the purity–impurity dichotomy, but women are nevertheless only seen as means to the ends of wealth, male progeny and the transformation of male sexuality into spiritual power. Moreover, women are valued for their ability to nurture children and to maintain the male lineage in the joint family.[11] Female sexuality is venerated 'as a source of ecstasy that is either paradigmatic of man–god relations (as in *bhakti* devotionalism) or as a means of achieving liberation (as in Tantrism)'.[12]

The interpretation of Hindu texts which was dominant in Bengal contained different concepts of femininity. Tantrism, the Vaisnava bhakti cult and Kulinism were part of Bengal's living tradition. As such they were influential in determining the position of women in Bengali Hindu society and the practice of purdah. All three religious philosophies were no longer as dominant as in past eras, but most families still followed the customs and rituals associated with them. Whereas Kulinism was a rigidly hierarchical system which enforced Brahmanical superiority based on the purity of the male lineage at the cost of women, Tantrism and Vaisnavism were anti-Brahmanical, esoteric and based on individual conviction and participation.

Tantrism can be traced over more than a thousand years of Bengali history. It is difficult to assess how far the position of ordinary women was influenced by the cult, but it is very likely that the Tantric notion of female power reinforced the idea of women in need of male control to the extent of making purdah women socially invisible, although this stemmed originally from the concept of dharma. Moreover, Tantrism propagated the strength of female sexuality which was taken as an argument for the necessity of child marriage in order to protect women from extra-marital sex to satisfy their desires.[13]

Tantrism was widely accepted in eastern India. In its early days the popularity of the cult was probably related to its similarities with certain aspects of Buddhism, which survived as the dominant religion in the north-eastern region of India longer than elsewhere on the subcontinent.[14] Bengali folk tales which were written between the eighth and twelfth centuries were influenced by Tantrism.[15] Since the fifteenth century even Krisna worship by orthodox and Sahajiya Vaisnavas showed a strong impact of Sakta Tantrism.[16] During the nineteenth century, Ramakrisna Paramahamsa, the priest of a Kali temple in the vicinity of Calcutta, preached neo-Saktism. His mystical union with the Great Mother, his esoterical rituals and his rejection of Brahmanic as well as western rationalism were extremely popular among the Bengali middle class.[17] His gospel paved the way for Sri Aurobindo and other nationalist leaders in Bengal, who focused on the alleged identity of the Mother and India in their propagation of Indian nationalism.[18] This was definitely not without significance for the position of Bengali women; often the gospel of Ramakrisna and his disciple, Vivekananda, was cited in support of a wide range of social reforms (see chapter 1).[19]

In Tantrism, as in Saktism, the Supreme Mother is worshipped as the chief god.[20] Sakti, female power, is the concept of divine energy in its dynamic aspect as compared to Siva who symbolizes the static aspect:

Siva and Sakti as Brahman, are inseparable and non-different from each other. Sakti is the supreme energy (Para Prakriti) of Siva, the supreme self... The Sakti creates, preserves, and destroys the world at the mere will of Brahman. In other words Siva creates, preserves and destroys the universe through his Sakti.[21]

The Sakta Tantric aims at the mystical experience of the 'union of male and female energy'.[22] The final goal is 'to achieve freedom from the miseries of worldly attachment'.[23] However, rather than renouncing the world he tries to go through the experience of all temptations and desires with the aim of relinquishing 'his own desire and self and convert[ing] the various pursuits of enjoyment into instruments of spiritual discipline'.[24] These desires are presented by the five 'm's, namely *madya* (wine), *mansa* (meat), *matsya* (fish), *mudra* (parched cereal) and, the most important, *maithuna* (sexual intercourse).[25]

The Tantric's sexuality is activated with the aid of the female partner but, as the ultimate goal is the retention of the semen and the transformation of sexual energy into spiritual energy, the woman is more of an assistant rather than a valued partner.[26] The goddess Parvati, the archetypical female consort, is furious 'because she is asked to join her partner in coitus not in order to activate her own reproductive potential by the gift of the semen, but to assist the male in first producing and then retaining the semen'.[27]

Tantric sources are contradictory regarding independent female participation in the ritual and mystic experience. Without doubt orthodox Tantrism leaves no space, as Allen puts it, 'for undue feminist hopes' and denies the necessity of any ritual performances by women 'except that which consists in the service of the husband'.[28] Less conformist scriptures, however, allow women to receive a mantra, to be a guru and to initiate other disciples. Here, women are perceived as the embodiment of the Devi, the supreme Goddess. 'For this reason all women are worshipful, and no harm should ever be done to them, nor should any female be sacrificed.'[29] Such differences depend on the extent to which the female principle is worshipped as a separate entity apart from its materialization as a woman.

A similar problem arises between the followers of orthodox and Sahajiya Vaisnavism (*sahaj*, easy). In Vaisnavism, bhakti (religious devotion for Krisna) is modelled on the ideal of the love of the Gopis and, in particular, Radha for Krisna. 'In Vaisnava-sahajiya thought', which was a coalescence of orthodox Vaisnava devotionalism and the esoteric teachings of the Tantras:[30]

women of course embody Radha, and as such are the means to realization. But because of the primacy of Radha in the thought of Bengal and probably also because of the Tantric tradition, women were highly esteemed among orthodox Vaisnavas as well.[31]

Followers of the Sahajiya school value real women in order to experience the intense feeling of 'love in separation' as the equivalent of the worshipper's relationship to Lord Krisna, whereas orthodox Vaisnavas take Radha's love for Krisna as the ideal they try to emulate in a spiritual experience. For Sahajiya Vaisnavas the separating line between the divine and the human does not exist and thus spiritual union with the god can be

experienced through a physical union with a woman, provided it
is done in the right state of mind. 'Thus, when one realises himself
as divine', as the key to the oneness of spiritual and carnal love,
'one experiences in union not the insignificant joys of human love,
but the perpetual divine joys of the love of Radha and Krisna.'[32]

The ideal final stage, however, is to feel the love of both Radha
and Krisna in one through the stimulation of a woman. This
feeling in its highest form is felt as true love, *prema*; it is free of
carnal desire, but is of utmost intensity. The feeling is increased
through a twofold separation: on the one hand, the woman is
unattainable because she is absent, and on the other hand she is
married to another man as were Radha and the gopis.[33] For the
most devoted worshipper of the Vaisnava belief women excel in
their absence. But they are essential and highly valued and not
inferior because of their innate impurity.

Abandoning the notion of purity—as orthodox Vaisnavas and
much more so Tantrics do—is a revolutionary action seen in the
context of the most oppressive Brahmanical tradition. Thus the
revival of Vaisnava faith at the turn of the fifteenth century in
Bengal through the inspiration of Caitanya must be seen as a
genuine protest movement which was unwelcome to the
dominant Brahmanical society; it cannot be marginalized as a
secondary channel of protest, 'a mechanism for devia-
tion...provided by the society itself'.[34] However, one can only
speculate over the causes:

the decay and subsequent 'corruption' of Buddhism, the prevalence of
extreme Tantric schools with their potential licentiousness, the aridness
and dogmatic rigidity of Brahmanism in both social and religious spheres,
and the impact of Islam, especially Sufi Islam with its emotionalism.[35]

The attitude of Vaisnavism towards women can be described
with only slightly more precision than its origins. While the guru
of Vaisnava revivalism, Caitanya (1486–1533), found 'that even
conversation with a woman is deluding and destructive to true
devotion', women were later accepted as worshippers and, among
Sahajiyas, as gurus because of their identity with Radha.[36]
Moreover, in contrast to orthodox Hinduism which excluded
women from reading and even citing the holy mantras, Vaisnavism favoured female education. In 1830, a government report
on vernacular education noted that 'the only exception to the

universal illiteracy among females was found among the mendicant Vaisnavas, who could read and write and instructed their daughters'.[37]

Vaisnavism was the religion of the vast majority of the Hindu peasantry in Bengal, whereas the bhadralok tended to be Saktas. In late nineteenth-century Bengal, Caitanya's Vaisnavism became a major target of the Hindu revivalist movement, which rejected the notion of love and supported strength as the most desired quality in men.[38] The sources on the influence of Saktism or Tantrism in Bengal are much more copious than on the influence of Vaisnavism, which can only be inferred in an indirect way. On the literary level the bhakti movement added a new emotional dimension to Tantric poetry.[39] On a spiritual level, Ramakrisna's neo-Saktism 'was blended with emotional bhakti'.[40]

An evaluation of the political impact of Vaisnavism may prove to be more fruitful in assessing the extent of the influence of the philosophy in Bengali society. It has been argued by A. K. Majumdar that even Aurobindo's veneration of Sakti, the Mother, had strong Vaisnava traits because of its emotionalism.[41] It is, however, more to the point to examine the bhakti influence on Gandhi. Broomfield suggests that one aspect of the conflict between the Bengali bhadralok nationalists and Gandhi was the spiritual differences between their respective nationalist ideologies. The Bengali elite insisted on individual action and the significance of a strong leadership, whereas Gandhi propagated passive mass involvement.[42] Judged by the latter's success, particularly with regard to female participation in Bengal, future research might ask whether Vaisnava ideals were also influential in the everyday lives of Bengali women.

Orthodox Vaisnavism and Tantrism focused on the disruptive and dangerous aspects of femininity. Such a focus cannot be blamed for the rigid seclusion of women in eighteenth- and nineteenth-century Bengal. Yet the value system underlying purdah which stresses chastity and modesty was shared by orthodox Vaisnavism and Tantrism to the extent of excluding women from participating in religious rituals.

Kulinism, however, with its stress on purity provided a straightforward endorsement of strict purdah. In Kulinist ideology the implementation of the concept of purity reached its high point; Kulin women suffered the worst oppression, particularly

through the custom of polygamy. According to Kulinism, the
successive Hindu kings of Bengal ranked Brahman and Kayastha
sub-castes and clans in order to uphold the hierarchical social
order. The Kulins, the group at the top, were considered particularly pure and thus enjoyed the protection and material support of the king. Historically this development coincided with
Muslim invasions and later the conquest of Bengal from the
twelfth to the sixteenth century.[43] Political developments rendered
collaboration with impure non-Hindus necessary for the Bengali
elite. Therefore, the strict code of conduct in the non-domestic
sphere was abolished and rank came to be assigned through
transactions in the domestic sphere, namely through the gift of
daughters. 'From now on', in Inden's view, 'marriage, which had
been considered the necessary but not sufficient act by which
embodied rank was sustained, becomes in and of itself the
primary act of worship by which rank is to be sustained.'[44]

While Hindu political authority was fading, Hindu society—in
this case Brahman and Kayastha sub-castes—assumed the duty of
worshipping and supporting the Kulins. Hypergamy into a Kulin
family was the only way for Bengali upper-caste families to improve their ritual status. They paid for their ritual status with large
sums of money, dowries, which expressed on the one hand the
purity of their intentions through the gift of their daughters, and
on the other hand the acceptance of their duty to support the
Kulins.[45]

The Kulin concept of marriage was based on the field (womb)
and seed (semen) theory. The Kulins were assigned the superior
power 'to transform inherited rank into superior fruits'[46] and,
simultaneously, to improve the ritual status of the girls' families.
This, however, was only possible if the bride's inherited 'bodily
substance' was 'considered to be suitably transformable by her
husband and his clan'.[47] The respective rules were numerous with
regard to the age and family background of the bride, but most
important was the regulation which excluded girls who had
reached puberty from transformation and thus excluded them as
marriage partners.[48]

Many social 'evils' for which nineteenth-century Bengal was
notorious—and which subordinated women—were closely related to Kulinism. The importance of 'the bodily substance' and
purity heightened the concern for female purity and chastity. The

rigidity of purdah had here, at least partly, its source. Polygamy was the logical outcome of a strictly hypergamous marriage system. By the middle of the nineteenth century, polygamy had lost its social acceptability. The most excessive examples of impoverished Kulins marrying up to 100 women belonged to the past.[49] These women had lived in their fathers' houses, virtually as strangers to their husbands who only visited them at irregular intervals to enjoy both their conjugal rights and the financial support of their wives' families.[50] But a milder form of polygamy, with two or three wives living in the husband's house, still existed at the turn of the century, a truncated legacy of the Kulinist extreme which did not conflict with other strands of Hinduism.[51]

Child marriage and child widowhood were the worst consequences of Kulin ideology. Both had existed before the emergence of Kulinism, but its obsession with hypergamy had increased the strain on parents of finding a suitable groom.[52] Parents of daughters were thus driven to accept matches whenever they were offered, virtually irrespective of their daughters' youthful age. Hence, age differences between husbands and wives were very wide. Elderly Kulins who needed money arranged to have other wives who would bring considerable dowries.[53] Due to the age gap, wives were very often still in their childhood or youth when they became widows.

A brief glance at different religious movements has indicated that there was a variety of traditions backing the sexual control and seclusion of women or their subordinate position as helpmates to men. We can only infer from the literature how important religious values were for the illiterate majority of the Bengali population. Any inferences drawn with regard to rural people on the basis of bhadralok norms must take into account general religious differences. The bhadralok were predominantly worshippers of Sakti, while the rural population venerated Krisna who symbolized a more lenient view of the dangers connected with femininity. Moreover, knowledge of the Sastras was transmitted in Sanskrit and therefore excluded the illiterate majority from knowing, for instance, the injunctions which prescribed child marriage. But the *Ramayana* was common knowledge. And there women's sexual weakness was implied when Sita's conjugal loyalty was only assumed while she was under her husband's or brother-in-law's control.

In addition, there is evidence to suggest that the purity–pollution dichotomy was as significant for male control of women at the bottom of the Hindu hierarchy as it was at the top. Based on fictional evidence, Rajat K. Ray has analysed patterns of sexual control in an untouchable community in West Bengal at the turn of the century. According to Ray, high-caste women were deprived of social freedom and kept as incarnations of ritual purity; low-caste women were seen by their men as the epitome of pollution which increased their vulnerability under conditions of economic scarcity.[54]

Marriage Manuals

Marriage manuals went into sexual details, where Hindu ideology only set the norms. Although their readership was class-specific, there was a buoyant market for marriage manuals in the late nineteenth century. This proves that, at least for the Bengali or English-educated middle classes, sex was of great private interest.[55]

At the close of the century, advisory books on marital life appeared in numerous editions. The most popular publication seems to have been *Yuvak-yuvati* by Bipradasa Mukhopadhyaya, first published in 1891, but reprinted seven times before 1922. The publication was a popular guide book on various subjects related to the development of the female body, sexual intercourse, pregnancy, birth and child rearing. It was written as a dialogue between doctor and patient, suggesting a western scientific approach to the problems. In addition, it contained many traditional Hindu rules regarding the times suitable for intercourse and the code of conduct for menstruating women.[56] The general emphasis was on the regulation of sexuality and the danger and disorder which would result if sexuality, particularly youthful sexuality, was not controlled.

In a number of examples the physical development of girls, it was suggested, would follow from socially acceptable behaviour. Breasts would grow, *Yuvak-yuvati* pronounced, if a girl did regular work in the household.[57] Incidentally, this causal connection was similar to the observation that educated urban women were weak because they missed the exercise rural women had while fulfilling their daily household duties.[58] Another assumption, widespread

in Bengali society, and mentioned in the guide book, referred to
the inducement of puberty. Girls in the company of their husbands
were said to be sexually stimulated and thus reached puberty
earlier.[59]

While menstruating, a woman was impure and dangerous. To
keep in physiological balance, a woman was advised to avoid any
additional burden, such as bathing, cutting nails, crying and loud
noises. The danger originating from a menstruating woman was
heightened, readers were told, by her allegedly increased sexual
desire before and after menstruation. The ideal time for sexual
intercourse was twelve days following the end of the period.
However, intercourse on the first three days of the period was
dangerous: if sex took place on the first the husband would die
early; on the second no child would be conceived; and on the third
the child conceived would be weak and retarded.[60]

The guide book underlined the idea that women were closer to
and more dependent on nature than men. 'Nature as destiny' was
more than a slogan when the day of the week on which a women
first bled was said to determine if she became a widow or a happy
wife. The month of the first period was important as well and so
were a woman's physical attributes: a woman with oval, veinless
and hairless thighs would become a queen.[61]

Yuvak-yuvati was not the only guide book on marriage. Others,
like Yogindranath Mukhopadhyaya's *Jiban Raksa* and Baradakanta Majumdar's *Naritattva* went into even greater detail regarding
the sexual facts of life, and were sometimes read by young men
instead of scarce pornographic literature.[62] Majumdar's *Naritattva*
expounded reformist views on medical questions and called for a
prolonged period of *gaona* (the bride's residence at her father's
house during the period between marriage and sexual maturity)
so as to delay the onset of the first menses.[63] Majumdar's idea of
female progress and health was less concerned with a woman's
happiness than with the advantages society would derive from
healthy and educated women. Women, he argued, did not have
inferior intellects, but they could not concentrate and think logi-
cally like men. Consequently, their ethical, religious and practical
education should emphasize their future responsibilities as
housewives and mothers.[64]

Jiban Raksa emphasized the necessity of controlling female
sexuality. Daily sexual intercourse was bad, the author believed,

as were sexual day-dreams which led to involuntary orgasms and the weakening of the body. Sex was acceptable provided it was practised at three-day intervals. Various times of the day, however, were said to be unsuitable for sex. Among them were the evening, the early morning and the middle of the night and day. In addition, the body was allegedly unfit for sexual excitement after meals, after a sradh ceremony, after the death of parents (for one year), on Sundays and on astrologically important days. Intercourse threatened both the bodily substance and purity; sex had to be avoided when both were otherwise endangered. Accordingly, sex—like vomiting, bad dreams, shaving and a visit to a burning *ghat*—had to be followed by a bath.[65] In these rules on when to have sex women were identified with pollution. Womanhood was presented as a punishment; a man who left a good wife would, the reader was warned, be reborn seven times as a woman and a wife.[66]

Apart from the regulation of sexual practices, the male orgasm was the unchallenged focus of the treatise. Couples were admonished not to delay the male orgasm because otherwise semen would enter the urinal tract and create physical disorder. Moreover, a man should not lie on his back while making love because this would lead to diseases.[67] This seemingly scientific discourse on sexuality did little to disguise the fact that the satisfaction of men was its purpose.

The notion of women as sexual servants was underlined by other issues in Bengali society. In the case of female attire women and their needs were subordinated to male assumptions regarding propriety. Traditionally women wore a thin, virtually see-through sari, without a blouse or a petticoat. The thin piece of cloth hardly covered their bodies. Although men and women were not supposed to meet or to speak during the day, the knowledge that there was a group of semi-dressed women in the zenanas was a source of pride for men. In addition, men could be sure that the women would not leave the zenana insufficiently dressed.[68]

Around the middle of the nineteenth century Brahmo women gradually started to leave the zenana modestly dressed in heavy saris, petticoats, long-sleeved blouses and veils over their hair which covered their whole bodies apart from their faces and hands. But Hindu women did not alter their dress habits to the Brahmo style until the turn of the century. Still, men continued to

criticize chemises and petticoats. Women, however, won this bat-
tle against male control, and the sari-cum-petticoat, blouse and,
for some, even shoes became the standard outfit.[69] A change in the
dress code was also a pre-condition for the liberalization of social
interaction between men and women or, to be more specific,
between husband and wife.

Affection

Courtship developed only gradually in middle-class families.
Even in the Brahmo community, where in the 1920s love marriages
were common, it was only in exceptional cases that pre-marital
courtship included unaccompanied excursions. This point is illustrated by the experience of Suniti Devi, a second-generation
Brahmo, whose father's friends included the Sadharan Brahmo
leader, Dwarkanath Ganguly, as well as Ramananda Chatterjee.
Due to such influences her education—she was a pupil of the
Maharani Girls' School in Darjeeling—was never in question. She
met her future husband, the eldest son of Hemlata Sarkar, at
school in 1910 and enjoyed his gallant attempts to see her before
they got married:

My husband's courtship might send the modern generation into gales of
laughter, because we were too shy to speak too much to each other and
the puritanic Brahmo code, which was somewhat Victorian, did not
permit any romantic outings together. However, my husband was an
excellent rider and he used to ride round and round the hilly track
overlooking our school and I made sure that I was out in the gardens,
with a copy of Shelley in my hands, to watch him and be watched by
him.[70]

In the early 1930s, in other Brahmo families, pre-marital
courtship went a little further. Prathiba Chatterjee was born in
1910 into a Navabidhan Brahmo family. Her parents had met
before their wedding and they regularly took their meals together,
then a common practice in Brahmo families. Before Prathiba's
engagement her future fiancé was asked to come for supper and
afterwards he took her to his friends' homes. They abstained from
such adventurous behaviour only after her mother-in-law raised
objections. After their engagement, however, they resumed their
social activities.[71]

Other Brahmo women showed puritanic attitudes to any public demonstration, not only of pre-marital, but also of conjugal affection. Thus, while Manilata Mazumdar and her husband co-operated in arranging marriages for poor, but respectable girls as part of their social work activities, Manilata considered it indecent to walk down a street with her husband. Courtship was accordingly virtually unheard of before marriage. In 1985 elderly women in their seventies and eighties still considered it offensive to be asked if they had ever fallen in love. To them marital love was beyond the sphere of individual preference and romantic love was immoral.[72]

Early marital relations were marked by emotional distance. A daughter-in-law's initial days with her in-laws did little to establish conjugal intimacy. During her first weeks in her new home she was welcomed as goddess Laksmi, the goddess of fortune, and spoilt with sweets and attention. Friends and relatives of her husband came to admire her and she had to endure their constant inspection with due modesty. The *bau bhat* (the bride's rice meal) was the climax of the introductory phase. The *bau* served a rice dish to her relatives and as food cooked in water could be extremely polluting if touched by an impure hand, this meal meant the factual acceptance of the bride into her in-laws' lineage.[73]

As couples were traditionally not allowed to see each other during the day and because there were few interests that they shared, love and understanding developed only over a number of years and were thus not a source of support during the initial period. Moreover, many mothers-in-law had a vested interest in their sons maintaining a conjugal distance because they were concerned with their own influence on and emotional closeness with their sons. Then, only childbirth liberated a wife from the stigma of being the youngest and most subordinate daughter-in-law. But as a mother a woman directed her attention on the child, not on her husband.[74]

Radharani Basu, who married shortly after 1900 at the age of ten, regretted the absence of her husband's support. Her mother-in-law, she recalled, 'was very proud, being the daughter of a rich family. She was not satisfied with all my ornaments although there was no demand of dowry'. Her husband did not protect her against his mother's temper. One day his elder brother ignored all rules and took Radharani out for a walk to cheer her up. 'After that my mother-in-law did not talk to me for fifteen days and my sister-in-law was also very angry with me.' Radharani's husband was of the old school which left young wives under the authority of the sasuri, but his elder brother's attitude was becoming more common.[75]

In the 1920s more and more middle-class husbands began to move towards liberating their wives from traditional gender roles. Young wives were then better able to argue their cases against the traditional behaviour of their mothers-in-law.[76] But not all young women could cope with these changes. The Brahmo poetess, Kamini Ray, depicted the variety of female reactions in some of her poems. Young women who insisted that the role of a wife and mother was not enough and that service for the country and society was necessary, were contrasted with women who felt lost in their husbands' changing worlds where idols were thrown away, where people of different castes met socially and where khadi was replacing silk.[77]

Generally, from the beginning of the 1920s, middle-class couples shared more interests than around the turn of the century and there was a basis for partnership. Girls often married at a slightly later age than they did twenty or thirty years earlier and were educated upto an elementary level. Advisory books flourished, which prepared young middle-class girls for their domestic duties. In *Grihasri*, published in 1915, women were encouraged to be the centre of the home and to feel responsible for all arrangements, not just for cooking; more detailed instructions were given about medical care, hygiene and household management. They were advised to show love and respect towards their husbands.[78] As time passed advice to women became increasingly pragmatic. In 1934, in Priyanath Basu's *Griha-dharma*, women could read of the dangers of employing young maid servants because they could get involved with the men in the family. Also, economic changes now loomed large. A poor man's wife was advised to renounce her ornaments and show sympathy with her husband by putting his hands around her neck and telling him that his hands were her most precious jewels.[79] Her advice should be such as to help her husband avoid loans. By sharing his woes she could keep his mind clear of worries.[80]

Men needed female support to cope with migrations or changing religious affiliations. Conjugal partnership was consciously

nurtured. During the gaona period between marriage and puberty, while the wife was with her parents, it became increasingly
popular among educated couples to maintain contact by writing
letters. Intimacy was forbidden in these letters and, besides, the
wife was never the first in her family to read them, but the practice
nevertheless helped to establish familiarity with each other. This
practice evoked a literary response in the form of advisory books
which contained letters between a husband and wife. These books
usually propagated educated, but self-effacing womanhood. Educated wives, it was feared, would use their knowledge to indulge
their own feelings. Thus novel-reading was condemned and so
were detailed emotional descriptions of their sorrows.[81]

For some couples letter writing continued after the gaona
period in cases where the husband lived by himself in Calcutta.
While he was a student or while his wife was very young, it was
impossible for them to move to Calcutta together.[82] In 1890,
Ramananda Chatterjee, a Brahmo from an orthodox family,
penned his emotional agony at being separated from his wife in
his diary. He was a college lecturer in Calcutta, while his wife,
Manurama, lived with his family in Bankura:

Wednesday, 1 January 1890 ...Did I love her before we were born or do I
love her now? Shall we love each other after we are dead? And so, is our
love endless? This beautiful feeling, I don't think I am able to relate to her
clearly...

Thursday, 2: I am supposed to study a hundred pages a day, but I could
not. I was supposed to write for the *Indian Messenger*, but I could not. All
the time, Manu's face came to my mind. I have not been able to do
anything for her today...

Friday, 3: ...I wrote a letter to Manurama. It was nothing except asking
her to answer my letter. I have written to her but have not been able to
express my heart's feeling.

Saturday, 4: ...I have written a letter to Manurama. I think there was a
rough tone in my letter. So at night I felt repentant and wrote to her again.
I don't know how much I have hurt her.

After four more days without a letter from Manurama,
Ramanada's anxieties grew worse:

Wednesday, 8: ...Even today she has not answered to my letter... I have
again written to her that I cried last night because she did not write to

me... I love her very much. Oh, my dear Manurama, please come to me. I think I can bring you by the sheer strength of my love for you.

Thursday, 9: ...I have received a letter from her. I am so happy that I cannot explain how joyful everything seems. I have written to her.[83]

Shortly afterwards Ramananda succeeded in bringing Manurama to Calcutta and later to Allahabad. She, however, never really managed to become familiar with life in a city without the security of the joint family.[84]

Other women were glad to escape their husbands' joint families, to be their own mistresses and to have time to do what they liked. They were the first generation of middle-class Hindu women who would talk to their husbands during the day and in front of their children. In the early 1920s Phulrenu Chanda was nearly 20; she was happy to learn sewing to keep herself busy because cooking just for herself and her husband did not fill her day. She had attended school up to class seven and, to continue her education, her husband arranged for a woman teacher at home. They were childless. But while childless women in joint families were often criticized for their infertility this couple developed a close relationship in coping with their situation. He adored his wife and together they travelled to many centres of pilgrimage, like Puri and Tarakeswar, offering prayers for a child. He took her to his best friend's house, other couples came to see them and he was always prepared to protect her against other people's remarks concerning her barrenness. Phulrenu Chanda thought their happiness and closeness was very much due to the fact that they were not so far apart in age as were her parents. Her mother and father never talked during the day and, because her mother always behaved like a child with her much older husband, she never lost her initial shyness.[85]

After the turn of the century patterns of conjugal life were more varied than they had been fifty years before. In the late nineteenth century conjugal partnership and a certain degree of female independence within the family was the prerogative of Brahmo families who had internalized Victorian values of partnership. After 1900 the strongest impulses for conjugal change came from female education and from the spread of nationalist consciousness. Abha Mukherjee, born in Rannaghat, but brought up in Calcutta, was married at the age of 17 to a man 13 years her senior.

Her relation with her husband and her in-laws was clearly marked
by the growth in romantic and emotional affection. Her mother-
in-law had been educated in school and the further education of
the 17-year-old daughter-in-law became a family affair. In such an
atmosphere, nobody minded that her elder brother-in-law ignored traditional customs and helped her pass the Matric and I.A.
as a private student from Victoria Institution. 'My husband and I',
Abha Mukherjee recalled, 'shared a lot of interests. My husband
saw me as his best friend and we went out walking together in the
streets to see our friends. Together we went to Congress lectures,
but we did not get involved actively.'[86]

Other couples became politically involved together. In 1930 in
Comilla, for instance, wives waited to replace their arrested husbands in picket lines;[87] and Shubarnaprabha Baksi from Barisal
district—married in 1921 at the age of 16 to a Swadeshi activist—
went picketing together with her husband. To block access to the
court they lay down on the road.[88] These were just a few examples
of a broad movement; such developments did not have the Mes-
sianic character that female emancipation had within the Brahmo
movement and many Hindu families continued to follow traditional practices.

Often girls from reformist families married into more conservative ones. They lived through the first years of their marriage
coping with harsher restrictions than in their baper bari. Renuka
Raychaudhuri, for instance, was born in a Bikrampur family
living in Calcutta. They were Hindus, but some of her uncles were
Brahmos and spread reformist ideas in the family. Thus men and
women would interact during the day, would eat together and her
parents would talk to each other in front of her *thakurma*, father's
mother, and travel together with their daughter by tram through
Calcutta. She was educated at the Victoria Institution up to class
ten and afterwards her musical education, specializing in
Rabindra Sangeet, was continued privately. In the early 1930s her
marriage into an orthodox family changed her life. 'In my sasur
bari there was a big joint family', she recalled:

My sasur was very conservative. I was a proper daughter-in-law and had
lost all my liberties I had enjoyed in my father's house. But I used to talk
to my husband during daytime. It was slowly changing, even in my sasur
bari. The new daughter-in-law and the change of society had an impact

on my sasur. After his death all the old rules and customs were broken, no restrictions were left.[89]

While living in Assam, Amiya Sen had seen her parents talking freely to each other as long as no relatives from Calcutta were visiting the family. But when she married in 1920 at the age of 14 she had to re-adapt: 'I myself did not talk nor see my husband during daytime. But I had an American lady teacher in my sasur bari in Allahabad.'[90] The breaking of traditional taboos in public was for many otherwise reformist-minded women unacceptable.

Adultery and Prostitution

While men and women began to meet socially with greater ease and while marital relations were based increasingly on individual affection, adultery acquired a new profile in Bengali society. What had once been an inevitable social evil was, after the turn of the century, more and more associated with personal tragedy for women.

In the nineteenth century polygamy was common in Bengal. Childlessness or conjugal friction encouraged a husband to arrange another marriage with a younger woman. Wives feared the *satin* (co-wife). In folk-sayings, bratas (female nursery rhymes) and numerous poems, a wife's agony over the arrival of a co-wife was depicted. *Sonar Satin* (Golden Co-wives) was the satirical title of a book which gave a detailed account of the problems raised by a man's second marriage. There were constant fights about where the man would spend the night and whom he liked best. After the second marriage the new wife was under great pressure to give birth to a child or be faced with the ultimate sanction of being sent home. She would probably suffer the same fate if the first wife unexpectedly became pregnant.[91]

After 1900 polygamy or men keeping mistresses in garden houses was no longer socially acceptable. Instead, adultery threatened conjugal harmony. Wives who were liberated from polygamy now feared other rival women from inside and outside the family. Left behind in their village-based joint families, wives worried about the faithfulness of their husbands who studied or worked in Calcutta or Dhaka.[92]

Love between male middle-class migrants and young widows or Brahman girls, for whom no suitable husband could be found, was the common subject of contemporary Bengali literature. In most cases it was not the betrayed wives who suffered most, but the girls involved in the love affairs. They hoped for marriage, but were disappointed. In fact, they were most often abandoned both by their lovers and their families and often had no alternative but to become prostitutes. After the turn of the century large numbers of women still lived the frustrating lives of widows, but the rigidity of sexual control in the zenana was decreasing and they were thus more easily available to men from inside and outside the family.[93]

Sexual promiscuity within the household was at all times difficult to detect, but nevertheless prevalent. Affairs between maidservants and male members of the family were notorious.[94] During the second half of the nineteenth century, the problem grew as an increasing number of families began to employ maids. Women who worked as servants outside their parents' or husband's area of control for the first time were ill prepared to defend themselves against sexual advances. While middle-class women valued chastity for their future marriage prospects, lowcaste and working-class women were not constrained by the same social pressure and control in strange households. It was not extraordinary for young men to misuse these women 'to collect experiences'. Young widows, in particular, were the target of men, as were daughters-in-law.[95]

While women had little chance of preventing their husbands' sexual adventures, men were by no means prepared to show leniency if married women were involved in adultery. In respectable circles, if an affair became public, a woman was regarded as a prostitute and treated as an outcast.[96] It was a measure of the inequality in gender relations that an unfaithful wife was more often murdered than an unfaithful husband. Murder is, in general, more often committed by a member of the victim's family than by a stranger. Compared to the West, women hardly ever murdered their husbands in Bengal, although there was much male promiscuity. While the classical female response to adultery was suicide,[97] only a few women resorted to poisoning their husbands. However, if a man became notorious for seducing women, on occasion the victims' relatives took the law into their own hands.[98] The most frequent causes of homicide were, according to police reports, intrigues with women, followed by domestic quarrels and land issues.[99]

Bengali society took a lenient view of crimes committed for the sake of honour. When a known seducer or a girl of disreputable character was killed, the village society refused to co-operate in the murder investigations. Thus, such crimes went unpunished. If a husband killed his unfaithful wife, a similar reaction by villagers was likely because an unfaithful wife forfeited society's protection. The lower courts sometimes had a similar attitude towards husbands and lovers who had killed their female partners. In 1901, in 24-Parganas, a wife who had denied having a relationship with her neighbour was stabbed to death by her husband. The jury acquitted her husband and, only after a review in the High Court, was he found guilty and sentenced to transportation for life.[100]

In early twentieth-century Bengal little distinction was made between female adultery and prostitution as can be seen in contemporary literature. Both were regarded as the outcome of women's natural weakness for which there was, once a woman had committed either offence, no cure and no pardon. Being called a prostitute was the worst misfortune which could befall a woman. An unfaithful wife or even her illegitimate daughter were marked as prostitutes and became outcastes.[101] There were different levels of prostitution in Bengali society, which need to be differentiated in order to understand otherwise contradictory assumptions concerning prostitutes in Bengal.

Prostitution was well established in Bengali society. In the eighteenth century courtesans and *nac* girls who catered to the rich were renowned far and wide. During the nineteenth century the decline of old money and the rise of a new professional urban elite changed the patterns of prostitution. Nac girls in garden houses were replaced by brothels, some of which especially catered to the rich. In 1853 there were, according to official estimates, more than 12,000 prostitutes in Calcutta and their number remained fairly stable at about 15,000 until the First World War. In 1921 and 1931 there were less than 10,000 and 7500 prostitutes respectively in Calcutta, including the suburbs in 24-Parganas.[102]

While prostitution was concentrated in Calcutta it was by no means uncommon in the mufassal. What little evidence I have suggests that prostitution in the countryside was regarded with a measure of connivance unheard of in Calcutta, Dhaka or Europe. A special report written by a police commissioner just after the turn of the century identified Mymensingh as an area of particular interest. Apparently there were more prostitutes around Mymensingh than anywhere else in East Bengal. The peasants were unusually rich due to the quality of their jute crops and the absence of a rent-receiving middle class.

The local prostitutes were at the bottom of village society. They were tolerated by the male (the police commissioner did not speak to women) villagers and were even essential for religious festivals. The earth from the front of a prostitute's house and a king's palace was required during Durga Puja. Moreover, the sight of a prostitute at the beginning of a journey was an auspicious sign.[103]

Mymensingh prostitutes enjoyed, the police commissioner discovered, the special protection of the local *zamindars*. On festive occasions or at jatra performances, special seats were reserved by the landlord for the prostitutes and they were allowed to pay their respects to the wives of their zamindars. The zamindars saw them as a valuable source of income without which no bazaar would flourish and no *mela* would be successful. In some places in the Mymensingh area, zamindars received *nazars* (money) when a young prostitute entered the profession or the zamindar himself auctioned her in the bazaar to the highest bidder.[104]

The position of prostitutes in the local community depended on their involvement with the men of the locality. In case of police prosecution, the commissioner heard, a country prostitute could count on four possible defences: if there were 'public men' among her clients, they could exercise their influence on the authorities; the community could take her side against arbitrary police action; the local pleader often defended her without a fee; but the most effective defence was from the prostitute herself—she could accuse the prosecuting officer of acting out of spite due to the denial of her favours.[105]

Like other occupations, prostitutes claimed that prostitution was a hereditary vocation. But several local studies in the early 1900s showed that many prostitutes came into the profession not as their mothers' heirs, but after traumatic experiences as widows, maltreated wives and persecuted daughters-in-law. On a smaller scale girls were sold by their impoverished parents, while illegitimate daughters were given away by their widowed mothers.

The claim by prostitutes to be in a hereditary vocation was there-fore an attempt to claim respectability, albeit at the bottom of the social and ritual hierarchy; they were ranked with sweepers or leather workers.[106]

The forces which compelled women into prostitution were familiar to any villager. On the one hand, they did not condemn them or hold them personally responsible for their fate. But on the other hand, following the concept of *karma*, they saw the fate of a prostitute as the consequence of sins in the woman's earlier lives. Accordingly re-integration into a family was impossible. But the social degradation inherent in prostitution in the mufassal was ameliorated by the paternalism of the zamindar who granted his protection, although for selfish motives, such as to ensure the profitability of his mela or to ensure his own access to prostitutes. Consequently prostitutes were tolerated by the local community as well, considering the latter's dependence on the zamindar and village 'notables', such as the local policeman and the pleader. Rural prostitutes were spared the extreme cruelties which their impoverished city counterparts suffered. However, what European observers perceived as the absence of 'stigma and shame' was not positive acceptance.[107] Rather, within a hierarchi-cal society which was based on complementarities, such as the pure and the impure, even the most low-ranking person was allocated a position.[108]

There were, in the view of reformers who made the subject one of special concern, two levels of prostitution in Calcutta. At the top there was a select group who enjoyed a regular income, more independence than 'respectable' women, and the protection and solidarity of colleagues. Below this group was the majority of the poor and exploited prostitutes. They were indebted to pimps and brothel-keepers, who advanced money for jewellery, clothes and liquor. They were unable to repay their debts due to the steep interest rates.[109]

The exact patterns of prostitute recruitment in Calcutta are difficult to trace. What we do know is that most prostitutes were born in Calcutta or had migrated over a short distance from the neighbouring districts of 24-Parganas, Hooghly, Midnapur and Burdwan. Fewer came from Bihar and UP to cater for Hindi-speaking men. There was, by some accounts, a high level of internal recruitment in prostitution. Mothers initiated their

daughters or other younger female relatives into the profession.
However, it was also true, although reformers disagreed over the
extent of the traffic, that girls were sold by their parents to prostitutes or abducted by brothel-keepers from their homes.[110]

There was also a considerable number of first generation prostitutes who fled their homes for a combination of reasons. As
stated earlier, many women were pushed into prostitution by
widowhood and/or poverty, by maltreatment or by seduction.
The importance of the various factors differed according to the
observer's interests. Missionaries usually stressed causes linked
with Hindu religion, such as child marriage and the prohibition
of widow remarriage. Widows left their homes to conceal a pregnancy, to live with a lover or to escape maltreatment. Despite what
the missionaries wrote, the consequences of poverty appear to be
more compelling. Widows were an economic burden on their
families; the seduction of unmarried girls was more common in
families which had just migrated to Calcutta and which lived in
overcrowded bustees. If a girl became pregnant, prostitution was
the likely outcome.[111]

One of the most detailed and realistic, albeit fictional accounts,
of high-class prostitution is provided by *Patitar Atma-carit*, the
life-story of an educated prostitute, written by a Calcutta lawyer
in protest against the Sarda Act. He made the book appear as the
autobiography of a first-generation prostitute, Manadasundari,
who attempted in her later years to rehabilitate herself. She had
been to Bethune School, and fell in love with a young man after
her mother died and her father married a young woman. She
eloped with her lover who then left her. On her return to Calcutta,
she was ashamed to return to her family and took to soliciting in
the streets. There a brothel mother picked her up and recognized
her to be from a good family. She soon did very well. She had a
doctor *babu* as a regular customer and became a member of the
well-settled community of prostitutes.[112]

Women like Manadasundari lived the lives of cultured courtesans. They had only two or three regular customers who knew
each other and came at fixed days of the week. They entertained
groups of men friends with singing and dancing, but only one
would stay the night. They asked their customers to put vermilion
on their foreheads as a symbol of a temporary marriage, which
they washed off once the customer had left. The housekeeper was

responsible for law and order, and for supplying betel nut and liquor; but the women were not dependent on a brothel mother because they had the strong backing of regular customers.[113]

Some of them accumulated substantial wealth. In 1907, for instance, Saudamini, the daughter of a prostitute, left immovable property in Calcutta worth 3000 rupees to her two sons and four daughters. Her will became public when it was contested in court. Whereas Saudamini's daughters became prostitutes as well, other wealthy and influential prostitutes provided a better future for their daughters. The most common career was the theatre, where girls from respectable families would not seek employment. In fact, around the turn of the century, the mothers of the most popular and successful actresses on the Bengal stage—Binodini, Tarasundari and Tinakari—were all prostitutes.[114]

City courtesans protected their interests by forming an association like other professional groups. The association celebrated community pujas and had a social fund to bail out arrested members. It also paid for medical as well as funeral expenses. Women who were temporarily out of work could borrow money from the fund. The association also hired minders to protect their brothels. Like other voluntary associations the prostitutes undertook charitable work. In the 1920s they collected money for victims of a cyclone in East Bengal. On another occasion they sang in the streets and collected money and old clothes for flood victims in North Bengal.[115]

Prostitutes saw themselves, like barbers and washermen, as an established professional group at the bottom of the Hindu hierarchy. They responded to Gandhi's campaign against untouchability and participated in the nationalist movement. Prostitutes in Rambagan in Calcutta, for instance, started spinning and wore khadi saris. Manadasundari's brothel community banned alcohol from its premises although this meant losing some regular clients. In 1924 ten prostitutes participated in the Tarakeswar satyagraha and the nationalist activist, Jyotirmoyi Ganguli, presided over a meeting of prostitute volunteers. She was criticized by other activists for such an alliance with 'vice' and Gandhi refused to visit a prostitutes' association in Barisal.[116] But what is clear from these incidents is the strong identity of prostitutes who saw themselves as a community integrated into Bengali society.

'Common prostitutes' were part of the bazaar economy. The difficulty of effectively controlling the 'native quarters' influenced the way a British police officer characterized prostitution. In 1920 E.C.S. Shuttleworth, Superintendent of Police, Rangoon, reported on Calcutta prostitution:

The Indian prostitutes live all over the native quarters of the city and its suburbs, but they are to be found in largest numbers in the northern portion, along the greater part of Chitpur Road, Beadon Square and the quarter known as Sonagachi. This part of the town is a seething mass of Indian prostitutes. The houses and balconies along Chitpur Road and Beadon Square are thronged with prostitutes sitting outside, and the narrow lanes and gullies at the back of these main thoroughfares form a veritable ant-hill of these 'unfortunates'. A very large number are also to be found in the labyrinth of tortuous narrow gullies and lanes at the back of many of the main thoroughfares and arteries in the very heart of the city. These Indian brothels and prostitutes are practically under no police control or supervision...

Prostitutes lived like other women trading in the bazaar economy. But to S.C.Mukherjee, a non-official member of the Bengal Legislative Council, every unmarried woman without her own means or with a lover was a prostitute. In his view, as a social reform activist and sharing the perspective of the British police superintendent, almost all bazaar women were clandestine prostitutes, as were European and Eurasian telephone girls and shop assistants. Mukherjee was not alone in this judgement. In 1916 a Brothel Special Committee of the Calcutta Corporation was unable to declare any streets free of brothels.[118]

S.C. Mukherjee represented a common male—and predominantly British—view of bazaar women. Bazaar women did make ends meet by occasionally taking money from lovers. In 1904 Reverend Anderson was appalled at the sight of a daughter watching out for her father, while her mother was with a client. These women, however, were part-time prostitutes and worked primarily in the local bazaar. They lived in very different conditions than full-time prostitutes. The former were married, had children, and were in arrears with the rent for their bustee hut; the latter had pimps and brothel mothers for whom they worked and to whom they owed money. The pattern of homicides underlined the differences between 'clandestine' and real prostitutes: unfaithful working-class wives were killed by their husbands; prostitutes were killed by strangers for a gold necklace and some cash.[119]

Single women who started as street walkers became brothel inmates when they could no longer pay their debts. A brothel mother advanced money for jewellery, saris and cosmetics and a pimp acted as an advertiser and brought clients. The price they charged depended on their youth and looks, but however much it was, it rarely covered their debts once the pimp had taken half and the brothel mother her share for the rent. When a prostitute grew old she could either become a brothel mother or live off her real or adopted daughter's earnings.[120]

Young girls were initiated into prostitution by a mock marriage. The spouse was either a *pro forma* husband who left after the ceremony, or a plant in case of a Hindu girl or a sword or knife for a Muslim. When the ceremony was over a Hindu girl wore a vermilion mark in the parting of her hair as a sign of her new status. 'The symbolism is carried so far', the Census report recorded

that the plant is carefully watered and the sword is kept locked in a box, in the belief that if the one dies or the other is lost the girl becomes a widow. In fact, when the plant dies, she wipes off the vermilion smeared on her head and removes the iron bangle from her wrist just as if she is a widow.[121]

The celebration of Hindu and Muslim rites of passage, such as marriage, and the efforts of prostitutes to establish a community identity through which they perceived themselves and were perceived by outsiders, determined their position in Bengali society. A woman's introduction to prostitution was as definite a determination of status as birth in a low caste. In 1912 the Honorary Secretary of the conservative British Indian Association explained this view with reference to the female character:

If a woman has been systematically trained in sexual aberrations from her youth upwards, all her ideas are concentrated on debauch and sexual intercourse; so that it becomes impossible later on to restore her to a life of social duty.[122]

Even if a prostitute was rehabilitated in an industrial school 'her life would still become unbearable as she would be despised by all respectable people for her past misconduct'.[123] The nature of women contained the root of evil. 'Excessive sexual passion', S. C. Mukherjee wrote

is an indirect cause for drifting of a woman to a life of shame. The force of sexual desire lies dormant in the bosom of most females until aroused by some outside influence… In a case of seduction the woman, though duped, is a willing victim. She, however, sins from weakness and love is therefore an object of weakness.[124]

The dominant Bengali gender ideology understood prostitution as a phenomenon rooted in female nature rather than in the economic and patriarchal structure of society.

Consummation, Colonialism and Women's Sexual Nature

Dominant interpretations of Hinduism and marriage manuals as well as discourses regarding affection, adultery and prostitution focused on the power of female sexuality and its need of control. Significantly, the relaxation of the code of public conduct for married couples coincided with the internalization of restrictive Victorian values, as has been highlighted by Borthwick in her study of the bhadramahila.[125] But Bengali and Victorian values did not always combine so smoothly. In fact, Bengali and British gender stereotypes, particularly regarding the sexual control of women, clashed on different occasions when western or westernized reformers and politicians tried to modify Bengali conventions of male control of women. Here we will look at two issues, namely at the legislation on the age of consent in 1890–91 and at attempts to reform and 'rehabilitate' prostitutes. Both were closely related to the activities of the movement for social purity in Britain and highlight the interdependence of discourses on gender in Britain and India.

In 1885 the social purity movement had secured the passage in Britain of the Criminal Law Amendment Act which raised the age of consent from 13 to 16 years. The social purity movement differed from earlier reformist organizations. In the 1870s the movement for the repeal of Contagious Diseases Acts criticized the double standard of legislation which institutionalized male domination and state control of prostitutes. In contrast, the social purity movement was less 'feminist' and more Protestant, aiming at the abolition of prostitution and the moral purification of society.[126]

The interventionist approach of the purity crusaders was linked with deep economic and ideological change. In the 1880s Britain's economic and imperial pre-eminence abroad was being challenged by the newly-industrializing nations, while at home the resurgence of socialism threatened the established social order. The danger of an uncontrolled proletariat with revolutionary aspirations posed a threat to the expansion of capitalism. Gareth Steadman Jones has shown how a 'wave of insecurity' swept over Britain in the 1880s. Reformers campaigned to alter the moral code of the working class. For social purity crusaders the path to success lay through the repression of youthful sexuality and the redemption of young girls from early sexual intercourse. They hoped to reform the working-class character by disciplining working-class children.[127]

The Age of Consent Act of 1891 in India, I suggest, was an illustration of Kenneth Ballhatchet's argument that English class attitudes at home changed into racial attitudes in an imperial setting.[128] The Act was an important British challenge to control by Bengali men over female sexuality. The controversy highlighted the power of gender ideology as a mobilizing factor in colonial politics for the British and Bengalis alike. The Act was, from the British point of view, part of the continual process of ideological domination that established the legitimacy of colonial rule. The argument for raising the age of consent was couched in an humanitarian concern for the health of young girls, endangered by early sexual intercourse. The argument against the Act was based on tradition, a nationalist resentment at alien interference with Hinduism and a denial of damaging consequences to young girls. Two different ideologies—men exercised patriarchal control over women's sexuality in both—were at the heart of the matter.

Similarly, in early twentieth-century Bengal social purity reformers failed in their attempts to 'rescue' prostitutes. Their rescue work, once again based on Victorian humanitarian values, was incompatible with both the organization of prostitution as a hereditary profession and with the general perception of prostitutes as an occupational, caste-like group at the bottom of Bengali society. Both these aspects were closely linked with the notion of purity and the Bengali Hindu view of female sexuality. In contrast to legislation on prostitution in Britain the reforms intended in Bengal did not affect male control within the family. Thus neither Bengalis nor Europeans became as involved in the matter as they did when the age of consent was at stake.

The Age of Consent Act raised the legal age of sexual intercourse for girls from 10 to 12 years. Sex with an under-aged girl was defined as rape in the Act and was punishable by a maximum of ten years' imprisonment or transportation for life.[129] While the previous age of consent, fixed at 10 in 1860, had not interfered with the custom of intercourse soon after a girl's first period, the new Act raised this as a possibility. Moreover, the political climate in 1890, particularly in Bengal, was more hostile to government legislation than in 1860.[130] What sharpened the debate over the passage of the Bill was the pronounced racism of the British public in Bengal towards the end of the century and the fact that this was the first major intervention into the private 'religious' sphere of Bengali life after the Mutiny.[131]

Lansdowne, the Governor-General, saw this intervention as unavoidable because he feared that the British social purity movement might criticize his government's record on social issues. But in India, the Age of Consent Act was an important departure from previous policies of social reform and the Government of India needed a suitable pretext for its new initiative.[132] 'Such an opportunity was afforded by the Hari Maiti case', wrote Lord Lansdowne, 'and we took advantage of it at once.'[133] Hari Maiti's 11-year-old wife, Phulmani, died as a result of premature sexual intercourse with her husband. The court regarded this as an accident rather than a serious offence and sentenced Maiti to one year in prison. However, the social reform lobby in Britain did not share the court's lenient view. Lord Lansdowne was encouraged to make a statutory statement of moral disapproval.[134]

Bengali opposition to Lansdowne's statement, namely the Age of Consent Act, was closely connected with the region's specific practices of ritual or practical marriage consummation, garbhadan, and of gaona, the bride's residence at her father's house during the period between marriage and sexual maturity.

Ritual purity as well as psychological considerations were at the basis of prescriptions regarding the actual consummation of marriage. Consummation was delayed for a couple of days after marriage or, if the bride had not reached puberty, until her first period. The delay allowed a young couple to become acquainted. The first night after the wedding was spent in the girl's home. It was, for him, an initiation into his wife's family. While the husband and wife sat on a bed, he was teased by the sisters and female cousins of the bride. The young women involved proved their friendship and concern for the bride; she was uneasy at her first acquaintance with her husband.[135] The peculiarity of the night was that gender roles were inverted. Women dominated the conversation and took liberties with the only male in the room.[136]

The bride was introduced to her husband's family in a different fashion. The first night in the the husband's home was regarded as inauspicious for beginning a new phase in life and the husband and wife were not supposed to see each other. Instead of spending the night with her husband, the bride slept in a room with other women of the family or, if she was a child, at her mother-in-law's side.[137]

The first night on which the couple was left alone was called the 'night of the flower bed'; the bed was covered with flowers and petals. The girl sat veiled in the dark and waited for her husband. Her shyness was exacerbated as she knew that her husband's younger sisters and female cousins were hiding in or outside the room to eavesdrop.[138] This was a stri achar or female marriage folk rite which was a safeguard for the immature wife who was physically unprepared for sexual intercourse. After 'the night of the flower bed' she left her room before dawn as she was not allowed to see her husband during the day. This routine—but without the female witnesses—continued for ten or fourteen nights, but sexual intercourse was not supposed to take place before the bride had reached puberty. In the case of pre-puberty brides, the girl's maternal uncle came to escort her back home after ten days. Thereafter, until she reached puberty, she was expected to pay only occasional visits to her sasur bari.[139]

Traditionally marriage was consummated soon after a girl had reached puberty. The opposition to the Age of Consent Act, which put the girl's age in place of her physical maturity, was based on this timing. The timing went back to Raghunandan's interpretation of a Hindu ritual in sex and marriage which highlighted the significance of garbhadan. This was the ritual consummation of marriage straight after the first 'menstrual flow' without regard to the wife's age. The related texts contained detailed rules about how to approach the wife, what to say while lying next to her, while touching her heart, and having intercourse. Without the ritual, *garbha* (conception) would be polluted and any son or daughter impure. An impure son would be unable to offer *pindas* (sacrifices) to his ancestors. It was the duty of every mother to give birth to a pure son. Marriage was, the pandits pointed out to British officials, a ritual ceremony and, unlike Christian marriages, the satisfaction of 'carnal desire' was only secondary.

It was this belief which led to child marriage because a girl's first period was expected to occur between the age of 11 and 12. By the early 1890s garbhadan was said to be fading and 40 years later it had definitely died out.[140] The practice of sexual intercourse on the first occurrence of a wife's menses was, however, still current in the first quarter of the twentieth century. It was less common among high-caste, middle-class families who preferred to educate their daughters up to the age of 13 or 14 before they arranged their marriages, but remained widespread among the uneducated and low-caste population, Hindus as well as Muslims.[141]

There is some evidence that in nineteenth-century Bengal gaona was not as strictly observed as in other Indian regions, and that under such circumstances some cases of sexual intercourse with immature girls occurred. In the early twentieth century pre-puberty marriages became less common and gaona more widespread.[142] Nonetheless, in the 1920s it was still difficult for parents to practise gaona if husbands did not consent, as had been the case when Phulmani died in 1890. The man was master once the marriage ritual had been celebrated; parents were reluctant to displease a bridegroom over whom they had spent much time in negotiation. In the mid-1920s in Sankharitala, Calcutta, a husband killed his ten-year-old wife for rejecting his advances. They had been married for two years and, while gaona was being observed, Jogendranath, the husband, went to stay at his in-laws' house. The mother ordered her daughter to spend the night with him. On the third night he tried to have sex with his child-wife. She refused and was then brutally killed. This was an unusual crime, but it highlighted the weakness of parents' positions who both wanted to protect their daughters and please their sons-in-law.[143]

Among educated families, the conflict between parents and in-laws regarding the observation of gaona took place in a different context. Whereas the in-laws' interest remained the same, namely to accustom the girl to the habits of the new family and to secure her smooth adaptation to the inferior position of a young daughter-in-law, her parents' concern was about her health and also her intellectual development. Many parents accepted offers for their daughters, who were as young as 11 or 14, but insisted that the girls stayed with them until they had finished their education.[144]

The customs of gaona and in particular of garbhadan were at the centre of the opposition's religious arguments against the Age of Consent Act. Following the introduction of the Bill by Sir A.F. Scoble in the Viceroy's Legislative Council on 9 January 1891, Bengalis were mobilized on a scale unknown before in the Province.[145] Opposition began with the presentation of religious and legal arguments against the Bill in the press, but this soon changed into mass agitation against British rule in India.

Bengali opposition was united in regard to the rejection of British interference in their private lives. There were, however, a number of distinct groups with different arguments and aims. The orthodox faction led by pandits of the Calcutta Sanskrit College defended the sanctity of Hindu religion and its ritual practices. The most radical political group centred around the two newspapers, *Bangabasi* and *Dainik-o-Samachar Chandrika*, both owned and edited by Jogendro Chandra Gosh and Krishna Chandra Banerjea.[146] This group used the religious argument in the Hindu Revivalist mode of the Maharashtrian nationalist, Tilak, in order to secure mass support and to establish an Indian sense of identity with the aim of challenging British rule in India. Finally, a diverse group of political moderates—including members of the British Indian Association, the Indian Association and Congress—accepted the theoretical concept of the law which was in accordance with the principles of their western education, but they questioned the 'facts' as had been presented by the British. The moderates denied the regular occurrence of premature intercourse and the brutality of husbands towards their young wives.[147]

Whereas the assertion of Hindu identity and the gradual removal of the British from India were the aims of Hindu

Revivalist opponents of the Act, what gave Bengali agitation its driving force was the desire to defend the traditions and rituals of their gender relations. Equally, the British social purity activists and, pushed by them, the Government of India argued for the necessity of individual protection to save girls from prostitution and premature intercourse. But the evidence with which they justified their intentions was permeated with late-Victorian gender ideology.

Victorian sexual stereotypes were linked with a world view which, according to Leonore Davidoff, 'often used a body metaphor in an effort to stress the organic nature of...society'. Social groups, sexes and classes were, she suggests, 'hierarchically ordered but interdependent parts' of the body, which was governed by the white middle-class or aristocratic male in the position of the head.[148] Women, that is middle-class ladies, were the heart and soul of the 'body politic'. Although women were identified with their bodies—which justified their subordination to men—they learnt to control sexual desire through sublimation inculcated by their upbringing. Their purity and asexuality helped their husbands in the arduous task of overcoming the male sex drive, which was perceived as a constant threat to male authority and the working of the entire social organism. While gentlemen mastered their sex-drive, women being too weak for such heroism had to repress it. The construction of feelings of guilt and the stereotype of female innocence fell into the mother's sphere of her daughter's primary socialization.[149]

The powerlessness of working-class or non-white people in the empire was visualized by their distance to the head, the organic centre of the body: working class people were the hands; prostitutes, homosexuals and criminals were located in the 'nether regions' of dangerous and polluting bodily functions. Prostitutes were those women whose upbringing had not prepared them to sublimate their sexual desire and who had thus fallen into sin.[150]

The *Rig Veda* also used the body metaphor to justify the hierarchical order of Indian society. Mankind originated from the body of the Primeval Man: Brahmans from his mouth, warriors (Ksatriyas) from his arms, merchants (Vaisyas) from his thighs, and artisans and peasants (Sudras) from his feet.[151] This metaphor differed in two important aspects from its Victorian counterpart. First, impure people, that is, social outcastes who were located in the Victorian 'nether regions', were not mentioned at all, because they were not regarded as originating from Primeval Man. By denying any connection between the origins of caste and casteless people Vedic racial prejudices were more radical than the Victorian bias against 'asocial' people. Second, in the Vedic model the difference between men and women was not made as explicit as in the body metaphor used by Victorians. Women, not being mentioned separately, stemmed from the same substance as men of their caste. Spirit and nature, or intellect and sensuality, were not evenly distributed among men and women, but, in contrast to the Victorian model, Vedic thought identified neither men nor women with just intellect or just emotions. Differences between men and women were not illustrated with the same image as social stratifications.

In the Victorian metaphor all subordinate groups—women, the working class and 'natives' in the colonies—were seen as being closer to nature than white middle-class males. Here, the political motives linked with racial stereotypes became obvious. From a non-racial viewpoint, 'ladies' had as much or as little in common as 'gentlemen' with working-class people, 'colonials' and social outcastes. English male-dominated ideology, however, identified women and other subordinate groups with nature in order to justify and stabilize the political and economic dominance of the English middle-class male. This legitimized the Victorian belief in a world-wide organic hierarchy in which everything and everybody was the object of control by the white middle-class or aristocratic male. The images with which Victorians portrayed subordinates at home and abroad were often female and the stereotype of the 'effeminate Bengali' is an exact illustration of this ideology. E. Said and some feminist historians have gone a step further by tracing in the European discourse on the South and East the 'feminization' of the whole Orient in contrast to the male dominant Occident. The parameter for imperial expansion was neatly outlined.[152]

In Victorian middle-class socialization the youthful sexuality of girls needed to be controlled more urgently than anything else. Accordingly, British medical doctors in Bengal were distressed when they observed how little privacy surrounded some intimate activities in the family. Dr Joubert wrote:

Owing to the complete want of privacy in an Indian house, the children are mixed up with all the functions of the married life of their seniors. At an early age, they know all about childbirth from actual observation, and they probably know a deal about what precedes childbirth.

He complained that Bengali children always stayed in the room when he was examining a patient and, even worse, that Bengali adults approved of their being present. He continued:

What is the result of this indifference on the part of the seniors to children knowing what is kept from their knowledge in European countries? At an early age they have little more to learn about married life, their thoughts dwell upon it, for the young human mind is full of curiosity, which easily takes a prurient direction if not checked or prevented.[153]

In British eyes, this openness about the everyday reality of sex, birth and death needed to be replaced by the control of youthful sexuality. Cotton, a former secretary of the Government of Bengal, believed that the only way to combat the 'great perversion' of child marriage was in the imitation of the sexual and moral practices of the British middle class. Sexual appetite among children or adolescents could only be overcome, he argued, by the strictest discipline and a life of labour; in his ideology sexual desire was the most selfish of all instincts.[154]

Bengali gender relations also centred around the control of female sexuality, but the concept of sexuality and the means of control were diametrically opposed to British ideas. Rather than repressing sexuality as the Victorians were supposed to have done, Bengalis celebrated the power of sex.[155] To Bengali men, women were unique products of nature and nurture. On the one hand, due to upbringing, the Bengali woman was a pure example of chastity and honour. On the other hand, due to nature, she burnt with sexual desire which had to be satisfied straight after menstruation. The means of control was sexual intercourse rather than repressive Victorian socialization. The absolute reign of the intellect, as symbolized by the superiority of the British middle- and upper-class male, did not exist to the same extent in Bengali culture.[156]

Bengali views of women being pure and sexual at the same time were not contradictory, but were two expressions of the male Bengali's concept of his own grandeur as guardian of a civilized nature. The image of his wife as a goddess flattered his ego and

corresponded with the ritual significance of marital consummation. This image allowed opponents of the Bill to portray British
plans as an attempt to undermine Bengali moral superiority, itself
based on the woman's purity in action and thought. It was
sacrilege that Bengali women, who were taught never to turn an
eye or to give a thought to men other than their husbands, could
be dragged in front of a court or to a medical examination. Premature cohabitation was pronounced an outrage and completely
alien to Bengali society. In fact, wives were protected and
honoured and did not need any special attention from the
British.[157]

Unsatisfied female sexuality was a common male fear in Bengali society. This fear appeared as *vagina dentata* in Bengali folk
myths.[158] Proverbs expressed such emotions more pithily: 'Fire is
never satisfied with fuel, the ocean is never filled by rivers, death
is never satisfied by living beings and women are never satisfied
with men.'[159]

Girls, once they had reached puberty, were described as feeling
the cravings of nature, or as waiting impatiently for a husband's
company.[160] Early sexual intercourse was obligatory, if the god-
dess-like chastity of a woman was not to be damaged. As a
consequence of the Bill becoming law, the *Bangabasi* painted a
picture of widespread, unsatisfied female sexuality: 'Females in
groups hurrying from door to door begging males to gratify their
lust.'[161] In short, the proposed law was perceived as a direct threat
to male sexual superiority.

Moreover, it was the loss of honour, rather than physical pain
or psychic damage, which was considered to be the main aspect
of rape. This, it was argued, proved that it was impossible to rape
one's own, even immature, wife since she could never lose her
reputation in this way.[162] Leaving aside the question of a woman's
experience of being raped, this view was based on the concept of
women being mere 'functions' in the family, mainly in relation to
their husbands. This concept supplied the ideal justification for a
complete female submission to father, brother, husband or son.
Those women who had violated this ideal and petitioned the
Queen in support of the law forfeited their femininity and Indian
identity. Arguing that 'our sex is solely dependent on the Government for the protection of our personal rights', women from all
over India, including Calcutta and Mymensingh in Bengal, chal-

lenged the joint family, patriarchy and the guarantee of respect and protection they were due according to Hindu religion.[163]

Male pride and fear determined the arguments of ruler and subject alike. The involvement of such unreflected feelings sharpened the discourse on sexuality beyond British expectations and led to the unprecedented radicalization and mobilization of a wide strata of Bengali society. It had been the intention of British officials in India to stabilize the Raj by pre-empting British criticism through legislation. But when this very legislation led to the opposite result by evoking a wave of Indian protest, Lansdowne changed his strategy and took refuge in a policy of appeasement. Five days after the Act was passed Lansdowne arranged for a circular to be sent to all local governments admonishing them to apply the Act 'with the utmost care and discrimination'. Enquiries should only be held by native magistrates, it stated, but if there were any doubts, prosecutions should be postponed.[164]

It was no wonder that there were very few prosecutions under the Act. As the opposition had argued— and known— all along, the Age of Consent Act was impossible to enforce in the political conditions prevailing in Bengal and in India as a whole. Between 1891 and 1893 there was an average of two or three cases a year per province which, however, were either dropped because of false evidence or ended with a one or two-year prison sentence if violence and cruelty were involved. In 1893 the Indian government asked the local governments to discontinue the submission of annual reports on the working of the Age of Consent Act, because it had turned into an empty bureaucratic exercise.[165] Educated families tended not to give their daughters in marriage below the age of 12 and the majority of people, in the absence of education, continued to follow the custom unaffected by legislation.[166] The arm of the law did not reach those girls who really needed help. In a number of cases, in Bengal's Rajshahi division, for instance, young wives under and over 12 were killed by their husbands for refusing them their so-called 'conjugal rights'.[167]

Attempts to reform prostitution aimed at both preventing girls being sold to prostitutes and being introduced to the profession. Such efforts met with the opposition of prostitutes who needed to recruit young women to secure their living in old age, and the apathy of Bengalis who saw no future for 'rescued' apprentice prostitutes. However, in 1893 Calcutta social purity activists—a coalition of missionaries, Anglican churchmen and Bengali social reformers—founded the Society for the Protection of Children in India.[168] The social purity reformers in Calcutta campaigned, like the British social purity movement, for the closing down of all brothels. After their demand for the abolition of brothels was rejected as impracticable in the 1890s, they resorted to those means which existing Indian laws provided. Any brothel could be put out of business by the police if members of the public complained. For decades to come an average of 20 to 30 Calcutta brothels were closed each year following complaints from neighbours. Closing, however, often simply meant re-location in another part of the town.[169]

Dissatisfied with ineffective police action, social purity activists wanted more decisive steps taken against the traffic in child prostitutes. In 1903 the Bombay Missionary Conference and the Calcutta Society for the Protection of Children in India proposed legal actions against prostitutes keeping girls under the age of 16 in brothels without being their lawful guardians. The government rejected major legislation against the practice of prostitutes but district magistrates were given wider powers to remove girls under 16 from houses of ill-repute.[170]

Still, in 1907 there were 1042 girls below the age of 14 living with Calcutta prostitutes and 142 of them with other than their mothers or next of kin. These girls, the Society for the Protection of Children claimed, had come to brothels by 'a regular traffic which goes on in the districts outside Calcutta, and which has for its object the procurement of female children by purchase from indigent parents and guardians'.[171]

The Society proposed a Bengal Protection of Minors Bill with a special police staff to remove girls from brothels and the establishment of rescue homes outside Calcutta. The Society hoped that the evidence presented—in particular a book by one of its members, the Reverend Herbert Anderson, on the extent of the evil in Calcutta's streets—would encourage government legislation, just as W. T. Stead's publication on the traffic in English girls had resulted in legislation on the Age of Consent.[172]

Once again government refused to legislate because there were no homes for the rescued girls. The Bengal government refused to finance a state-run home and considered a missionary-run home politically unacceptable. Removing girls from brothels to missionary control came close to a forced conversion which would have evoked strong protest from the Bengali press and Hindu Revivalists.[173]

In 1912 two bills were introduced in the Indian Legislative Assembly to fight the 'social evil' of prostitution. The first was a bill making trade in white women for the purpose of prostitution illegal, and the second was to prevent the sale of Indian girls into prostitution, mainly under the religious cover of dedicating them to a temple. But British Indian officials were not convinced of the necessity to legislate against these aspects of prostitution. In 1913 there were apparently only 234 European prostitutes in India, largely in Bombay (125) and in Calcutta (50), and they had allegedly come as mature women of their own will. The men who had arranged their trips were foreigners living outside India and outside the reach of Indian law. Thus legislation, they argued, would be futile. As for *devadasis*, they were a regional problem of South India and outside the scope of all-Indian legislation.[174]

Faced with a lack of Indian co-operation in the field of 'anti-vice' legislation, government officials in Delhi and Calcutta were extremely reluctant to act. Western missionaries and some social reformers were the only ones who demanded legislation to stop further recruitment of girls for prostitution, apart from the women's organizations which lobbied in favour of legislation to curb the dedication of devadasis to temples from the 1920s onwards.[175] But it was mainly international pressure reinforced by the India Office and political considerations which made the Indian government agree to all-India and provincial legislation. In 1912 the British parliament ratified the International Convention for the Suppression of the White Slave Traffic. Whereas the Delhi government had rejected non-official bills, which took up the issues of white women's and devadasis' prostitution, in 1914 the government introduced a bill for the protection of minors. Further action on this bill was postponed because of the war, but in 1915 an act was passed to expel foreign prostitutes from India. White prostitutes, said one official, 'have no claim to come here and they lower the prestige of the white races'.[176]

In the 1920s questions of social welfare were discussed in a less moralistic and more pragmatic manner. The First World War and the strengthened nationalist movement in India focused more attention on questions of national, including juvenile, health. In

1922 the Bengal Children Act was passed and in 1923 the Calcutta Suppression of Immoral Traffic Act. The acts arranged for the removal of girls under 14 and 16 respectively from brothels and their location in suitable custody. The Calcutta Act also increased the power of the police to close brothels, penalize procuration, and interfere with pimps and the importation of girls for prostitution.[177]

The main problem with such legislation was the future of rescued girls. As re-integration into their families was impossible, the alternatives were homes and industrial schools. But the only agencies which volunteered to run such institutions were the missionaries, and government would have evoked severe Bengali criticism if Hindu girls, even prostitutes, had been forced by law into Christian homes. The Bengal government itself refused to open a rescue home as demanded in several bills because they believed this to be an object of community funding.[178]

Once it was legally possible to remove girls below the age of 16 from brothels, the Vigilance Society campaigned for private subscriptions to a rescue home. Lord Lytton, the Lieutenant-Governor of Bengal, actively supported the cause. However, after his first public address in 1924 only 12 men subscribed Rs 1000 each by 1927. By then, the Vigilance Society had realized that buying a house was beyond their means and they rented a home for thirty girls in Cossipur. There were other homes run by the Women's Friendly Society and the Young Women's Christian Association. But as the common aim of these homes was to place women as servants or to marry them off, the response from prostitutes was limited. These initiatives liberated women temporarily from work, but ignored that alternative employment was often worse paid, did not re-integrate the girls into society, and deprived women and children of the support they had had while they were with other prostitutes.[179]

British and Bengali attitudes to prostitution highlighted the differences regarding the perceptions of female sexuality in their respective gender ideologies. Moreover, the British view of Bengali prostitutes was biased by prejudices against a society which was beyond foreign means of control. Prostitutes were identified with the hostile environment of narrow and almost impenetrable bazaar lanes. Confronted with the political and economic problems of the 1920s, interference with this network for the sake of some 10,000 women or a reformist image of British rule lacked political feasibility.[180] Conservative Bengalis—in harmony with the Bengali social structure—viewed prostitutes as irredeemable among other low-caste people. Consequently, the reformist debate on prostitution in Bengal was conducted almost exclusively by British men. The issue proved to be one of the last resorts of social reform. It was not contested by Indian nationalists and was even supported by the Indian women's organizations.

Differences in British and Bengali attitudes to prostitution were only of cosmetic relevance for the women who worked as prostitutes. Both Bengali passivity and British theoretical activism accepted the sexist and economic background of the age-old trade. In 1926 the Madras women's journal, *Stri Dharma*, asked in an article, 'Where are they that accuse thee?' Four young women had been charged in a Bengal court with soliciting and each was fined Rs 8. But neither the names nor addresses of the men had been taken by the police. In the 1930s prostitution was to become a feminist issue.

Conclusion

Discourses on female sexuality have been traced in a number of different, seemingly unrelated, contexts. At first sight marriage manuals and conjugal affection have little to do with colonial policies on rescue homes for reformed prostitutes. However, all these discourses share the notion that female sexuality was the means to an end, namely male superiority. The ideology of male dominance in Bengal was based on the nature of women's sexuality and not on women's physiological and psychological vulnerability during, say, pregnancy and motherhood. There were two central elements in this discourse on female sexuality. One was the danger/impurity combination associated with women's sexual desire and the other was the hierarchy within the joint family. The concept of purity required women to be initiated into sex early; the principle of seniority amongst women reinforced the hierarchy of gender relations within the household. While the ideology of impurity in relation to sex and childbirth remained as strong as ever in the period under study—slightly modified regarding the age of marriage for educated girls—seniority was weakened by the intensification of conjugal partnership.

The discursive construction of female sexuality implied female weakness versus male strength, female sensual nature versus

male intellectual culture, female chaos versus male structure.
Bengali interpretations of Hinduism and contemporary marriage
manuals carried these notions as hidden agenda suggesting that
they were universally valid. However, the analyses of patterns of
conjugal affection, of adultery and prostitution and of colonial
policies regarding marriage consummation and prostitution
showed that the construction of female sexuality depended as
much on class and culture as on race and political power.

NOTES

[1] J. Hoch-Smith and A. Spring (eds.), *Women in Ritual and Symbolic Roles*, New
York, 1978, 'Introduction', p.1.

[2] Ibid., p.2.

[3] M. Allen, 'Introduction. The Hindu View of Women', in M. Allen and S.N.
Mukherjee (eds.), *Women in India and Nepal*, Canberra, 1982, p.4.

[4] Ibid., p.6.

[5] Ibid.

[6] Ibid., p.17.

[7] S.S. Wadley, 'Women and the Hindu Tradition', in D. Jacobsen and S.S. Wadley,
Women in India, New Delhi, 1977, pp.114–19.

[8] L. Dumont, *Religion/Politics and History in India: Collected Papers in Indian
Sociology*, Paris, 1970, p.78; quoted in Allen, 1982, p.17.

[9] Allen, 1982, p.8.

[10] Ibid., p.9.

[11] Ibid., p.18.

[12] Ibid., p.11.

[13] 'Glorifications of Goddesses', in D. Zbavitel, *Bengali Literature* (J. Gonda, ed., *A
History of Indian Literature*, vol. IX); Wiesbaden 1976, pp.159–69; India Office Library
and Records, P/3951, *Sudhakar*, 30 January 1891 and *Burdwan Sanjibani*, 13 January
1891, *Report on Native Newspapers in Bengal (RNNB)*, 17 and 31 January 1891.

[14] S.B. Dasgupta, *Obscure Religious Cults*, Calcutta, 1962, 1st ed., 1946, pp.9–10;
H. Sastri, *Discovery of Living Buddhism in Bengal*, Calcutta, 1887, p.1; M.M. Bose,
Post-Caitanya Sahajia Cult of Bengal, Calcutta, 1930, pp.134ff.

[15] P.K. Maity, *Historical Studies in the Cult of the Goddess Manasa*, Calcutta, 1966,
p.68.

[16] E.C. Dimock, jr., *The Place of the Hidden Moon*, Chicago, 1966, pp.43, 83.

[17] S. Gupta, 'Tantric Sakta Literature in Modern Indian Languages', in T.
Goudriaan and S. Gupta, *Hindu Tantric and Sakta Literature*, Wiesbaden, 1981 (J.
Gonda, ed., *A History of Indian Literature*, vol. II), p.200.

[18] N.N. Bhattacharyya, *History of the Sakti Religion*, New Delhi, 1974, pp.152–65;
N.S. Bose, *Indian Awakening and Bengal*, Calcutta, 1976, p.179.

[19] Interview with Abha Mukherjee, Calcutta, 7 March 1985.

[20] P. Kumar, *Sakti Cult in Ancient India*, Varanasi, 1974, p.151.

[21] Ibid., p.168.

[22] Maity, 1966, pp.63–4.

[23] Allen, 1982, p.13.

[24] Kumar, 1974, p.166.

[25] Ibid., pp.165–6.

[26] Allen, 1982, pp.13–4; Bose, 1930, pp.76.

[27] Allen, 1982, p.13.

[28] Ibid., p.15.

[29] J. Woodroffe, *Shakti and Shakta*, Madras, 1951, p.540; quoted in Dimock, 1966, pp.98–9.

[30] L. Siegel, *Sacred and Profane Dimensions of Love in Indian Traditions as Exemplified in The Gitagovinda of Jayadeva*, Delhi, 1978, p.25.

[31] Dimock, 1966, p.99.

[32] Ibid., p.15.

[33] Ibid., pp.16–8.

[34] Ibid., p.105.

[35] Ibid., p.26.

[36] Ibid., p.101.

[37] M.T. Kennedy, *The Chaitanya Movement*, Calcutta, 1925, p.85.

[38] J.H. Broomfield, *Elite Conflict in a Plural Society: Twentieth Century Bengal*, Bombay, 1968, p.148.

[39] Gupta, 1981, pp.179, 194–201.

[40] Ibid., p.200.

[41] A.K. Majumdar, *Bhakti Renaissance*, Bombay, 1965, p.77.

[42] Broomfield, 1968, pp.148–9.

[43] R. Inden, *Marriage and Rank in Bengali Culture*, New Delhi, 1976, pp.51, 60–3, 73–6; S. Sen Gupta, *A Study of Women in Bengal*, Calcutta, 1970, p.15.

[44] Inden, 1976, p.76.

[45] Ibid.

[46] Ibid., p.104.

[47] Ibid., p.96.

[48] Ibid., pp.96–7.

[49] S.C. Bose, *The Hindoos as They Are*, Calcutta, 1883, pp.232–41; COI, 1891, VII, p.208; Chakraborty, 1963, pp.8–10; Sen Gupta, 1970, pp.16–18.

[50] M.M. Urquhart, *Women in Bengal*, Calcutta, 1926, pp.31–2; C. Deb, *Antahpurer Atmakatha*, Calcutta, 1984; B. Banerji, *Pather Panchali*, Bloomington, 1968, p.37.

[51] S.C. Bose, 1883, pp.232–41; Amarendranath Ray Caudhuri, *Sonar Satin*, Calcutta, 1898; Bhuvanacandra Mukhopadhyay, *Ami Ramani*, Calcutta, 1880.

[52] 'The rule that brahmana girls were to be married between 8 to 10 years became general from about the 6th or 7th century and continued down to modern times.' P.V. Kane, *History of the Dharmasastra*, 2, 1, Poona, 1974, p.445.

[53] S.C. Bose, 1883, p.238.

[54] R.K. Ray, 'The Kahar Chronicle', *Modern Asian Studies*, 21, 1987, pp.711–49, 745ff.; for a critique of the essay, see D. Engels, 'History and Sexuality in India: Discursive Trends', *Trends in History*, 4, 1990.

[55] M. Borthwick, *The Changing Role of Women in Bengal 1849–1905*, Princeton, 1984, pp.18–9.

[56] Bipradasa Mukhopadhyaya, *Yuvak-yuvati*, Calcutta, 1922, 1st ed. 1891, pp.42–51.

[57] Ibid., pp.30–7.

[58] Dinescandra Sen, *Grihasri*, Calcutta, 1915, p.134.

[59] Bipradasa Mukhopadhyaya, *Yuvak-yuvati*, Calcutta, 1922, p.42.

[60] Ibid., p.51.

[61] Ibid., pp.87–9.

[62] Jogindranath Mukhophadyaya, *Jiban Raksa*, Calcutta, 1887; Baradakanta Majumdar, *Naritattva*, Calcutta, 1889.

[63] Ibid., pp.40–1.

[64] Ibid., pp.30–5.

[65] Jogindranath Mukhophadaya, *Jiban Raksa*, Calcutta, 1887, pp.24–8.

[66] Ibid., p.32.

[67] Ibid., p.33.

[68] Borthwick, 1984, pp.243–5.

[69] Borthwick, 1984, pp.243–56; Usha Prabha Sen, 'Comment', *Prabasi*, 1325, 2, p.239; Joges Candra Ray, 'Semij', ibid., p.532; Krisna Bihari Caudhuri, 'Naridiger Upanat Bybahar', *Bharat Mahila*, 6, 1911, p.52–3.

[70] Suniti Devi, 'Oh Calcutta', *Eve's Weekly*, Oct. 24–30, 1981, pp.52–8.

[71] Interview with Prathiba Chatterjee, Calcutta, 11 February 1985

[72] Interview with Manilata Mazumdar and Puspa Sengupta, Calcutta, 2 February 1985.

[73] Interview with Pansy Ganguli; Bose, 1883, pp.73–7; G. Forbes (ed.), *Sudha Mazumdar. A Pattern of Life. The Memoirs of an Indian Woman*, New Delhi, 1977, pp.99–103.

[74] S. Kakar, *The Inner World*, Delhi, 1981, 1st ed., 1978, pp.73–9; M. Roy, *Bengali Women*, Chicago, 1972, shows the continuity of these problems in present-day, middle-class Bengali society.

[75] Interview with Radharani Basu, Calcutta, 7 March 1985.

[76] This development seemed to threaten the cultural norms of Bengali society. A fictional conversation between a sasuri and bau ma was even used to ridicule women's liberation, see Priyanath Samkhyatirtha, *Nabina o Prabina*, Sibpur, 1935.

[77] Kamini Ray, *Thakurmar Cithi*, Calcutta, 1924.

[78] Dines Candra Sen, *Grihasri*, Calcutta, 1915. This essay collection was extremely popular and had thirteen editions between 1913 and 1935.

[79] Priyanath Basu, *Grihadharma*, Calcutta, 1934, pp.39–48, 75–8.

[80] Saudamini Gupta, *Kanyar Prati Upades*, Dhaka, 1918, pp.76–84.

[81] Yadunath Cakravarti, *Kayekkhani Patra*, Calcutta, 1902; Forbes (Mazumdar), 1977, p.106.

[82] Girija Prasanna Raycaudhuri, *Griha Laksmi*, Calcutta, 1887, pp.57–63.

[83] Translation of Bengali MSS (in family possession) by Paramita Viswanathan, granddaugthter of Ramanada Chatterjee.

[84] Interview with Paramita Viswanathan and Shyamasree Lal, Ramanada Chatterjee's granddaughters, Calcutta, 27 January 1985.

[85] Interview with Phulrenu Chanda, Calcutta, 3 February 1985.

[86] Interview with Abha Mukherjee, Calcutta, 7 February 1985.

[87] WBSA, GOB, Poll/Poll, 526 (1–18), 1930.

[88] Inteview with Subarnaprabha Baksi, Calcutta, 3 February 1985.

[89] Interview with Renuka Raychaudhuri, Calcutta, 9 February 1985.

[90] Interview with Amiya Sen, Calcutta, 9 February 1985.

[91] Amarendranath Raycaudhuri, *Sonar Satin*, Calcutta, 1898; Bhubana Candra Mukhopadhyaya, *Ami Ramani*, Calcutta, 1880.

[92] M. Bandhopadhyaya, *The Puppet's Tale*, New Delhi, 1968, 1st Bengali ed., 1936, tells as a side story the suffering and social disgrace of a co-wife who is kept like a mistress. Bhabani Caran Ghose, *Parinaya-Kahini*, Calcutta, 1903, contains the story of sisters who discuss an absent husband's faithfulness.

[93] Under the headline 'The Dangers of Industrialisation', *Modern Review*, August, 1921, 244, an anonymous author warned of male infidelity when couples lived separately because of work or studies. The author described social life in the small town of Bolpur: 'I have found an increasing moral breakdown, not only in those who have come in for trade purposes and left their wives behind them in the villages, but also in the student life which has been obliged to congregate in different bazar quarters.' Although such reports often painted a negative picture of social conditions to serve their own social reformist ends, such a specific account of a small town probably contains some facts. This view is supported by evidence that refers to conditions in Calcutta: Sudhir Candra Bandhapadhyaya, 'Kalikatar Natik Abastha', *Prabasi*, 1316, pp.427–35; Manadasundari Debi, *Patitar Atmacarit*, Calcutta, 1929.

[94] Priyanath Basu, *Grihadharma*, Calcutta, 1934, pp.75–8, advised women not to employ young maidservants for this reason.

[95] 'Narir Upar Atyacar', *Prabasi*, 1330, 1, pp.559–61; interview with Naina Debi, New Delhi, 12 December 1984; interview with Aroti Ganguli, Calcutta, 3 March 1985; 'Nari Kirtti', *Bharat Mahila*, 6, 1911, pp.126–8.

[96] Sarat Chandra Chatterji, *Chandranath*, Bombay, 1969, 1st Bengali ed., 1916. The novel shows the far-reaching consequences of a woman's promiscuity.

[97] In 1884 the suicide of Kadambari Debi gained prominence. She was the sister-in-law of Rabindranath and committed suicide because her husband neglected her and had affairs with other women from inside and outside the family, Subrat Rudra, *Kadambari Debi*, Calcutta, 1977.

[98] IOLR, V/24/3203, 1901, p.27; 1902, p.17 (four wives in Backerganj poisoned their unfaithful husbands); 1903, p.20 ('There were as usual several cases of faithless wives or their paramours poisoning husbands'). Future police reports, however, contained no further evidence.

[99] IOLR, V/24/3203, *Report on the Administration of the Police of the Lower Provinces, Bengal Presidency*, 1901, p.26; 1903, p.21; 1904, p.23.

[100] IOLR, V/24/3203, 1900, p.35. Although this particular case occurred in Bihar the pattern was not unusual as lynch justice happened in Bengal as well, V/24/3203, 1901, p.27.

[101] For instance, Sarat Chandra Chatterjee, *Chandranath*, Bombay, 1969, 1st ed., 1916.

[102] F. Henriques, *Prostitution and Society*, London, 1962, pp.140–203, 235–6. For British attitudes to courtesans, V. Talwar Oldenburg, *The Making of Colonial Lucknow 1856–1877*, Princeton, 1984, pp.134–42, 200–2. I am not going to discuss the dedication of girls, devadasis, to temples because this was a predominantly South Indian practice which hardly occurred in Bengal. For a contemporary account, A.R. Caton, 'Two Social Evils', in Caton, 1930, pp.177–85 (article by M. Reddy); U. Chakraborty, *Condition of Bengali Women around the 2nd Half of the 19th Century*, Calcutta, 1963, p.25; COI, 1931, VI, 1, p.62.

[103] IOLR, P/8954, GOI, Home/Judl., 145/1912 (September), pp. 2055–8.

[104] Ibid., pp.2057.

[105] IOLR, P/8954, GOI, Home/Judl., 145/1912 (September), p. 2057.

[106] IOLR, P/7891, GOI, Home/Judl., 174–6/1908 (July–December), pp.1838–78.

[107] NAI, GOI, Home/Police, A, 24–29/1920 (January), 'Extent, Distribution and Regulation of the "Social Evil" in the Cities of Calcutta, Madras and Bombay and in Rangoon Town' (hereafter 'Memorandum'), p.1.

[108] See L. Dumont, *Homo Hierarchicus*, Chicago, 1980, 1st ed., 1966, p.191.

[109] Interview with Dr Panchanan Ghosal, Calcutta, 6 January 1985; from the 1920s onwards, Dr Ghosal worked as a psychologist with the Indian Police Service in Calcutta; Caton, 1930, p.187.

[110] IOLR, P/10596, GOI, Home/Police, 175/1919 (April), pp.390, 394; 'Memorandum', p.5; K. Ballhatchet, *Sex, Race and Class under the Raj; Imperial Attitudes and Policies and their Cities 1893–1905*, London, 1980, pp.130–1.

[111] 'Memorandum', pp.22–4; Sudhir Candra Bandhapadhyaya, 'Kalikatar Natik Abastha', *Prabasi*, 1316, pp.427–35; H. Anderson, *The Social Evil*, Calcutta n.d.

[112] Manadasundari Debi, *Patitar Atma-carit*, Calcutta, 1929, pp.1–104. I am grateful to the anonymous reader of my manuscript for informing me about the fictional character and political background of the book.

[113] Interview with Dr Panchanan Ghosal.

[114] I.L.R., 38, 1911, Calcutta, pp.493–501; I.L.R., 25, 1898, Calcutta, pp.254–8; Binodini Dasi, *Amar Katha*, Calcutta, 1912; Upendranath Vidyabhusan, *Binodini o Tarasundari*, Calcutta, 1919; Upendranath Vidyabhusan, *Tinakari*, Calcutta, 1919; Chakraborty, 1969, pp.31–4.

[115] Interview with Panchanan Ghosal; Manadasundari Debi, 1929, pp.105, 128.

[116] Ibid., pp.129–41.

[117] 'Memorandum', p.5.

[118] S.C. Mukherjee, *Prostitution in India*, Calcutta, 1934, pp.124–5; IOLR, P/10596, GOI, Home/Police, 175/1919 (April), p.394.

[119] Anderson, n.d., 29–30. On 7 September 1890, a durwan 'suspecting his wife of infidelity, cut her throat with a clasp knife which he had newly purchased'. At midnight, 13 October 1890, a prostitute was found lying strangled on her bed in Jorasanko, Calcutta. Gold and silver ornaments worth Rs 164 had been taken. The murderer left the house unseen. 'All efforts to trace him failed.' IOLR, P/4120, GOB, Judl./Police, 19–20/1892 (January), p.5; IOLR, V/24/3215–16, GOB, *Annual Report on the Police Administration of the Town of Calcutta and its Suburbs*, 1891–1907, and IOLR, V/24/3203–05, GOB, *Report on the Administration of the Police of the Lower Provinces, Bengal Presidency*, 1900–26, contain several cases which underline the pattern.

[120] IOLR, P/10596, GOI, Home/Police, 175/1919 (April), p.392; Manadasundari Debi, 1929, 144–53.

[121] COI, 1911, v, 1, pp.324–5.

[122] IOLR, GOI, Home/Judl., 276/1913 (July), p.2429.

[123] Ibid., p.2430.

[124] Mukherjee, 1934, pp.56–7.

[125] Borthwick, 1984, pp.108–50.

[126] J.R. Walkowitz, *Prostitution and Victorian Society. Women, Class and the State*, Cambridge, 1980, p.245.

[127] G. Stedman Jones, *Languages of Class. Studies in English Working Class History 1832–1982*, Cambridge, 1983, p.190; G. Stedman Jones, *Outcaste London*, London, 1984, pt. III. See also D.J. Pivar, *Purity Crusade. Sexual Morality and Social Control, 1868–1900*, Westport, Conn., 1973, pp.255ff, for a comparison with the USA.

[128] Ballhatchet, 1980, p.121.

[129] GOI, Legislative Department, *The Unrepealed General Acts of the Governor General in Council, 1891–98*, vol. VI, Calcutta, 1899, p.25.

[130] S. Sarkar, *Modern India 1885–1947*, New Delhi, 1984, pp.71–3.

[131] J.M. Compton, 'British Government and Society in the Presidency of Bengal, c. 1885–c. 1880: An Examination of Certain Aspects of British Attitudes, Behaviour and Policy', unpublished. D.Phil., Oxford, 1968; N.S. Bose, *Racism, Struggle for Equality and Indian Nationalism*, Calcutta, 1981.

[132] IOLR, Lansdowne to Northbrook, 6 September 1890, MSS. Eur. D 558/12.

[133] IOLR, Lansdowne to Bailey, 10 October 1890, MSS. Eur. D 558/19.

[134] Queen Emperess *v.* Hurree Mohun Mythee, *ILR*, Calcutta, XVIII, 1891, 49–68; IOLR, Cross to Lansdowne, 16 October 1890, MSS. Eur. D 558/3; Lansdowne to Cross, 1 and 23 September, 8 October 1890, ibid.

[135] L.B. Day, *Bengal Peasant Life*, Calcutta, 1969, 1st ed., 1874, pp.67–70; S.C. Bose, *The Hindoos as They Are*, Calcutta, 1883, pp.68–9.

[136] Ibid.; N. Zemon Davies, *Society and Culture in Early Modern France*, London, 1975, 'Women on Top', pp.124–51, analyses sexual inversions which, however, were more far-reaching than the modest Bengali example, although the underlying principle was identical.

[137] Interview with Pansy (Pankojini) Ganguli, Calcutta, 12 January 1985.

[138] S.C. Bose, 1883, pp.79–80; G. Forbes (Mazumdar), 1977, pp. 102–4.

[139] Ibid., p.105.

[140] *Bangavasi*, 10 January 1891, *RNNB*, week ending 17 January 1891, p.57; B.N. Saraswati, *Brahmanic Ritual Traditions*, Shimla, 1977, pp.91–5. He argues that garbhadan was celebrated in the case of an immature bride by reciting the mantras after the wedding ceremony without practising intercourse. IOLR, P/3951, GOI, *India Legislative Proceedings*, April 1891, Appendix U; GOI, *Report of the Age of Consent Committee 1928–29* (hereafter *AoC Report 1928–1929*), Calcutta, 1929, p.97. None of the women I interviewed about their weddings could remember the garbhadan ceremony.

[141] *AoC Report 1928–1929*, pp.67–8; GOI, *Report of the Age of Consent Committee, 1928–1929. Evidence, Bengal*, vol. 6. Calcutta, 1929 (hereafter *AoC Evidence*), answers to questions 6 and 7. Day, 1969, 57, argues that financial difficulties led to the postponement of marriages.

[142] *AoC Report 1928–1929*, pp.67–8; *ILR* 1905, p.28, Calcutta, 49; IOLR, Lansdowne to Bailey, 10 October 1890, MSS D. 558/19; NAI, GOI, Home/Judl., 1892,July, 278–91; IOLR, P/4351, GOI, Home/Judl., 1893, July–December, 187–96; *AoC Report 1928–1929*, p.97.

[143] 'Sisupatni-hatya', *Prabasi*, 1332, 1, pp.439–41.

[144] Interview with Amiya Sen. Amiya Sen who was married at the age of 14 in 1920 was 'demanded' by her in-laws nine months after the wedding although her father had been assured before the wedding that she could stay with him until the age of 18.

[145] IOLR, P/3951, GOI, Legislative Proc., April 1891, Appendix E; IOLR, Elliott to Lansdowne, 5 January 1891, MSS. Eur. D 558/21.

[146] S. Banerjee, *National Awakening and the Bangabasi*, Calcutta, 1968; in 1891 the *Bangabasi*, a weekly, had 20,000 subscribers, the daily *Dainik-o-Samachar Chandrika* had 1500. They were thus the largest selling Bengali newspapers, both of which were founded in 1881, IOLR, L/R/5/17, *RNNB*, 1891.

[147] For a detailed analysis of these developments, see A. Sen, 'Hindu Revivalism in Action—The Age of Consent Bill Agitation in Bengal', *Indian Historical Review*, 7, 1980–81; M. Sinha, 'The Age of Consent Act: The Ideal of Masculinity and Colonial Ideology in Late 19th Century Bengal', *Proceedings of the Eighth International Symposium on Asia Studies*, Hong Kong, 1986; D.A.E. Engels, 'The Age of Consent Act of 1891: Colonial Ideology in Bengal', *South Asia Research*, 3, 1983.

[148] L. Davidoff, 'Class and Gender in Victorian England', in J.L. Newton, M.P. Ryan and J.R. Walkowitz (eds.), *Sex and Class in Women's History*, London, 1983, p.19.

[149] Ibid., p.25; P.T. Cominos, 'Innocent Femina Sensualis in Unconscious Conflict', in M. Vicinus (ed.), *Suffer and Be Still: Women in the Victorian Age*, Bloomington, 1972, pp.155–72; P.T. Cominos, 'Late Victorian Sexual Respectability and the Social System', *International Review of Social History*, 8, 1963, pp.18–48, 216–50, 242ff.

[150] Davidoff, 1983, p.19.

[151] A.L. Basham, *The Wonder that Was India*, London, 1985, 1st ed. 1954, pp.240–1.

[152] Davidoff, 1983, p.20. For the close connection between racial attitudes and the 'cultural division of labour', that is the economic and political interests of the dominant classes, see M. Hechter, *Internal Colonialism. The Celtic Fringe in British National Development, 1536–1966*, London, 1975, pp.39–42, 73. For the orientalist debate, see E.W. Said, *Orientalism*, Harmondsworth, 1986; M. Alloula, *The Colonial Harem*, Minneapolis, 1986; R. Kabbani, *Europe's Myths of the Orient*, Bloomington, 1986. (See the review of both books, M. Badran, 'Beyond the Mirage', *The Women's Review of Books*, 4, January 1987, pp.7–9.)

[153] Dr Joubert, 'Discussion on the Nubile Age of Females', *Indian Medical Gazette*, December 1890, in IOLR, P/3951, GOI, Legislative Proceedings, April 1891, No 34, p.51.

[154] *Statesman*, 14 February 1891, p.5.

[155] R.C. Mitter asked social reformers to understand the temptations with which married men had to cope. 'Puritanic reformers, who, viewing the world in the light of their own iron-heartedness, fail to sympathize with the weakness and imperfect nature of their fellow-beings, may say that these men ought not to marry, ought not to bring to their solitary homes girls under age.' IOLR, P/3951, GOI, Legislative Proc., April 1891, Appendix A20, 'Report of the Select Committee'.

[156] *Sudhakar*, 23 January 1891, *Banganibasi*, 30 January 1891, *RNNB*, 31 January and 7 February 1891.

[157] *Banganibasi*, 23 and 30 January 1891, *Bangabasi*, 21 March 1891, *Dainik-o-Samachar Chandrika*, 19 January 1891, *RNNB*, 24, 31 January, 7 February, 28 March 1891. Dainik reminded its readers of the Contagious Diseases Act which had rendered medical examination obligatory.

[158] S. Kakar, *The Inner World*, 2nd ed., Delhi, 1981, p.92.

[159] Ibid., p.93.

[160] *Burdwan Sanjibani*, 13 January 1891, *Sudhakar*, 30 January 1891, *RNNB*, 17 January, 7 February 1891.

[161] *Bangabasi*, 7 March 1891, *RNNB*, 14 March 1891.

[162] This argument was brought up by the Sobha Bazar Committee and in the Memorial of the Inhabitants of Kalighat. Sahachar, 18 February 1891, *RNNB*, 21 February 1891; IOLR, P/3951, GOI, Legislative Proc., April 1891, Appendix W3.

[163] *The Times*, 29 November 1890, quoted by Heimsath, 1962, p.501; *Dainık-o-Samachar Chandrika*, 4 February 1891, *RNNB*, 7 February 1891; Abstract, 1891, pp.80–2.

[164] IOLR, P/3889, GOI, Home/Judl., April 103–04/1891, p.884; Lansdowne to Elliott, 24 March 1891, MSS. Eur. D 558/20.

[165] IOLR, P/4351, GOI, July–December 187–96/1893, 1781–85, p.1269.

[166] NAI, GOI, Home/Judl., July 278–91/1892, p.3.

[167] Ibid., p.7.

[168] IOLR, GOI, P/6587, Home/Judl., 34/1903, March, p.1665. The apathy of village relatives was repeatedly blamed for the lack of success in tracing the traffic in girls, IOLR, P/7891, GOI, Home/Judl., 174/1908, July–December 1828, p.1835. Even after Sections 372 and 373, Indian Penal Code, had been amended in 1923 (NAI, GOI, Home/Judl., 591/1929, Deposit, 12), the traffic still continued, A.R. Caton (ed.), *The Key of Progress*, London, 1930, p.182.

[169] Ballhatchet, 1980, pp.130ff; 'Memorandum', p.5; Bengali newspapers regularly published complaints about brothels, *RNNB*, 1895–1920.

[170] IOLR, GOI, P/6587, Home/Judl., 34/1903, March 1665; NAI, GOI, Home/Judl., A, 88–9/1911, April, Notes.

[171] IOLR, GOI, P/7891, Home/Judl., 174/1908, July–December 1835.

[172] NAI, GOI, Home/Judl., A, 88–9/1911, April, Notes; H. Anderson, n.d.; Ballhatchet, 1980, p.130; J.R. Walkowitz, 1980, pp.246–56.

[173] IOLR, GOI, P/7891, Home/Judl., 176/1908, July–December 1878.

[174] IOLR, P/8953, GOI, Home/Judl., 337/1912, March, pp.503–7; P/8954, 148–50/1912, November, pp.2070–95; 245/1913, July, pp.2399–411; 276/1913, July, pp.2425–8; 101/1914, March, pp.503–5; NAI, GOI, Home/Judl., A. 337–8/1912, March, Notes, 1/1914, Deposit, February.

[175] 'It is only an infinitesimal minority—mostly Brahmans and educated men of culture living in the cities—who are desirous of rescuing minor girls from prosititution.' IOLR, P/8954, GOI, Home/Judl., 145/1912, September, p.2057. The campaign was led by Dr Muthulakshmi Reddi; see Caton, 1930, pp.177–85.

[176] NAI, GOI, Home/Judl., A, 100–27/1914, Notes, 6; 820/1922, p.20.

[177] NAI, GOI, Home/Judl., 820/1922, 10; Home/Police, F24/3, 1923.

[178] In 1908, the opening of rescue homes was discussed in depth and rejected, IOLR, P/7891, GOI, Home/Judl., 174–6/1908, July–December 1837, 1877–78.

[179] *Lord Lytton in Bengal, Being a Selection from his Speeches as Governor of Bengal, 1922–1927*, Calcutta, 1929, pp.396–9, 445–8; 'Memorandum', p.20.

[180] See chapter 9. For the connection between political feasibility and British reform policies in India, see L. Mani, 'The Production of an Official Discourse on Sati in Early Nineteenth-century Bengal', in F. Barker *et al.* (eds.), *Europe and its Others*, vol.1, Colchester, 1985, pp.107–27.

4
THE POLITICS OF CHILDBIRTH[1]

Successful biological reproduction, that is a son by a pure mother, was the fulfilment of any man's existence and the ideological justification of male control over women. However, birth itself was highly polluting. The purity of conception and of offspring on the one hand and the impurity of birth on the other demonstrated quite clearly the ambiguity of Bengali perceptions of women.

In the last chapter, Bengali and colonial discourses centring on marriage consummation and conception were examined in order to highlight the underlying assumptions of male or European superiority. The organization and reform of childbirth were considerably less contentious from the point of view of the Bengali male as—due to the purdah-related separation of male and female spheres—birth was an entirely female concern. This also influenced the official colonial approach to birthing and women's health.[2]

The poor image of birth in Bengali culture, underlined by high infant and maternal mortality rates, provoked contradicting explanations and ideas for reform. Whereas the Bengali nationalist approach blamed colonial economic exploitation and poverty, western observers complained about poor hygiene and bad birth management stemming from the alleged impurity of birth. On the whole, male reluctance to address the issues left more space to reforming agencies, mainly run by women, once the notions of impurity were overcome.[3] I will examine how British and Indian women differed when they used this discursive vacuum to initiate reforms.

Customs, debates and reforms regarding childbirth were part of the wider discourses on health.[4] In fact, few exceptions apart, it was only with regard to childbirth that women's health was

explicitly and officially dealt with in colonial Bengal. In the light
of recent studies on colonial medicine this comes as no surprise.
In particular David Arnold's work has emphasized the instrumen-
tality of state intervention in the field of medicine and public
health. This implied that health measures were targeted towards
the focal points of imperial concern, namely barracks, urban
centres, industrial estates and plantations, while the rural areas,
and the majority of the population, were ignored.[5] In most cases
imperial interests in childbirth cannot be explained by straightforward references to economic or military engagements. But as
Arnold and Jeffery have stressed, many aspects of British health
policy in India were part of the ideological enterprise which was
set up to justify the Raj.[6] However, such hegemonic strategies only
worked when the cultural assumptions of the receivers, that is the
Bengalis, were respected. Otherwise colonial health policy was
regarded by the Bengalis as proof of imperial incompetence from
the last decades of the nineteenth century onwards. Moreover, the
British reformist effort was doomed to failure because childbirth
was regarded in isolation from the mothers' socio-economic environment.

Giving Birth

Although the cultural assumptions relating to childbirth were
widely shared by all classes of Bengali Hindu society, the extent
to which religious prescriptions and customs were followed
depended on a family's caste and, more importantly, class background. Details regarding the management of birth, for instance,
were published in early twentieth-century census reports and in
reports on women in the organized economic sector. The first
tended to stress what seemed to be the ethnographically curious
and the second measured birthing according to principles of
modern western medicine. In contrast, Bengali octogenarian
women who spoke in 1985 of their mothers' confinement con-
firmed some of the details, but differed in their assessment.

Once a young wife had moved into her in-laws' house, pregnancy was anxiously awaited. Economic circumstances permitting, every indulgence was shown during her pregnancy in sharp
contrast to her strict diet and seclusion after birth. During her first
pregnancy, at least, a young wife travelled back to her baper bari

and stayed there until after her confinement. The idea was that she needed special care and emotional support, which was guaranteed in her father's house. During and after birth a woman had to cope with the implications of her ritual impurity, but while pregnant she was spoilt. A number óf rituals were performed during pregnancy, involving the participation of women, aimed at her physical and psychological contentment. Other rituals were aimed at the health of the baby.[7]

Even women in employment tried to spend the period of pregnancy and birth with their family rather than at their place of work. Tribal women miners, for instance, who were mainly part-time workers took extended leave before and after birth: Santhal women usually two to three months, other women, like Bauris, as long as they could afford, often up to one year. However, women whose labour migration had taken them further away from their homes and whose wages were proportionally more important to the family budget, could take off less time from work. Thus, most women in tea plantations continued to work almost until the day of delivery and returned about a fortnight afterwards.[8]

The management of childbirth was determined by the ritual pollution that stemmed from the separation of the child and mother through the cutting of the umbilical cord.[9] The loss of blood increased the impression of impurity and was a real problem for very poor women. Women who worked in jute mills, for instance, took left-over bits of fibre home when delivery was approaching to have something to lie on and to clean up with.[10]

Childbirth took place in a special room, *athurghar* or *sutikagriha*:

The character of the room depends on the means and the enlightenment of the family, but generally it is one of the worst rooms in the house, or a shed is erected outside the compound. Among the poorer classes, the woman's accommodation is wretched. A portion of one of the living rooms may be screened off, or she may have to use the verandah; some doctors even state that the cowshed or kitchen is occasionally used. As a rule, when a separate room is assigned, it is small, dark and ill-ventilated.[11]

The ventilation was worsened by 'windows and apertures being closed with mud or stuffed with old rags'.[12] This was done to prevent evil spirits from entering the room, and the mother and child from catching a cold. For the same reason a small fire was kept burning in an earthen pot irrespective of the year's season,

filling the tightly-insulated room with suffocating smoke and
heat.

In middle-class families with educated daughters who had
abandoned the strictest orthodoxy, the conditions of childbirth
were similar. Abha Mukherjee, whose father was a clerk in the
Upper Court and whose mother had been to the Mahakali Pathsala, a respectable middle-class girls' school along the lines of
Hindu Revivalism, remembers the family's athurghar as 'dirty
because the midwife was not trained to keep it clean. It was smoky
though the fire was essential to keep mother and baby warm',[13]
Rather than blaming customs and traditions, as western observers
did, she gave reasons why, compared with the clinically clean
conditions prescribed in medical textbooks, the conditions in the
athurghar were poor.[14]

In the late nineteenth century women gave birth in a kneeling
or sitting position. Written in the Census in a disapproving tone,
for the late twentieth-century reader the description of giving
birth reads like a contemporary statement on natural birth (apart
from the hair in the woman's mouth):

When the pain begins the patient is either made to kneel down on all fours
and to hold a basket, pillow or some similar article to her breast, or she
sits on the lap of the dai who presses her knees against her loins and
kneads her abdomen with her hands... In order to facilitate delivery the
passage is anointed with castor oil, the abdomen is rubbed with mustard
oil, and nutmeg and betel leaves are given internally as a stimulant, while
an effort is made to promote nausea by stuffing a handful of the patient's
hair into her mouth...[15]

Around the turn of the century western practices were emulated and women started to give birth lying on their backs. In
emergencies middle-class women consulted western-trained doctors. Renuka Ray-chaudhuri's mother, for instance, wife of a
government servant, gave birth at home to seven children before
she was 25 years old. After Renuka's birth, exhausted by the
frequency of pregnancies, she became so ill that she was taken to
hospital. At home, however, she had lain, as was customary, in the
smoky athurghar for a whole month after giving birth.[16]

After delivery the umbilical cord was cut with a knife, a bamboo stick or a shell disinfected with cow dung. From then on the
child was regularly massaged with a mixture of turmeric and
mustard oil, as well as sun-bathed to strengthen the cranial bones

and to adapt the child to the hot climate. Sometimes the midwife massaged the mother as well and, during the cold season, applied hot compressions to the mother and child.[17]

The period of strict maternal rest started once the placenta had come out.[18] It was also a time of impurity which was shorter for a twice-born woman than for a Sudra, and shorter after giving birth to a son rather than to a daughter. It lasted up to 30 days in the case of a girl's birth and 21 for a boy's. It ended with the mother's ceremonial bath.[19] If families could afford orthodox rules, no member was allowed into the room for the entire time of confinement. On the fifth or sixth day the mother had her first bath after delivery and the room was cleaned.[20]

During the mother's confinement the family celebrated the arrival of the new member, more extensively in the case of a son than a daughter, with a number of rituals including a ceremonial feeding of children.[21] In Anupama Chatterjee's baper bari many people were fed, and dust, which had been touched by the feet of at least six Brahmans, was scattered in the athurghar.[22] Sasthi puja, a ritual to evoke the goddess Sasthi's blessing for the child, was performed on the sixth day after birth. During the night ink and pen were left in the child's room, and the dai or a priest stayed awake, at a safe distance, because Bidhata Purusa, the creator god, was expected to enter the room and to write the child's future in indelible, but invisible, letters on his or her forehead.[23]

This birth system, named Sasthi after the goddess invoked, was followed by high-caste women. It inflicted a good deal of suffering, centrally concerned as it was with the concept of purity. There was an alternative system, the Krisna or Harilot system, which was more rational, easier to follow and more comfortable for women. It was said to be 'gaining popularity among more enlightened Bengalis' by 1911:

No fire is kept burning in the room; no...concoctions of spices are administered. The woman is allowed cooling drinks, and given ordinary food. She is not regarded as unclean, and need not therefore be banished to an outhouse and left to the midwife's mercies, but is attended by women of the household during the period of her confinement. She and the child are also bathed in cold or tepid water soon after delivery.[24]

The Krisna system was followed by culturally-marginalized groups, who had either, like Vaisnavas, abandoned the purity ideal of Brahmanical Hinduism, or had never been affected by it, like the Bauris and other *adivasis* living at the western fringe of Bengal.[25]

Irrespective of any birth system, many families who depended on female labour could just not adhere to the prescribed period of confinement and women were back at work after one or two days. Unless an older child or a relative was able to stay at home to look after the baby, women in employment took their infants with them. Women who picked tea went back to the plantations, 'carrying the child slung in a basket or cloth over the shoulder'.[26] Women in jute mills laid their new-born babies on jute fibre next to their place of work.[27]

Infant and Maternal Mortality

Until the 1920s and, to a limited extent, even thereafter western observers of high infant and maternal mortality rates in Bengal blamed the region's cultural and religious customs. However, as in the case of childbirth, class, not caste or religion, was more important in determining life or death.

The statistical basis for any assessment of maternal and infant death is uneven and weak. Census data suffered from changing terms of reference from one census to the next and from incomplete compilation. Nevertheless, the available data was used in contemporary discourse to compare conditions in Britain with those in Bengal and to draw political conclusions regarding the state of civilization in the countries and the beneficiary effect of public health measures. Moreover, findings which contradicted the official line were at times simply ignored.

Available data suggests that the infant death rate was considerably higher in Bengal than in England. During the decade ending 1885 the infant mortality rate in England was 142 per 1000.[28] The rate improved rapidly after 1900 and in 1920 was as low as 80 per 1000. In contrast, during the first two decades of the twentieth century in Bengal, one in five babies died before their first birthday. In 1921 infant mortality rates were still on the increase and were, even among the bhadralok, double the corresponding proportions in European countries.[29]

The blame for high infant mortality was mainly laid on incompetent midwives and poor hygiene in the athurghar. The 1911 Calcutta census noted that

the practice of cutting the umbilical cord with dirty instruments (e.g. a piece of split bamboo, or a conch shell) and of applying cow-dung ashes to the freshly cut end commonly results in tetanus neonatorum and causes a very large number of deaths among healthy infants every year.[30]

But a closer look would have shown that, had traditional customs been strictly followed, Bengali mothers and babies were not at greater risks than Europeans.[31]

Early-twentieth century western observers focused on the poor standards of traditional Indian midwifery. Dais belonged to low castes, usually Dom and Bagdi, because higher-caste women would not stand the ritual pollution of childbirth. In 1901 the editors of the census commissioned a special enquiry into the methods of indigenous midwives. 'The curious information' collected differed little from contemporary European folk practices:

the dais' resources are very limited. The occupation is usually hereditary, and the young woman who aspires to follow this occupation must first go through a course of attending delivery cases, as a spectator or assistant, before she is allowed to practice on her own account. But there is very little obstetric skill to be acquired from her elders, and her proficiency seldom becomes very great. In ordinary cases everything usually goes off satisfactorily, but when a cross birth occurs, the dai rarely attempts to turn the child. More often she seizes the arm or leg presented and endeavours to attain the desired end by force. If successful the limb is usually dislocated and the mother terribly lacerated, but more often the effort ends in failure and death ensues.[32]

Before 1900 midwives in Europe interfered with the process of giving birth to a greater extent. It was, according to one authority, a common practice to reach into the vagina and the uterus with unclean hands to speed up labour, a practice which was unheard of in Bengal. Moreover, the isolation of mothers in uncomfortable surroundings was, in nineteenth-century Europe, as widespread as in Bengal.[33]

High infant mortality was, according to British critics of Bengali sexual practices, decisively caused by the early consummation of marriage. From what we know, early consummation did not take place in England where the age of consent had been raised to 16 years of age in 1885. Criticism of early consummation was, from a British point of view, a better stick with which to beat the Bengalis; in the case of dirty athurghars and untrained dais, men were, at best, negligent observers. In 1909, Major W.W. Clemensha, Sanitary Commissioner of Bengal, claimed that: 'Out of 2700 children that die within the first month (in Calcutta), more than 1200 or nearly 50 per cent, come under the hands of premature birth and debility at birth...probably early marriage is the preponderating factor...'[34]

High maternal mortality in Bengal was also due, according to British critics, to child marriage and consummation immediately after puberty. 'There is a phenomenal excess of female mortality in Bengal during the first part of a woman's reproductive age-period',[35] it was noted in the Bengal census in 1921:

Much has been said and written of the evils of infant marriage, resulting in the survival of child-widows condemned to a life of austerity and very often of drudgery and so on, but to the critic of these statistics the evil which does far more harm to other women of this country is the custom that ordains, that a married woman must not only be married but live the life of a married woman immediately she attains puberty.[36]

This, the official view, was adopted in the Report of the Age of Consent Committee, 1928–1929. The Committee found that the birth rate in Bengal was lower than in any other province; it implied that this was due to early sexual intercourse and the subsequent emaciation of women.[37] The Bengali witnesses, however, among whom were women doctors and health workers, denied such a link. They were convinced that the low birth rate accompanied by a high infant mortality was due to the malnutrition of overworked women and the economic decline of the province. In addition, they argued, it was not the mothers' age at birth which exhausted women, but the high frequency of births. The latter phenomenon could clearly not be dealt with by legislation or education, but only through a combination of economic improvement and education. Only if the rate of infant mortality were reduced through the better nutrition of mothers and children, would it be possible to educate people about birth control. As it was many children were necessary to guarantee the survival of a few.[38]

British administrators, who emphasized poor hygiene and 'curious' practices, admitted that poverty was important among the causes of infant and maternal deaths:

Among the labouring classes many of the mothers are poorly-fed cooly women, who continue to work to the very end of their pregnancy, with the result that they give birth to weakly, and not infrequently premature, infants, who succumb during the first few hours, days or weeks of external life...owing to poverty and malaria, the failure of nursing powers is not uncommon. In such cases unsuitable substitutes for proper artificial food help to undermine the health of the infants.[39]

By this account, then, women who were malnourished and overworked could not give birth to, nor bring up, healthy and strong children. Anaemia during childbirth and a chronic calcium deficiency resulting from a strenuous pregnancy were major problems.[40] Moreover, any downswing in the economy increased mortality. Whereas the mortality rate decreased during the jute boom created by the First World War, inflation and the influenza epidemic in the wake of the war took their respective tolls.[41]

In addition, there was a clear link between the survival of infants and the occupation of the father. Children of professional fathers had a 'clearly higher chance of survival' than did children of peasants.[42] Among the non-middle-class people direct access to land and food was important for infant health. Those without access, such as artisans and, in particular, domestic servants, suffered considerably higher rates of infant mortality—20 per cent higher than average in the latter case.[43]

The health of women in jute mills, coal-mines and tea planta-tions was under closer scrutiny than the medical welfare of other women in Bengal. This could imply that in these areas statistics were more favourable because data were more complete. It could also mean that companies and colonial authorities influenced the statistical results in order to show the effectiveness of colonial health intervention. However, while such considerations might put in question the reliability of evidence from villages or provin-cial towns it should not hamper the comparison between mills, plantations and mines because in all three areas official health intervention occurred in the 1920s. The statistical results suggest that relatively small efforts in support of young mothers and babies had a significant effect. The data also show that any support by large-scale employers or the colonial state for mothers and babies was solely dependent on the former's political and economic concerns.

In the Darjeeling and Jalpaiguri tea plantations the birth rate was higher and infant mortality lower than in the mining or mill areas. But both also compared positively with the figures for rural Bengal or the province as a whole. Details are given in the table at the end of this chapter. Why were conditions in tea plantations so much more congenial to birth and a baby's survival? Without underestimating the poverty of the women, exploitation by the sardars and planters, and chronic diseases such as malaria and hookworm, work in the plantations was less strenuous than mine or mill labour and the natural environment healthier. Thus women at the childbearing age were stronger and more likely to conceive and give birth to children with a chance of survival. In addition, the fact that workers were settled as family units gave rise to conditions under which a woman could be supported during pregnancy and lactation by other family members.[44] The relatively regular wages earned by women probably accounted for the positive picture compared to rural areas or the entire province. But financial support by planters may well have made the decisive difference.

As almost every child was employed around the age of five or six, planters had an immediate interest in the reproduction of their labour force. They paid a small reward at childbirth and on the child's first birthday. The 'birthday reward' was to motivate careful mothering to nurse the child through its most dangerous period till the end of the first year. All payments were irrespective of a woman's marital status and irrespective of whether or not she attended work. Thus the money was not to replace wages but to supply an additional income to be spent on food for the sake of maternal and infant health. As a result, throughout the 1920s the birth rate in Jalpaiguri plantations was 50 per cent higher than in the whole of Bengal.[45]

Such 'success' was relative in a country where the conditions at birth were marked by the ritual impurity of the event and the absence of sanitary or medical provisions. Midwifery in the tea plantations, at least according to the British doctor, Dagmar Curjel, was as unsophisticated as anywhere else among the lower classes of Bengal:

On most tea estates there were a certain number of the plains women who acted as dais when required. Their scale of fees were lower than those charged near Calcutta, but usually not less than Rs·1/- was paid. Some of these women were relatively cleanly in person and had fairly successful results, others were dirty and I heard of deaths among the women attended. They usually considered that abnormal cases were foredoomed to die... None of the indigenous dais I met in Bengal appeared to have any outside training, in no case did they own a pair of scissors, but used the ordinary household knife or, in the country, the sickle to be found in each home.[46]

In the coal mining area conditions at birth were more difficult to investigate because the labour force was less permanent than in plantations and only semi-proletarianized. Most women miners were part-time workers and often lived at some distance from the mines. As mines were less dependent than tea plantations on women's labour and because many mining women were supported by larger families, only a small maternity benefit of up to one rupee was paid by a couple of mining companies. But even without such support the majority of women giving birth, not in the lines but in the family homes, had enough food while they were absent from work. For assistance during birth these women depended on their families, whereas women who gave birth in the lines employed midwives; some 400 dais worked in the area.[47]

In jute mills women became an increasingly unwanted minority. The jute companies neither paid family wages in order to support dependent wives in the mill towns, nor did the architects of factory lines consider the social needs of a working wife/woman. Accordingly, the sex ratio and the birth rate in these towns were very low. As migrant male workers left their families in the villages and only entered temporary relationships in the mill areas, pregnancies and children by their 'mill wives' were unwanted. In spontaneous anger workers often beat their female companions when they got pregnant. Consequently, the fertility rate was low and it was doubtful if maternity benefit in cash could have improved a woman's situation; the money was likely to 'wander' into male pockets.[48]

Despite these class-specific differences, infant mortality was high among all classes compared with Europe or compared with parents' expectations. Under such conditions a large number of children was seen as an asset by everybody and birth control was not an issue of widespread importance.[49] Still, British officials suggested that birth control explained varying birth rates. In 1901 it was argued that 'there is no reason to suppose that in ordinary years the conditions under which the labouring classes live are unfavourable to child bearing'.[50] Instead, fluctuating birth rates were attributed to unknown methods of birth control. By the 1920s, however, when the province's economy had deteriorated, fluctuating birth rates were explained by growing poverty.[51]

While contraception was not common, infanticide was practised by some women. Infanticide was, however, never directed exclusively against baby girls.[52] Infanticide was reported among labouring women in jute mills and tea plantations where women could not spare the time for child-rearing. Mill managers suspected that infanticide occurred, but could not specify how widespread the crime was. In plantaions, in contrast, mechanisms of social control were more developed, as planters had an economic interest in children.[53] Consequently, infanticide was more likely to lead to prosecution. In 1926, in a case in point, a woman labourer killed her baby and was sentenced to transportation for life. As this was an unusually harsh sentence, taking into account the social conditions which had compelled the woman into crime, the Session Judge recommended a reduction in the punishment.[54]

Abortion was also practised, but not talked or written about. Like infanticide, abortion was not a form of constructive family planning, and both practices were the last resorts of women in desperate situations. Abortions apparently were arranged by village women. Although there is only circumstantial evidence, particularly from castes which prohibited widow remarriage, many sexually mature women faced this option. But abortions were not frequently prosecuted because of the political complications which official interference with matters of female sexuality implied in most cases.[55]

Due to the generally high level of infant mortality and the importance of a male heir, there was virtually no class- or occupation-specific pattern of fertility. Twice-born castes with relatively easy access to education and the professions, such as Brahmans, Baidyas and Kayasthas, seemed to be more fertile only because their children had better chances of survival. In particular, diseases such as lung infections, bronchitis, diarrhoea and measles— which caused most of the deaths of children between one month and one year—were clearly related to poverty, especially to inadequate housing, clothing and sanitation.[56]

British and Bengali observers explained infant and maternal mortality in ways which suited their political interests. Since the days of the Swadeshi movement, the nationalist press in Bengal had consistently drawn attention to the inequities of the colonial economy. Foremost among the conditions which were, they argued, the cause of high infant and maternal mortality was the supply of low-quality milk. The poor milk was blamed on a lack of official care and control as well as on bribery. Semi-scientific articles complained about the lack of rich and pure milk and advised consumers on the importance of milk for gaining nutrition and ways to test its quality.[57] In 1920 the Calcutta paper *Hitavadi* wrote that milk in the Calcutta Medical College Hospital was virtually undrinkable and asked why there was no special milk supply for patients as there was for soldiers in army barracks.[58] But even in the villages the level of poverty was said to be so low that cows could neither be properly fed nor milked with satisfactory results.[59]

Bad housing in Calcutta was also blamed in the nationalist press for high mortality rates. There was ample empirical evidence to support the point, but the argument was also shaped by criticism of the purdah system. Purdah was depicted by British critics as the origin of respiratory diseases that resulted in the deaths of mothers and infants.[60] Whereas both the British and the Bengalis had, in this case, some justification for their respective views, the disagreements were ideologically charged, using infant mortality rates, sticky zenana quarters and dilapidated bustee houses for colonial or nationalist ends. In 1920, in reaction to British instructions on child welfare, the Calcutta newspaper *Dainik Basumati* criticized the government for their reluctance to do anything about bad housing and food adulteration despite the existence of appropriate legislation. 'The poor and middle-class families in the city', it was argued,

are forced to live in such houses as are bound to impair their health... Scarcity of drinking water, the want of proper drainage, the absence of medical men and the prevalence of malaria are the leading features of life in the villages of Bengal.[61]

All parties agreed on the necessity of improving the conditions of childbirth. The choice of means for improvement, however, as well as success and failure, depended to a large extent on the political context.

Reforming Childbirth

The discourses on the reforms of childbirth in Bengal highlight the position of this issue at the crossroads of gender, race and class. During the closing decades of the nineteenth century efforts at reform were inspired by the spirit of European medical and scientific progress and superiority. Soon, however, Bengali public opinion criticized the Eurocentric and imperialist undertones of such reforms.Three discursive strands can be identified. First, white women doctors were the target of criticism by the Bengali press and by rival Indian women doctors. Second, influenced by international and particularly American concern over the conditions of chilbirth in India, the nineteenth-century patterns of imperial social reform were revived in the 1920s in the shape of social legislation and social work organized by Vicereines. Third, Indian reforming agencies combined the reform of birth conditions with nationalist politics. Indian reformers focused on education and the continuing supervision of dais within the villages avoiding the spatial split of reform and birth, or theory and practice, which had doomed British reformist initiatives to failure. However, while Indian activists largely overcame the racial bias of their European predecessors, their gender stereotypes were influenced by their middle-class background and were thus highly inappropriate for mothers and dais from a rural or industrial working-class background.[62] The professionalization of housewifery which went hand in hand with the reforms of childbirth had serious economic consequences, particularly for some women in the organized economic sector.

Imperial efforts to improve the conditions of childbirth and of female health in general were closely connected with the training and employment of British and Indian women doctors. But for middle-class Bengalis, women doctors gave rise to various problems. Cultural stereotypes hampered the acceptance of Bengali women in the profession, while British women doctors met with Bengali political and racial reservations.

While westernized Bengali families gradually accepted their daughters' teaching careers in the 1880s, medical studies remained a taboo for middle-class girls. Consequently women doctors were rare in Bengal and very few of them were Bengalis. A number of Brahmo women embarked on medical studies in the 1880s. Among them Kadambini Ganguli was highly successful, working at both the Lady Dufferin Women's Hospital and at Eden Female Hospital in Calcutta. She managed to combine professional success with marriage and a family life. She was, at the time, a rare example. Her colleague, Jamini Sen, was less unusual. In 1897 she began her successful medical career but remained unmarried throughout her life.[63]

The enrolment lists of Calcutta Medical College did not differentiate between Hindu and Brahmo women, but during the first decades of the twentieth century, there were never more than a handful of Hindu women as students.[64] Even for European and Bengali Christian women acceptance by the medical profession was more difficult in Bengal than elsewhere. While women were accepted at medical colleges in Madras and Bombay, the council of the Calcutta Medical College rejected female medical students. It was only in 1885 that Lieutenant-Governor Rivers Thompson overruled the College.[65] But the gap remained. In 1912, when there were two and three Hindu women students respectively at medical colleges in Madras and Bombay, there was none in Calcutta. There were eight Hindu women at the Medical School, Agra, but there was only one Baidya woman and one Kayastha woman at the Campbell Medical School, Calcutta, and the Medical School, Dhaka, respectively.[66] In the 1920s, compared with other Indian provinces, there was 'a paucity of women's medical work either on part of Missions or Government' in the eastern region of India.[67]

Why, in particular, were there so few women doctors and female medical students in Bengal? In 1912 an enquiry by experts on female and medical education reached the conclusion that medical colleges would have to provide separate classes and well-maintained hostels for women only, if they wanted to attract well-educated women students. Moreover, additional jobs for women doctors needed to be created and salaries increased so that female medical students could look forward to a post which would make them financially independent.[68]

Gender ideology rendered the study of medicine an unsuitable occupation for a woman. Western medicine and science—complete with dissections during anatomy lectures—was incompatible with orthodox Hindu teachings.[69] Women were more vulnerable than men because their purity was more important and more violable. Moreover, young women were not used to social contact with men from outside their families. They found it difficult to sit with unrelated young men listening to medical lectures that dealt with the functions of the human body. Renuka Biswas recalled this as a major problem when she started her medical studies at the Campbell Medical School in Calcutta in the early 1930s. She was one of six women students in her year and, to avoid problems, she was ordered by her father not to speak with any of the men. After six months, however, the situation became intolerable and she gave up medicine.[70]

The problem of women doctors in Bengal was closely connected with the associated politics of the colonial state. In the 1880s one of the most important Victorian responses to the conditions of female health and childbirth in India was the foundation of 'The National Association for Supplying Female Medical Aid to the Women of India', commonly known as Lady Dufferin Fund. It encouraged the establishment of maternity hospitals as well as baby clinics. The fund was a lucid example of British paternalism in India. In British eyes Bengali women were oppressed and anything done for them merited publicity at home. But while in Europe the struggle against midwifery was about to be won by the male-dominated medical sciences, in India no such development took place. State interference in childbirth, as the Dufferin Fund was perceived, was rejected because of the strong ritual injunctions that surrounded childbirth.[71]

Bengali opposition to the Dufferin Fund was explicitly political. The Dufferin women doctors were compared with female missionaries who had come to India with the aim of destroying the indigenous cultural system. In 1890, only a few years after the Fund's foundation, a Bengali newspaper attacked them as 'half-educated good-for-nothings' who would profit from the raising of the age of consent because it would allow them to medically examine women involved in the expected court cases.[72] The newly-founded zenana hospitals were denounced as an insult to the art of Indian childrearing. Since very few women attended hospitals, teaching midwifery and gynaecology in Calcutta was hardly possible due to 'very few opportunities for practical demonstration being available'.[73]

The Hindu Revivalist newspaper *Bangabasi*, which fostered cultural identity in the form of protest against colonial domination, spearheaded the criticism. It blamed the Dufferin Fund for a singular lack of knowledge: 'The Zenana Hospital is the outcome of a movement which was started without duly gauging the conditions of native life.'[74] The Dufferin Fund's regret that respectable women did not attend their Calcutta hospital was met with cynicism: 'Well, the promoters of the Zenana Hospital movement ought to have considered before establishing the hospital that this province is inhabited by Bengalis.'[75] During the 1890s the focus of Hindu Revivalism was on Bengali cultural identity; women who refused to attend a hospital affirmed their adherence to Bengali culture. After 1910 criticism was formulated with reference to the Dufferin Fund's shortcomings, for example, its racial politics with regard to appointments and treatment of patients.[76] In 1923 a Calcutta newspaper alleged that Indian women, including middle-class women, were treated worse than dogs in the Lady Dufferin Hospital, whereas European and Eurasian patients were treated well.[77]

Besides, Bengali men were, in general, dismissive of female health care. Some women, interviewed in 1985, had vivid memories of how their husbands and relatives had ignored their gynaecological problems during the 1920s; visits to doctors were delayed for months or never took place. Recent research into Indian attitudes to female health care supports the evidence; women's health was and is regarded as secondary to men's. Any expenditure of time or money on female health was either avoided or delayed until the disease could no longer be ignored.[78] Any money poured by reformist Indians or Europeans into the Dufferin Fund was seen by many Bengalis as a waste. Moreover, it should be remembered that while medical reforms in nineteenth-century Europe had a particular attraction for male doctors who experienced a rapid widening of their sphere of influence and domination, in Bengal birth was so impure that indigenous male co-operation in the process of birth management was out of the question.[79]

For British and Indian women doctors who competed for jobs, the Dufferin Fund and other state initiatives had additional dimensions. Initially, it had been difficult for British women to get jobs in the male-dominated world of medicine. In India they were paid less than men for the same work. But opportunities improved gradually with the foundation of the Dufferin Fund and the Association of Medical Women in India in 1907. The latter organization successfully lobbied for jobs, better payment and social security for medical women in India. In 1914, the Women's Medical Service was established which was administered through the Dufferin Fund and subsidized by an annual government grant.[80]

The reluctance of the British Indian government to attribute the Women's Medical Service government status, as well as the slowness with which they reacted to parliamentary lobbying, showed that women doctors were low on the list of government priorities in India.[81] Government officials made it clear that they would prefer more efficiency through privatization, regardless of the insecurity this meant for women doctors.[82] The male medical establishment in India had just asserted its position against traditional Ayurvedic and Unani medical practitioners by reducing their influence through various medical acts passed between 1912 and 1917 'to the position of unrecognized, unqualified laymen'.[83] Similarly, they were not prepared to share their legally-confirmed dominance with women colleagues.

An Indian woman found it difficult to secure a hospital job not only as a result of male prejudice but because European and some Eurasian women doctors had monopolized the posts supported by the Dufferin Fund, the major donor agency in India with regard to female medical aid. Unable to get a hospital appointment, some Indian women doctors went into private practice and opened their surgeries in remote districts. In 1902 the 'Malda Lady Doctor's Case' was publicized in the press. The doctor had been called out at night by a local zamindar under a false pretext and sexually assaulted. In court the zamindar was found guilty and fined Rs 1000.[84] Similar cases were reported in the 1920s. They discouraged Indian parents from sending their daughters to medical schools and colleges.[85]

In Bengal there was greater hostility to European women doctors than in other provinces of India. Certainly, white women doctors thought little of the competence of their Indian colleagues.

In the absence of high-caste middle-class women, they came from Christian families who were often low-caste converts. Margaret Balfour, founder member of the Women's Medical Service in India, for instance, described the 'oral and intellectual standard' of Indian women students as 'second class'.[86] In turn, Bengalis identified racist attitudes with white women in particular. English women doctors were accused of investing their work with a missionary zeal.[87] Moreover, at the time of the greatest expansion of female medicine, after the foundation of the Women's Medical Service, western medicine became a target of criticism by the nationalist movement.[88]

In the 1920s discourses on childbirth and health took place against a changed political background. Motherhood and fertility were no longer condescendingly regarded as predominantly moral issues, but as social problems linked with women's health and living conditions.[89] Poverty, health and physical degeneration were burning public issues. The First World War had shown the need for a more healthy and sturdy physical stock. Moreover, the new political climate as well as pressure from England and the International Labour Organisation directed public attention 'towards the improvement of the physique of the nation and the reduction of causes, which contributed to abnormal fertility'.[90] Infant and maternal health were the most important of all these concerns. Hospitals for women were opened all over the country and baby shows became regular events. Although only a few women were affected by these activities, the initiatives were a sign of the times.[91] During the early 1920s so-called 'female issues' had gained prominence because middle-class women's campaigns for female enfranchisement had attracted attention in Bengal as in other Indian provinces.[92]

The concern for public health and infant and maternal mortality was not restricted to India, but was expressed throughout the world. Anna Davin, in her essay, 'Imperialism and Motherhood', has analysed the increasing British interest in the politics of birth and childcare during the first decades of the twentieth century. In post-war Britain the activities culminated in the 1918 Maternity and Child Welfare Act 'which envisaged the provision of a network of infant welfare centres'.[93] In India the recommendations and conventions of post-war international organizations, such as the League of Nations and the International

Labour Organisation, were influential in condemning the issues of child marriage and poverty that British or Indian social reformers had raised. As the nationalist movement had an internationally renowned leader in Gandhi, the British Indian authorities in London, Delhi and Calcutta were sensitive to their image in the outside world. Nevertheless the reforms which were initiated in Bengal were limited and few. They either coincided with the interests of the Indian nationalist movement or had a clear bias towards western middle-class gender stereotypes which were emulated by Indian women's organizations.

The international lobby for women's health was most active with regard to women in the organized economic sector apart from campaigns against child prostitution and white slave trade. The debate on maternity benefit and maternity leave was initiated by the Convention of the International Labour Conference which met in October 1919 in Washington. The Draft Convention suggested six weeks leave before and after childbirth accompanied by sufficient benefits for women in commercial and industrial undertakings. On resuming work women were to be entitled to two extra breaks of thirty minutes each during their working hours while they were breastfeeding their babies. Throughout the 1920s the convention was not honoured in Bengal. Legislative initiatives were rejected with the argument that they were modelled on conditions in the Bombay cotton mills where the female labour force was said to be numerically more important and more permanent. Moreover, workers in Bombay were said to live in regular families and were thus worthy of support.[94]

In Bengal a laissez-faire policy on maternity benefit and leave was adopted. Women in tea plantations who needed and deserved support received benefits from the planters on a voluntary basis; mining women, being part-time workers and backed by agricultural families, were not regarded as being in need, and women jute workers received nothing:

The type of labour, moreover, must be kept in mind, particularly with respect to female labour in jute mills. Normal family life is notoriously absent among the labourers in jute mills... The peculiar type of the female labour in the jute mills does not conduce to the creation of schemes which presuppose normal family relations.[95]

Women were regarded as victims of unfavourable conditions and not directly responsible themselves. Still, what they needed was education, not money. Women were said to have 'abused' benefit schemes, such as those set up in the early 1920s by the management of the Baranagore and Kelvin Jute Mills, by taking the money and going to work elsewhere. Moreover, money alone would have implied that even child-mothers of 12 or 13 years of age would have been supported.[96]

Although malnutrition and hard factory labour placed the heaviest burdens on mothers and babies, the schemes which were introduced largely ignored these problems. A scheme that was different was started at the Titaghur Mills in March 1923. Its 'Maternity and Child Welfare' centre offered a qualified health supervisor, classes for indigenous midwives, instruction classes for expectant mothers, baby clinics and sewing-classes in which mothers learned how to tailor baby clothes. The centre provided soap for babies, but no food for mothers or milk for babies. During the 1920s this model scheme was imitated in many mills: though the women suffered from low wages, imminent unemployment and insufficient housing, they were asked to learn hygiene and modesty before they would gain the right of maintenance during maternity.[97]

Reforms which led to the abolition of women's underground labour in mines reflected the equally moralistic attitude of middle-class reformers. The reforms were mainly introduced to cut down the number of miners after the coal slump of 1926. But the ideological justification for the reforms concentrated on the alleged need to improve the conditions of childbirth and family life. In the 1920s the figures concerning the birth rate and infant mortality were favourable in the case of the mining population. As these workers had a more regular income than most people in Bengal and as their housing allowed some privacy, the fertility rate there was higher than in mill towns, Calcutta, rural areas or in the province as a whole. Nevertheless, the lobby which opposed female underground work argued that this was not the case. The Women's Indian Association urged the Government of India to prohibit underground labour and to

restore women to their normal functions and health and lessen the evil of intemperance among the men-miners, ensure a higher standard of domestic life, save the life of the infants and improve the physique of the new generation.[98]

A reason for the men's excessive drinking, they argued, was that husbands had to wait for their meals too long. Thus they asked for the domestication of women:

If the comforts of the house are guaranteed by the presence of wives there to perform the domestic duties under reasonable conditions, the whole standard of living will be raised, even if there be a temporary decrease in wages...[99]

The debate on female underground labour and its impact on women's health and fertility continued until the prohibition of female underground labour in 1929. The gradual decline of female underground labour was a questionable achievement, in respect to the poverty of the women and their lack of an alternative income. But another outcome of the campaign, namely an increasing concern with birth and maternity, improved the conditions of mining women. In the early 1920s the Asansol Mines Board of Health employed three trained midwives who were, however, only gradually accepted by the women workers. By 1929 training classes for indigenous midwives were opened and the latter were given fully equipped midwifery bags.[100]

Outside the organized economic sector, state initiatives to reform childbirth became increasingly marginal after 1920. Reforms and debates were politically significant with regard to British effort to contain the nationalist movement and prove the beneficial effect of British rule in India to the international community. In autumn 1925, for instance, the efforts to raise the age of consent, and thus to delay motherhood, profited from this new awareness. Act XXIX of 1925 raised the age of consent to 13 and 14 in marital and extra-marital cases. However, by 1928 only a few Indians knew about this Act. The Indian government was more concerned with possible protest against the act than with its publication and implementation. Consequently, as a safeguard against protests from the orthodox community, only a minor punishment was prescribed if the wife was between 12 and 13 years old.[101]

Outside India, it was American public opinion which worried the Indian government most. Attempts were made to improve the British Indian image by arranging visits to India for journalists, academics and businessmen. In the mid-twenties the Viceroy, Lord Reading, tried to give all of them the best possible impression of British administration in India.[102] While most of these visitors did not attract much attention outside British Indian government circles, the New York journalist, Katherine Mayo, visiting India in 1925, had an important impact on international public opinion and also on Indian politics. Her book, *Mother India* (1927), covered all aspects of Indian life, but particularly those which were guaranteed to horrify American readers. It was 'a devastating attack on Indian social customs'.[103] Mayo's account used the bare facts of population growth, infant mortality and death rates to justify British rule and Indian subordination. But the book became a major political event because it linked Indian sexuality with politics. It was this connection which Indians rejected more than the lurid description of misogynist practices on the sub-continent. There was no doubt that there was much room for improvement in the situation women faced at work and at home, but the cultural absolutism of *Mother India* was a questionable way of inducing social reform in Indian society. Besides, the book continued the British Indian tradition of singling out Bengal for moral condemnation.[104] She etched a provocative description of sexual perversions and used the deep inequalities of the patriarchal system in Indian society to spread the message that India lacked political maturity. While the book did not have a major impact on improving the conditions faced by Indian women, it did focus attention on the urgency of reforms.

The publication of *Mother India* put the British record in India on the line and the Viceroy called for action. Alexander Muddiman of the Legislative Department informed his colleagues:

His Excellency spoke to me about this case and was anxious that I should put down my views as to the way in which this Bill would be dealt with... It is naturally most desirable to avoid in any way conveying to the Assembly and to the world at large that we were opposed to beneficient social legislation and Government must avoid as far as possible being put in that position. The subject is likely to be pretty fully ventilated as Miss Katherine Mayo's book will doubtless drag cranks in many part(s) of the country and at home into the discussion.[105]

As proof of their concern the Indian government decided to set up a commission to investigate the state of affairs in the country and in June 1928 the Age of Consent Committee was established under the chairmanship of M. V. Joshi, who had till recently been Home Member of the Executive Council of the Governor of the Central Provinces.[106] There were five other initial members including two women, Rameshwari Nehru and the Englishwoman, M. O'Brien Beadon, Superintendent of the Victoria Government Hospital in Madras. On 25 September the appointment procedure was completed by the addition of four members of the Legislative Assembly. The Joshi Committee's terms of reference were to examine all questions surrounding the age of consent and to enquire into the effects of the 1925 amendment. In summer 1928 they formulated a questionnaire which was sent directly to 6000 selected people or public bodies and to a further 1930 persons through local governments.[107] The questionnaire was an unusual sociological document in the history of social reform in India. Apart from questions which probed the witnesses' attitudes and solicited their views on sex and marriage, the questionnaire was aimed at collecting as much information as possible about sexual practices and their religious or cultural backgrounds. It set out to determine if sex took place within marriage before puberty and why; it also wanted to find out when the garbhadan ceremony was celebrated. Other key questions probed the effects of early intercourse on girls and their future progeny, and women's attitudes to the custom and the existing legislation. Altogether, the committee and the questionnaire illustrated the scientific spirit which had dominated the issue of health policy since the end of the First World War.[108] But while a majority of witnesses pointed to the significance of socio-economic improvements, the committee stressed both the educational effects of future legislation and the recent 'emancipation' of urban middle-class women in order to justify their recommendation of raising the age of consent to 15 for wives and to 18 for unmarried women.[109]

The discourses surrounding the Age of Consent Committee showed that the colonial British and the nationalist Bengali approaches to reforms with regard to childbirth differed significantly. Childbirth was a contentious issue, as an examination of Viceregal baby-shows on the one hand and the reform of village athurghars on the other will show. After the First World War baby-shows were part of the schedule of Dufferin hospitals and of some Vicereines, particularly Lady Reading. The concept of these 'Child Welfare Exhibitions' was aimed at individual women.

Their purpose was to encourage better childcare by offering material prizes and moral rewards.[110]

Lady Reading, for instance, who as Vicereine founded the 'Lady Reading all-India Hospital Fund' and raised money for the 'Lady Reading Hospital for Indian Women and Children' in Shimla, expressed a particular mixture of well-meaning condescension and self-righteous zeal which evoked nationalist resentment. During her 1921 Christmas stay in Calcutta she visited a zenana hospital, a child welfare centre, a health school, a nurses' home and a fund raising occasion every second day. Yet these activities were unconnected with her own concerns in life, and she perceived these visits almost as outings to the zoo.[111] In February 1924, after a visit to the Baby Welfare Centre in Delhi slums, she admitted to what she called a perverse affection for Indian slums and a particular attraction to brown babies.

The Vicereine's excitement over racial attributes was heightened by class differences. Low-class mamas were referred to as chattering and pushing around her with the 'frank enthusiasm one misses in the semi-sophisticated', the latter being obviously in her eyes the highest grade attainable by Indians.[112] Her experience in the Delhi slums was surpassed by a visit to the Infant Welfare Centre in Bangalore where the babies were described as 'darker, but happier and more attractive than in the north'.[113] Moreover, in Madras where 'the light heartedness of Southern India is everywhere apparent and so refreshing',[114] she was not confronted with the harshness of Indian survival as in Delhi where women, at the prize-giving event of a baby-show, hardened by permanent scarcity, gave their tickets for winning cups to their best friends with babies who came to collect a prize a second time.[115]

The British and Bengalis drew different conclusions from these and similar events. 'And these are the people', Lady Reading cynically commented at the Delhi prize-giving session, 'we declare unfit for self-government', implying that they were indeed not able to look after themselves.[116] The Nationalist Bengali press expressed the opposite conviction, namely that child welfare exhibitions proved the inability of the British to cope with the material problems of India. The *Amrita Bazar Patrika* depicted the shows as an insult to Indian motherhood, while the real need was for alleviating malnutrition and providing pure and nutritious milk.[117]

Earlier, but comparable, efforts by British educators and vicereines to reform the conditions of birth had also failed because they were as unconnected with the lives of Indian women as were Lady Reading's baby-shows. In 1883 a nursing and midwifery course was started at the Campbell Medical School. The course was welcomed, more students enrolled than expected, and soon qualified midwives began to advertise in the *Brahmo Public Opinion*. Bengali district boards appointed qualified midwives in preference to European women doctors.[118] Yet due to traditional prejudices against the impurity of birth, this initiative only produced a limited number of midwives. In addition, they asked for such high fees once they were qualified, that they were out of the reach of most women. The next step was a training scheme for traditional midwives. In 1903 Lady Curzon organized the Victoria Memorial Scholarship Fund for this purpose. But as follow-up supervision was not catered for, village midwives who had attended classes for a couple of weeks soon returned to their old habits.[119]

However, efforts by Bengalis to reform the athurghar and child-rearing practices were welcomed in villages and in the press. Latika Basu, for instance, informed the Age of Consent Committee that she was the Secretary of the Chittaranjan Seva Sadan, a maternity hospital with a public health section, founded in 1926, for the special purpose of training nurses and midwives for village work.[120] She was part of a wider movement that linked reforms in childbirth with nationalist politics rather than with colonial 'improvement'. In 1925, Gurusaday Dutt founded the Saroj Nalini Dutt Memorial Association (SNDMA), an umbrella organization for mahila samitis, village or municipal women's groups. In 1913, following the days of the Swadesi movement, the first such group had been founded by his wife, Saroj Nalini, in Patna. This and subsequent groups had provided the social space for middle-class women—who ventured to leave their zenanas, albeit still in purdah—to exchange recipes and gossip with, and impart instruction on health and hygiene to, women in the local district towns and surrounding villages. The movement aimed at mobilizing middle-class women with the ambition of improving the situation of women of all social classes. The political framework was provided by Gandhi's and Tagore's village reconstruction programme.[121]

Calcutta nationalist celebrities such as Jyotirmoyi Ganguli and Latika Ghose were among the founding members of the SNDMA, as were Lady Sinha and Maharani Adhirani of Burdwan. The groups which were founded by local women—although with some Calcutta connections—in villages or urban neighbourhoods provided and encouraged self-help, and tried to attract lower middle-class membership. They stressed training programmes and individual participation that aimed at female literacy, reviving village crafts, teaching needle work, but most importantly, improving traditional midwifery and conditions in the lying-in-room. Female co-operation was regarded essential for village reconstruction, and improving the conditions of birth was a priority among the members.[122]

Some of the early members at district or village levels excelled at midwifery. Nalinibala Devi, for instance, the daughter as well as the wife of a medical doctor, learnt midwifery from her family. In Sylhet, she founded a Mahila Samiti and a clinic where she herself arranged forceps deliveries.[123] Hermangini Sen, founder member of the Tala Mahila Samiti, taught and practised midwifery.[124] Charusila Devi, Secretary of the Jaduboyra Samiti, provided a light and well-ventilated room in her own house to be used as an athurghar by poor local women. She came from an orthodox Brahman family but this did not prevent her from acting as midwife to low-caste women.[125]

In more usual cases a newly-founded mahila samiti set up maternity clinics or installed clean maternity wards in local hospitals. These were managed by women only to liberate mothers from the depressing conditions in traditional athurghars. Classes on maintaining hygiene during birth were also arranged for traditional midwives. By 1929 there were over 250 samitis all over Bengal and almost all had worked towards improving the conditions of birth, including the organization of baby-shows which were now, in connection with nationalist politics, welcomed and successful.[126] In 1925 the Bankura Samiti organized a baby week which also included the screening of a film, 'The Cry of the Baby', to stimulate improvement among local women and midwives. Subsequently, they arranged a midwifery training programme and successfully lobbied for the addition of a women's ward at the Bankura Medical School.[127]

Each year the SNDMA report listed more clinics, maternity centres and midwifery training centres.[128] In 1929, in Kidderpur, near the Calcutta docks, a lying-in-room was opened where local women factory workers could come free of charge for their deliveries.[129] As each activity was conducted by an autonomous women's group which was only affiliated to the umbrella organization in Calcutta, the movement was basically democratic and lacked the patronizing undertone of colonial baby shows or the Dufferin Fund. The means available to the Dufferin Fund were more extensive, but it was the nationalist impetus and the involvement of women in district towns and villages that contributed to the popularity of the SNDMA.

Conclusion

Childbirth was one area of 'impurity' where attempts to improve the conditions of women were crowned, at least as far as middle-class women were concerned, with success. Due to the stricter separation of the sexes in Bengal than in the West, male-dominated medical science was less involved in improving the conditions of mothers and babies, upper middle-class families apart. In Europe the introduction of medical improvement was accompanied by the displacement of female birth assistance. In Bengal, however, at least in the initial period of reform, the ritual injunctions and the impurity connected with birth paved the way for improvements which did not alter the gender structure of attendance at birth.

The conditions of childbirth in Bengal were under constant scrutiny by varying interest groups. From the middle of the nineteenth century, reformist bhadralok and bhadramahila read western medical books about childbirth and midwifery and some of them put their reading into practice. But for the majority of women childbirth remained unchanged before 1910 and British observers expressed horror at the unhygienic conditions. It was improvement in these conditions, rather than the introduction of sophisticated birth management, which women's groups aimed at after 1910. Their efforts gained in popularity when, in the wake of the First World War, maternal and infant health became matters

of world-wide interest. Their success was particularly important
in contrast to the relative failure of imperial reform initiatives,
such as the Lady Dufferin Fund. Childbirth became embroiled in
a range of political issues which were unrelated to the medical
questions involved.

Similarly, the dai training scheme failed while it was managed
by highly-qualified, but foreign women, and succeeded once Indian middle-class women took over in the name of nationalism.
This example suggests some interesting points with regard to the
issue of professional work by Bengali women. The women's
groups were widely recognized and appreciated in Bengali
society. The contributions of middle-class women in these groups
were very similar to the duties of a doctor or teacher with the
exception that it was unpaid work that improved the birth conditions of other women in the name of nationalism.

Two conclusions follow from this. One is that men were more
concerned to monopolize the wage-earning capacities in their
families in support of their dominance than to assert their patriarchal power by keeping their wives at home for the sake of purdah,
husband worship (pati devata) and childcare. The other is that—
as in the case of female education, reforms of the dowry system
and changing conjugal relations—the connection with the
nationalist struggle was vital for the development of new ideas on
the position of women. In 1931 a summary of Hindu public
opinion on women professionals explained recent changes with
reference to 'the way in which zenana women have participated
in the national movement'.[130]

Birth Rate and Infant Mortality per 1000, Decennial Average, 1919–1929

	Calcutta areas	Rural towns	Province mines	Mill	Asansol	Tea gardens	England Wales
BR	18.4	29.3	28.7	16.9	26.7	40.2	-
IM+	318	182	193	173	146	96	117

NOTE: BR = Birth Rate; IM = Infant Mortality
Source: Royal Commission of Labour in India, Report, vol.v, Part 1, p.341;
Government of India, Report of the Age of Consent Committee, 1928–
1929, Calcutta, 1929, p.333.

NOTES

[1] A version of this chapter has been published as 'The Politics of Childbirth', in Peter Robb (ed.), *Society and Ideology. Essays in South Asian History presented to Professor K.A. Ballhatchet*, Oxford, 1993, pp.222–46.

[2] For comparison with birthing conditions in present-day India, see P. Jeffery, R. Jeffery and A. Lyon, *Labour Pains and Labour Power*, London, 1989.

[3] Significantly, western-trained Indian doctors did not really become involved in these issues, but were more concerned with their career prospects *vis-à-vis* European colleagues. See R. Jeffery, 'Doctors and Congress: The Role of Medical Men and Medical Politics in Indian Nationalism', M. Shepperdson and C. Simmons (eds.), *The Indian National Congress and the Political Economy of India 1885–1985*, Aldershot, 1988.

[4] For recent studies on the discourses of health, see D. Arnold (ed.), *Imperial Medicine and Indigenous Societies*, Manchester, 1988; R. Jeffery, *The Politics of Health in India*, Berkeley, 1988; R. MacLeod and M. Lewis (eds.), *Disease, Medicine and Empire*, London, 1988.

[5] D. Arnold, 'Introduction: Disease, Medicine and Empire', D. Arnold, 1988.

[6] Ibid., p.16; Jeffery, 1988, pp.3–10.

[7] S.C. Bose, *The Hindus as They Are*, Calcutta, 1883, pp.305–12; G. Forbes (ed.), *Shuda Mazumdar, A Pattern of Life*, New Delhi, 1977, pp.127–9.

[8] WBSA, Comm./Comm., April 1923, B77, 'Report of Dr D.F. Curjel on the Conditions of Employment of Women before and after Childbirth' (hereafter 'Curjel Report'), Report 7–10, Appendix A, p.xvii, Appendix D, Appendix E, 7; RCLI, iv, 2, pp.1, 19–20, 5, 1, p.41.

[9] R. Inden and R. Nicholas, *Kinship in Bengali Culture*, Chicago, 1977, pp.106–7.

[10] 'Curjel Report'.

[11] Census of India (COI) 1911, v, 1, p.328.

[12] Ibid.

[13] Interview with Abha Mukherjee, Calcutta, 7 February 1985.

[14] E. Shorter, *A History of Women's Bodies*, London, 1983, pp.48–68.

[15] COI, 1901, vi, 1, p.479.

[16] Ibid.; Interview with Renuka Raychaudhuri, Calcutta, 9 February 1985.

[17] COI, 1901, vi, 1, 480; COI, 1911, v, 1, 329; Interview with Phulrenu Chanda, Calcutta, 3 February 1985; interview with Renuka Biswas, Calcutta, 3 February 1985.

[18] COI, 1901, vi, 1, p.480.

[19] Interview with Abha Mukherjee; Inden, Nicholas, 1977, pp.107–8.

[20] Interview with Puspa Sengupta, Calcutta, 2 February 1985; interview with Phulrenu Chanda.

[21] L.B. Day, *Bengal Peasant Life*, Calcutta, 1969, 1st ed., 1874, p.30; S.C. Bose, 1883, p.25.

[22] Interview with Anupama Chatterjee, Calcutta, 2 February 1985.

[23] Day, 1969, p.29; S.C. Bose, 1883, p.25; Interview with Amiya Sen, Calcutta, 9 February 1985; Interview with Phulrenu Chanda. All the women I interviewed, apart from those with a family connection to the Brahmos, remembered the observation of Sasthi puja.

[24] COI, 1911, v, 1, pp.329–30.

[25] For an analysis of the ideology of purity, see M. Douglas, *Purity and Danger*, London, 1985, 1st ed. 1966; L. Dumont, *Homo Hierarchicus*, Chicago, 1980, 1st ed. 1966, 'Pure and Impure', pp.46–61.

[26] 'Curjel Report', Report, p.8.

[27] Ibid., Appendix A, pp.XVIII–XIX.

[28] COI, 1921, V, 1, p.209.

[29] Ibid., pp.209, 230.

[30] COI, 1911, VI, 1, p.30.

[31] Gangaprasad Mukhopadhyaya, *Matrisiksa*, Calcutta, 1871, 'English Introduction' mentions the deterioration of the customs and explains that the lack of hygiene is not a cultural phenomenon.

[32] COI, 1901, VI, 1, p.479.

[33] Shorter, 1983, pp.58–68.

[34] COI, 1911, VI, 1, p.31.

[35] COI, 1921, V, 1, p.255.

[36] Ibid.

[37] *AoC Report*, 76, COI, 1911, V, 1, p.269.

[38] *AoC Report, Bengal Evidence*, pp.28–45, GOI, Report of the Age of Consent Committee 1928–1929, Evidence, vol. 6, Bengal, Calcutta, 1929, pp.38–45.

[39] COI, 1911, V, 1, p.269.

[40] GOI, *AoC Evidence 1928–1929*, pp.14–5, 40.

[41] COI, 1921, VI, 1, pp.53–4; COI, 1931, V, 1, pp.164–5.

[42] Ibid., p.65.

[43] Ibid., p.171.

[44] 'Curjel Report', Appendix A, p.XXIII; Nepali women in Darjeeling, for instance, were helped at the time of childbirth by their husbands and a women relative.

[45] RCLI, V, 1, p.41; 'Curjel Report', Report, pp.7–8 and Appendix A, p.XVII, Appendix D, p.8.

[46] 'Curjel Report', Appendix A, p.XXIII.

[47] Ibid., pp.XVII–XVIII, and Appendix E, p.7.

[48] 'Curjel Report', Appendix A, pp.IV, V; Appendix B, S. Nos. 2, 3 and 5, 6.

[59] COI, 1891, III, p.173.

[50] COI, 1901, VI, 1, p.217.

[51] COI, 1921, VI, 1, p.53.

[52] Infanticide was generally rare in Bengal, IOLR, V/24/3203, *Report on the Administration of the Lower Provinces, Bengal Presidency 1900*, p.37; COI, 1921, V, 1, p.231.

[53] 'Curjel Report'.

[54] IOLR, V/24/3205 1926, p.27.

[55] IOLR, L/P&J/3/211, Emigration letters from India and Bengal, 1891, 'Special Report on the Working of the Act I of 1882 in the Province of Assam During the Years 1886-1889', Calcutta, 1890, pp.707–9; contraception, abortions and infanticides are mentioned as being practised by women working in tea plantations. National Archives of India (NAI), GOI, Home/Judl., 416/24 1924, p.39.

[56] COI, 1931, V, 1, p.165; COI, 1911, V, 1, p.269.

[57] In England, the debate on maternal and infant health was equally preoccupied with death rates and institutional management rather than with the connection between social conditions and health. The debate had taken off in the wake

of the African War which stimulated national interest in a healthy and strong progeny and in healthy soldiers. See J. Lewis, *The Politics of Motherhood*, London, 1980; A. Davin, 'Imperialism and Motherhood', *History Workshop Journal*, 5, 1978, pp.9–65; for the Bengal criticism, Dvijadas Datta, 'Milk and Milk-testing for Adulteration', *Modern Review*, February 1909, pp.114–20.

[58] *Hitavadi*, 9 April 1920, *RNNB*, 17 April 1920.

[59] Prabhat Sanyal, 'Banglar Svastha', *Banga Laksmi*, 1334–35, pp.18–21.

[60] GOI, *Report of the Age of Consent Committee 1928–1929*, Calcutta, 1929, p.166; Nayak, 23 June 1914, *RNNB*, 27 June 1914.

[61] *Dainik Basumati*, 30 March 1920, in *RNNB*, 10 April 1920.

[62] As Geraldine Forbes has recently argued, many Indian middle-class women agreed with the colonial establishment and white women doctors that Indian traditions and customs, epitomized by the uncleanliness of the low-caste and low-class dais, were to blame for bad birthing conditions. Accordingly dais were the foremost target of reforms. G. Forbes, 'Managing Midwifery in India', in D. Engels, S. Marks (eds.), *Contesting Colonial Hegemony. State and Society in Africa and India*, London, 1994, pp.152–72.

[63] Borthwick, 1984, p.324; Murshid, 1983, pp.105–7, provides plenty of details on the marriage patterns of professional or educated Bengali women around the turn of the century.

[64] Murshid, 1983, p.102; GOB, *General Report on Public Instruction in Bengal for 1899–1900*, Calcutta 1900, pp.108–9; GOB, *Education 1902–03 to 1906–07*, p.123; GOB, *Progress of Education in Bengal 1907–08 to 1911–12*, pp..1 19; NAI, GOI, Home/Medl., Deposit, July 1912, 1, pp.3–6, gives the religious affiliation of female medical students in Calcutta.

[65] Borthwick, 1984, p.323.

[66] NAI, GOI, Home/Medl., Deposit, July 1912, 1, pp.3–6.

[67] M.I. Balfour, R. Young, *The Work of Medical Women in India*, London, 1929, p.81.

[68] NAI, GOI, Home/Medl., Deposit, July 1912, 1, the experts in Bengal were attached to Bethune College, Calcutta Medical College, Eden High School for Girls, Dhaka and the Zenana Mission School, Calcutta.

[69] The general suspicion felt by Hindu society towards what was seen as violent interference by western medicine with the self-regulation of the body was felt more strongly when Hindu women became involved: S.N. Sen, 'The Introduction of Western Science in India during the 18th and 19th Century', S. Sinha (ed.), *Science, Technology and Culture*, New Delhi, 1970, p.34; as in Europe, the medical establishment in India doubted women's aptitude for the profession: *Indian Medical Gazette*, 4, 1869, p.274, quoted in O.P. Jaggi, *Impact of Science and Technology in Modern India*, Delhi, 1984, pp.74–5.

[70] Interview with Renuka Biswas, Calcutta, 3 February 1985.

[71] A.R. Caton (ed.), *The Key of Progress*, London, 1930, pp.54ff; M. Balfour and R. Young, *The Work of Medical Women in India*, London, 1929; Lewis, 1980, pp.120–1, 126–8.

[72] *Dainik-o-Samachar Chandrika*, 17 November 1890, *RNNB*, p.29, November 1890.

[73] *Amrita Bazar Patrika*, *RNNB* (English Papers), 17 April 1920; IOLR, P/6812, GOI, Home/Medical, July–December 1904, No 155, 1795.

[74] *Bangabasi*, 21 January 1893, *RNNB*, 28 January 1893.

[75] *Bangabasi*, 26 August 1893, *RNNB*, 2 September 1893.

[76] *Tripura Hitaishi*, 21 March 1905, *RNNB*, 25 March 1905; the Brahmo paper, *Sanjibani*, however, writing for a community in which female education was more widespread, had complained about racial employment patterns a decade earlier: *Sanjibani*, 19 September 1893, *RNNB*, 23 September 1893.

[77] *Hitavadi*, 21 September 1923, *RNNB*, 29 September 1923.

[78] During the 1920s and 1930s, one of the women I interviewed suffered from extended bleeding while she was in her twenties. While her husband had taken her to see a doctor, her relatives were reluctant to organize medical care once she became a widow at the age of twenty. For a contemporary analysis, see B. Agarwal, 'Women, Poverty and Agricultural Growth in India', *The Journal of Peasant Studies*, 13, 1986, pp.171–2.

[79] Lewis, 1980, pp.120–1, 126–8.

[80] On male medical opposition to women doctors in England, see Lewis 1984, p. 195. After the First World War they experienced a particular backlash which partly explains their interest in India. On the organization of British women doctors in India, K.A. Platt, 'Health and Sanitation', A.R. Caton (ed.), *The Key of Progress*, London, 1930, p.55; Balfour, Young, 1929, pp.50–6; M.I. Balfour, 'Co-operation', *The Journal of the Association of Medical Women in India*, 11 June 1923, pp.17–19. On Bengali criticism of allegedly racially-biased appointments, *Sanjibani*, 16 September 1893, IOLR, L/R/5/ 19, *RNNB*, 23 September 1893; *Sahachar*, 3 January 1894, IOLR, L/R/5/20, *RNNB*, 13 January 1894; *Bangabasi*, 24 March 1894, IOLR L/R/5/20, *RNNB*, 31 March 1894; *Sanjibani*, 17 December 1898, IOLR L/R/5/24, *RNNB*, 24 December 1898.

[81] Home Department papers testify to five years of lobbying in India and Britain as well as parliamentary debates before the Women's Medical Service was established: Balfour, 1923, p.17; IOLR, GOI, Home/Medl., A, January 1911, pp.109, 133–5; NAI, GOI, Home/Medl., B, 1912, 22 June, 16 July, p.79; Home/Medl., B, February 1914, p.32; Home/Medl., A, March 1914, pp.28–33. The last file deals with a petition by Bombay-trained Indian women doctors to show less partiality to English-trained doctors when women doctors are employed.

[82] NAI, GOI, Home/Medl., A, June 1911, pp.107–8.

[83] Jaggi, 1984, pp.68–9.

[84] Borthwick, 1984, pp.325–6. See K. Ballhatchet, *Race, Sex and Class under the Raj*, London, 1980, for the reshaping of British class-based prejudices into racialist attitudes in India.

[85] *The Indian Ladies' Magazine*, 2, 1903; Balfour, 1923, p.18, reminded the members of the Association of Medical Women in India of their duties to lobby against injustice done to their Indian women doctor colleagues.

[86] Balfour, Young, 1929, p.111.

[87] White nurses were accused of ill-treating Bengali patients in the Prince of Wales Hospital, Calcutta. Also, when a Bengali woman non-cooperator was injured by the police, the authorities in the Sambhu Nath Pandit Hospital refused to co-operate with the unofficial Bengali enquiry committee. Bengali newspapers compared the two cases to emphasize the underlying racial bias of Europeans in Bengal, *Dainik Basumati*, 22 February 1922, NAI, *RNNB*, 4 March 1922. But it was, in particular, the alleged aloofness of white women and their efforts to maintain a

social distance which infuriated Bengalis. In 1901, an Oriya boy watering the street in Ballyganj wet a white woman. The case was taken away from an Indian judge and the European assistant magistrate sentenced him to ten days' rigorous imprisonment. The High Court reduced the sentence to a fine of Rs 5. In later years, the case was several times referred to by Bengalis as an example of British racial attitudes. *Sri Sri Vishnu Priya-o-Ananda Bazar Patrika*, 8 May 1901, IOLR, L/R/5/27, *RNNB*, 18 May 1901. White women in India were said to be increasingly racial because they were surrounded by more and more Indians in jobs which had formerly been undertaken by Europeans. As example, *The Englishwoman* mentioned the employment policy of the Indian Medical Service: on small stations no white doctor was available any longer. English women were said to dislike Indian doctors with white wives the most, Bahadur, 'The Englishwoman in India', *The Englishwoman*, 10, 1911, pp.181–5. For the missionary-like impetus of European women doctors in India, see Balfour, Young, 1929; F.E. Hoggan, 'Medical Women for India', *The Girl's Own Paper*, 2 February 1884, pp.281–3.

[88] Jaggi, 1984, pp.69–70. Since the turn of the century, some vicereines followed Lady Dufferin's example by founding an organization to improve female health care: 1903 Lady Curzon's Victoria Memorial Scholarships' Fund to train indigenous midwives; 1918 Lady Chelmsford League for Maternity and Child Welfare. Lady Reading and Lady Hardinge set up women's hospitals in Simla and Delhi, Caton, 1930, p.54. But from 1920 onwards, particular stress was laid on reaching Indian women rather than organizing the services provided by Europeans: for instance, 1920 Delhi Maternity and Child Welfare Exhibition; 1924 All-India Baby Week, Balfour, Young, 1929, p.68.

[89] NAI, GOI, Education Department, Sanitary Branch, August 1919, B53; WBSA, Comm./Comm., July 1921, pp.38–9.

[90] *AoC Report 1928–1929*, p.10.

[91] IOLR, Letters by Lady Reading, 1921–1925, MSS. Eur. E316; J. Coatman, *India in 1927–28*, Calcutta, 1928, pp.153–8; see also chapter 3.

[92] For a comprehensive account of women's agitation for their right to vote, see B. C. Pal, *Narir Nirvacanadhikar*, Calcutta, 1921; also N.N. Mitra (ed.), *The Indian Quarterly Register*, vol. II, July–December 1925, p.300.

[93] A. Davin, 'Imperialism and Motherhood', *History Workshop Journal*, 5, 1978, p.43.

[94] WBSA, Comm./Comm., April 1921, A1–13, July 1921, A38–39, December 1924, A40–54, July 1925, A32–68; R. Kumar, 'Family and Factory'.

[95] WBSA, Comm./Comm., December 1924, A54.

[96] WBSA, Comm./Comm., December 1924, A48 and July 1925, A47, p.68.

[97] Ibid. and July 1927, A6–8, 6–7; 'Curjel Report', Appendix A, pp.xiv–xxv.

[98] Anonymous, 'Against Underground Labour from Women', *Modern Review*, November 1922, p.660.

[99] Ibid.

[100] 'Curjel Report', Appendix A, pp.xvii–xviii, Appendix E, 7; RCLI, v, 1, pp.32, 35, 181.

[101] *AoC Report 1928–1929*, 10; NAI, GOI, Home/Judl., 382/1927, Notes, pp.5–6.

[102] Winterton to Reading, 5 June 1923, ibid.; Peel to Reading, 13 January 1923, MSS. Eur. E238/17.

[103] G. Forbes, 'Women and Modernity: The Issue of Child Marriage in India', *Women's Studies International Quarterly*, 2, 1979, p.412.

[104] K. Mayo, *Mother India*, London, 1927, p.118.

[105] NAI, GOI, Home/Judl., 382/1927, Notes, p.8.

[106] Ibid., pp.9–10.

[107] *AoC Report 1928–1929*, pp.1–3.

[108] Ibid., pp.287–8.

[109] Ibid., pp.157, 169–70, 184, 195.

[110] Lewis, 1980, p.100; Davin, 1978, traces modifications and continuities of the patronizing and individualizing concepts.

[111] IOLR, MSS. Eur. E 316.10, Lady Reading Papers, Schedule for the Calcutta Visit, 3 to 22 December 1921.

[112] IOLR, MSS. Eur. E 316.8, Delhi, 26 February 1924.

[113] Ibid., Bangalore, 28 November 1923.

[114] Ibid., Madras, 16 December 1923.

[115] Ibid., Delhi, 2 February 1924.

[116] Ibid.

[117] *Amrita Bazar Patrika*, RNNB (English Papers), 17 April 1920.

[118] Borthwick, 1984, pp.327–8; Murshid, 1983, p.101; IOLR, P/6812, Home/Medl., July–December 1904, No 155, p.1795. In 1901–02, 45 'native dais' received approval certificates from Calcutta Medical College, GOB, Review of Education in Bengal (1897–98 to 1901–02), Second Quinquennial Report, Calcutta, 1902, p.50.

[119] Balfour, Young, 1929, pp.130–2.

[120] Ibid., pp.67–9, *AOC Report 1928–29, Evidence*, pp.67–9.

[121] Caton, 1930, p.123, 149; Saroj Nalini Dutt Memorial Association for Women's Work in Bengal: *Annual Report of the SNDMA, From the Year 1925 to 1931*, Calcutta, n.d., Report 1925, pp.1, 2.

[122] Ibid., pp.2, 9.

[123] 'Nalinibala Devi', *Banga Laksmi*, 1334–35, pp.691–2.

[124] 'Hemangini Sen', ibid., pp.615–8.

[125] *SNDMA Report*, 1927, p.50.

[126] Ibid., pp.8–11.

[127] *SNDMA Report*, 1925, p.12.

[128] *SNDMA Report*, 1926, pp.23–4, 35; 1930, pp.17–8; 'Mahila Samiti Sangbad: Madaripur', *Banga Laksmi*, 1334–35, p.142; 'Barisal', ibid., p.522; Miscellaneous information, *Banga Laksmi*, 1335–36, pp.306, 310.

[129] 'Notun Prasuti Agar', *Banga Laksmi*, 1334–35, p.299.

[130] COI, 1931, v, 1, p.417.

5

WOMEN'S EDUCATION

Changes in the domestic and political spheres were closely
connected with the spread of female formal education.
Political participation by women, reforms in birthing and
changing marital relations resulted in the implications of purdah
being re-negotiated to give women more control over their lives.
Education was not always a pre-condition for these developments, but it enabled women to gain self-confidence and argue
their case against male opposition which until then had profited
from being more eloquent and better informed. Moreover it was
the *sine qua non* for women's entry into the professions and other
white-collar jobs. Female education was also important with
regard to the significance attached to seniority by the women in a
Bengali family. Educated young daughters-in-law had a stronger
leg to stand on against their mothers-in-law, which explains resistance by older women to formalized female education.

In this chapter discourses on female education are placed in a
broad political and social context with no attempt at a detailed
analysis of the effects of education on the lives of elite women who
went to schools and colleges.[1] The main idea is to relate the
progress of female education to the changing social composition
and economic basis of middle-class families and to the development of the nationalist movement. Starting with traditional informal female education, developments informed by Hindu
Revivalism, Swadesi and nationalist radicalization in the 1920s are
traced. Individual efforts, schools, curricula and adult education
programmes combined to establish female formal education in
Bengal which, however, hardly touched the rural and urban masses between 1890 and 1930. During this period female education
was not promoted for the sake of employment or entry by women
into the professions. When this occurred it was a side-effect rather

than the main purpose and, as we shall see, was connected with considerable problems for those who attempted to leave the domestic sphere as adult women.

The motives for male and female education in nineteenth and early twentieth-century Bengal have been widely analysed.[2] After initial controversies regarding western or Indian education, Macaulay's Minute on Education in 1835 reserved state sponsorship for western education for the élite to introduce Indians to western civilization and qualify them for co-operation with the Raj. Later in the century Indians began to criticize colonial education for its lopsided focus on the arts and its neglect of science and technical subjects. Indian initiatives, particularly during the Swadeshi period, tried to make up for such shortcomings.[3] However, all these educational activities shared common goals, namely to prepare aspirants for jobs and to develop political consciousness for the sake of either colonialism or nationalism.

Education for women was, however, a different process from education for men.[4] Meredith Borthwick, who focused on the education of the bhadramahila from the Brahmo Samaj, has analysed how during the second half of the nineteenth century bhadralok reformers paid attention to the education of middle-class women. 'Woman's emancipation gradually became a matter of self-interest', Borthwick wrote, 'as the bhadralok internalized new social norms under the influence of British rule'. By 1900 the desirability of women's education was accepted by most reformist middle-class families. But women were educated to make better mothers and housewives rather than to earn money. The reform ideology of the Brahmos shaped the education of women. Borthwick has captured the limitations and contradictions of what she has called the bhadramahila ideal, which she claims was widely emulated by other Bengali women by the turn of the twentieth century:

The stereotype was created to suit the purpose of an elite under colonial rule, combining the self-sacrificing virtues of the ideal Hindu woman with the Victorian woman's ability to co-operate in the furtherance of her husband's career.[5]

Yet Borthwick also argues that, despite united bhadralok support for female education, 'conservatives' believed educated women would uphold the traditional values of Bengali society, while 'progressives' hoped that educated women would bring about 'social change'.[6]

These labels, 'conservative' and 'progressive', shifted in meaning in the late nineteenth century under the impact of the Hindu revivalist and nationalist movements. Politically 'progressive' opponents of British rule were not socially progressive in the sense of advocating social reform. The conservation of Bengali traditions and values in the face of 'progressive' colonial culture became one of the key cutting edges in Bengali opposition to British rule. The new 'progressives' adopted the old 'conservative' view on female education. The preservation of traditional Bengali elements in women's education was encouraged at the expense of 'progressive' colonial values. The spread of schools informed by such principles far exceeded anything achieved by earlier reformists.

In orthodox families, however, female school education, or merely the acquisition of literacy skills, was inhibited by cultural values. Girls were prevented from going to school by the common belief that a girl who could read and write would never find a husband or would soon become a widow.[7] After 1900 such views did change, but the formal education of many girls was delayed until their seniors, usually their grandparents, had died.[8] For the latter, even rudimentary intellectual independence acquired through education was incompatible with Bengali Hindu womanhood, which was true to the self-effacing ideals of Sita and Savitri.

Bratas

Traditional education was based on the rote learning of mythological epics and ritual texts. A mother seldom took part in her daughter's basic education, as she was generally too busy with her housework or looking after her husband's needs. Instead, the *thakurma*, the paternal grandmother, and in particular widowed sisters of the father, the *pichima*, would tell a daughter folk tales and stories from the *Mahabharata* and *Ramayana* as well as instruct her in the ritual duties of a young girl.[9]

Childhood rituals were accompanied by the recitation of bratas (vows) which gave religious affirmation to the daily order of life in a household. Most bratas were connected with alpanas (ornamental floor-drawings made with rice paste). Girls thus combined two duties, namely worship and the beautification of the house. Moreover, the alpana lasted for a day or so and bore witness to the completion of her household duty. Whereas Sanskrit prayers could be recited only by priests, bratas were in simple Bengali and were recited by children to themselves. Bengali girls, who received little further education, remembered these vows all their lives.

There was a wide range of bratas which varied according to region and season. Most bratas referred to a rural environment, to animals, in particular the cow, and to plants. Even families who had migrated to the cities still regarded the countryside, especially their ancestral villages, as their true homes and points of reference. Women celebrated pujas, during which they bathed and fasted to secure sufficient rain for their families' fields, to ensure a good harvest or to keep away snakes, a constant threat to villagers during the rainy season when all paths were water-logged.[10]

Young girls were generally proficient in only a few bratas, whose major intention was to prepare a girl for a happy married life. The most common rite was the *sib puja* in which a girl prayed to Shiva to bless her with a kind husband like Shiva himself. During Baisakh (the first month after the Bengali New Year and, according to the western calendar, after 14 April), girls as young as five years old would perform sib puja. In some families sib puja was started in Caitra, that is one month earlier. Where many girls lived in the same household, the rite was performed together. They rose before sunrise, had a bath, dressed in a special sari and then went into the garden to pick flowers and *durva* grass for the puja.

The actual ceremony varied slightly from family to family. Amiya Sen, for instance, born in Calcutta in 1905, used to sit on the floor with her sisters and cousins, each forming a *lingam* out of Ganges mud. After the older women in the house had recited the brata, the young girls were allowed to plunge their 'miniature penises' into the pond.[11] The ritual that Sudha Mazumdar, born in 1899, remembered was somewhat different. She started her sib puja at the age of eight:

In the puja room, Mother taught me how to make the necessary arrangements for the ritual with a set of small copper utensils I had been given. In the little water vessel I poured out some Ganges water and first washed the flowers, the *durva* grass, the leaves from the *bael* tree so loved by Shiva and *aconda* which was difficult to obtain in town, but sometimes supplied by the *mali* (gardener)… The grass and the fresh flowers I picked from our garden were separately placed on the little copper flower plate. Crimson and cream sandalwood would then be separately rubbed with water on a stone slab and the paste thus formed scraped up into tiny little bowls. Finally, a handful of uncooked rice was carefully washed and heaped on another plate, and on this I placed a peeled banana.[12]

Then Sudha would mould her symbol of Shiva and 'was often in despair, for (her) Shiva would insist on being a crooked one, which boded no good for (her)'.[13] The god was then bathed by sprinkling him with water, a prayer was said and an offering made of petals and bael leaves. Taking into account that Sudha had to finish the puja and her breakfast before the school bus came to pick her up at half past eight in the morning, it was only a very conscientious girl who continued the ritual after she went to school.[14]

The subject of the bratas of a young girl (*kumari brata*) was not solely her future husband, but covered all facets of her future married life. In the Yampukur brata a little girl prayed for her mother-in-law's soul;[15] in the Punyipukur brata she prayed to be spared widowhood.[16] In the Sejuti brata a girl hoped for a happy family life, but also feared a possible co-wife. This was one of the few bratas which was not based on a harmonious wish fulfilment, but called for the worst possible death for a co-wife.[17] The Magh-mandal brata, which was particularly popular in East Bengal, was recited to inculcate the demure qualities which were much admired in a young daughter-in-law in a joint family.[18] Another group of bratas encouraged an associated character trait, namely a gentle temper in general. Sudha Mazumdar, whose mother feared that her temperament was too lively, had to perform the Madhu-sankranti brata for two successive years. On the last day of each month she had to give a silver coin and a bell-metal bowl filled with *madhu* (honey) to a *sadhu* (holy man), and then salute him by wiping the dust off his feet.[19]

At least until 1920 bratas were a vital part of female education although their importance is difficult to assess with precision. The weight of ideological and anthropological literature on bratas suggests that the underlying values represented Bengali society's expectations and norms of female behaviour.[20] There is also some historical evidence to show the social relevance of bratas. During the Swadeshi period, when nationalists started to integrate women into the boycott movement, they chose the form of a brata for the vow women took to express their allegiance.[21] Moreover, in contemporary periodicals bratas were regarded as a living tradition, and a similar view can be found in some women's autobiographies. In addition, a number of middle and lower middle-class women, born in east and west Bengal between 1900 and 1910, remembered the brata rituals, in particular the sib puja, when they were interviewed in the 1980s. They thought, however, that they were the last generation of women to have been brought up in such a way When their daughters reached the age of brata learning, formal education at school had replaced many aspects of former middle class home education.[22]

The Era of Clandestine Learning

The beginnings of female school education go back into the nineteenth century. In the 1820s and 1830s there were some missionary initiatives, but formal female education in Bengal effectively began only in 1849 with the opening of the Bethune School. It was followed by the founding of the Hindu Mahila Bidyalaya and the Victoria College in 1873 and 1883, respectively. In the countryside individual members of the bhadralok had founded two small girls' schools (Baraset and Nibadhai) in 1847 and 1848 and others in increasing numbers from the 1860s. But the pupils of these schools came, almost without exception, from the three factions of the Brahmo Samaj or the Christian community, and not from orthodox Hindu families. In 1883 Candramukhi Basu, a Christian, and Kadambini Basu, a member of the Brahmo Samaj, were the first two women graduates from Calcutta University.[23]

For the Brahmo reformers female education was 'the key that would open the door to all other social progress'.[24] In 1878, due to their pioneering efforts, over 20,000 girls were receiving instruction, mostly at home, in Bengal. This number, however, was poor in comparison with literate men. In 1881 only 4 in 1000 women were literate, but a much higher proportion of men, namely 137 out of 1000, could read and write in Bengali.[25]

In the 1890s, when Brahmo and Christian girls had already been attending schools for some time, orthodox middle class Hindu girls only gradually began to learn to read and write at home. Some were taught in the zenana by women missionaries, but this never became very popular because of their proselytizing verve.[26] In other cases men in the household were the first teachers of their women.[27] Still, at the turn of the twentieth century young Hindu husbands with educated wives in orthodox families were rare. In the normal course of events a Hindu husband was not allowed to talk to his wife during the daytime. This was a serious impediment to any attempt at teaching wives to read and write. In conservative families it was often the young wife's mother-in-law who objected most to the rudiments of education. She feared a loss of control over her daughter-in-law. Moreover, an educated husband and wife threatened to intensify the emotional bond of marriage at the expense of their attachment to the joint family. In the early 1900s it was not unusual for a woman to wait until the death of her mother-in-law before she learnt to read and write.[28]

In a girl's parental home the situation was sometimes reversed. Radharani Basu, born in Calcutta in 1891, was educated by a private tutor. She was taught in Bengali, but whereas her mother encouraged her to learn English, her father was opposed to it. Her mother gave her English books which she hid inside her Bengali texts. When her father discovered this, he threw her English books away. Her mother supported an English education because of the increased value it placed on her in the marriage market, whereas her father objected to her learning the colonial language.[29] Such conflicts were the result of tensions aroused by the emergence of the nationalist movement. English-medium education was a particularly sensitive issue. The common belief was that once a woman could speak and read English she would become alienated from the ideals of Bengali womanhood. English novels were regarded as particularly pernicious; they were thought to be full of love stories containing an alien sexual morality dangerous to a Bengali woman's chastity. On a more profound level women were seen as wardens of Bengali identity and cultural purity.[30] Thus, it was generally the case that in the same family the women were educated in Bengali and the men in English. Hemangini Sen, for instance, who became a well-known social worker and campaigner for social progress, was kept in strict purdah during her childhood. She was not allowed to speak to men from outside the family and was not sent to school. Born in 1890, she received her Bengali education through her parents. Her father was an engineer and had been educated in an English-medium school. He was an enlightened man who arranged for her marriage at the comparatively late age of 14 years. Nevertheless, he neither sent her to school nor taught her to speak English. The path to her later career as a social worker was prepared by her husband, Sailendranath Sen, who continued her education. He taught her in English and appointed an English governess for her who also taught her to tailor blouses and baby clothes.[31]

On occasions illiteracy presented orthodox husbands with obstacles to courtship, as meetings had to be arranged through oral messages conveyed by maidservants. Amiya Bhaduri and her husband faced this problem early in their married life. She was given into marriage as a ten-year-old, illiterate child-wife in 1910. Her husband rejected his family's views on female seclusion, and wanted to see her during the day. However, he found it difficult, if not impossible, to arrange meetings with her. He could not entrust a servant to convey a message into the zenana, as secrecy was of the essence. Thus Amiya was taught to read and write by her husband, so that she could decipher his messages and turn up in time at their secret meeting place—a dark corner underneath the staircase.[32] The arrangements and motives for female literacy were not always as romantic, but before the Swadeshi period (1905–11) and the opening of girls' schools, it was only the individual efforts of men that enabled daughters in orthodox families to be educated.

Usually the education of sons received paternal attention, but in the absence of sons, daughters became the sole object of their fathers' love and attention. Educating a son was an important aspect of male identity in a patriarchal family. Men who perceived of themselves as intellectual beings in contrast to emotional women considered education to be a means of perpetuating not the lineage of blood, but the lineage of spirit and intellect. The common focus on a son's education reinforced the prejudice in favour of the superiority of male intellectual capacities which in turn justified the patriarchal structure of the family. In the face of such bias it was difficult for women to attain intellectual accomplishment. Significantly, the majority of women, known for their social reformist activities or for intellectual refinement, came from families without sons where daughters were not second to their brothers. Nagendrabala Devi was an only child in a Kayastha family. Her mother died when she was a child and she was

brought up, almost as a boy, by her father. 'Don't think of her as
my daughter', explained her father, 'she is my son'. As an adult
she became a well-known social worker and a supporter of Sister
Nivedita's school.[33]

Later, the period preceding widespread school education was
called the era of 'clandestine' learning because of the ambiguous
attitudes towards female education.[34] On the one hand, the increasing intellectual accomplishment of the Brahmo women impressed the Hindu community. On the other hand, female
education made traditional Hindus fear the loss of their cultural
identity and male dominance.[35] This attitude was most prevalent
in Calcutta, the centre of European power and influence. School
education, practices of reformist and westernized families apart,
started here later than in East Bengal. A family would keep its
daughters at home in Calcutta, but when it moved to the mufassal
or outside Bengal, daughters were allowed to go to school until
they were married.[36] Rural families, who followed traditional
norms, but were in favour of female education, sent their girls to
school at least until they were eight or ten years old. Prabhavati
Devi, for instance, born in 1875 in Debhatta village, went to the
village school until she was married at the age of ten. Thereafter,
while she was still living with her parents, her father appointed a
private tutor. Even in village conditions the social norms of the
sasur bari triumphed over the more liberal values of the baper
bari.[37]

Hindu Revivalism and Girls' Schools

After 1900 many Hindu girls were sent to school for the first time.
The idea of social progress had become acceptable and was no
longer identified with giving up Hindu religion and becoming a
Brahmo. In the second half of the nineteenth century the debate
over the curriculum had become increasingly critical of 'male'
education for women. Gradually a compromise was struck between 'male' and 'female' curricula, between an academic education for boys and a domestic education for girls. Women were
prepared for household work and, through cultural and national
orientation, for their role as guardians of Bengali culture and
tradition. This has been depicted as a development without
qualitative ruptures and as a virtually organic progressive

process. But Borthwick's view that the reformist bhadramahila ideal was widely emulated and was fast becoming the dominant model of social behaviour pre-empts social and political developments after the end of the nineteenth century, which encouraged female education for reasons different from those of early Brahmo reformers.[38]

The cultural innovations which prepared the ground for political developments during the Swadeshi period are known as Hindu Revivalism (see chapter 1). With regard to female education the influence of Hindu Revivalism was best illustrated by the foundation of the Mahakali Pathsala school in 1893. Started by the wealthy female ascetic, Mataji Maharani Tapaswini, it aimed to provide formal but traditional education for Hindu girls. A decade earlier the Brahmo leader, Keshab Chandra Sen, had undertaken a similar project in opening the Victoria College as an institution where higher female education would not be based on a 'male' curriculum. But in the Brahmo school the academic curriculum was only supplemented by ethical Hindu education; it was not set up to systematize the traditional education middle-class girls had, until then, received at home. Maharani Tapaswini, however, herself a Sanskrit scholar and 'well-versed in the Shastras', based her curriculum on orthodox Hindu norms.[39]

That orthodoxy and female learning were no longer contradictory, as had been the case only half a century ago, was a measure of the ideological shift orthodox Bengali Hindu society had undergone. Purdah girls arrived at school in closed carriages and horse-drawn buses, which were provided by the Pathsala, to be instructed about 'the strict observance of Shastric injunctions in matters of domestic life' and about *patibrata dharma*, devotion to their future husbands.[40] The novelty was not the closed carriages—before the 1920s no girl would walk or use public transport to reach school—but the cultural similarity between school and home education. In a six-year course girls learnt about their moral, practical and economic duties within the family and the community. They were taught Indian history, arithmetic, cooking, how to read and write and, most importantly, their minds were shaped by the epic images of Sita and Savitri. For this purpose the Mahakali Pathsala published its own text-books in Bengali and Sanskrit. To begin with the pupils learnt to read the Sanskrit texts of Bengali stories they were familiar with, such as the *Ramayana*.

At a more advanced stage, they had to cope with moral and philosophical texts which required a high standard of Sanskritic knowledge. However, the heart of the curriculum was a simple extension of home education. The girls read, for example, the *Shiva Puja Paddhati*, a text explaining the sib puja which all of them were familiar with through the teaching of the senior women in their families. During Baisakh, sib puja was celebrated at school, as were the Saravasti puja and the Virastami brata.[41] The school enjoyed British support. In 1906, for instance, Lady Minto distributed the Pathsala's annual prizes in the Town Hall. Little girls in pink saris were rewarded with gold and silver medals for their proficiency in the culinary arts, and for good conduct and modesty.[42]

The growth and decline of the school reflected the development of female education in the early 1900s. It opened with 30 students in 1893 and by 1903 had an enrolment of 450 which increased to over 600 in 1912. Moreover, there were 23 branch schools in Bengal. The Mahakali Pathsala was thus the biggest girls' school at the time, with considerably more pupils than the Bethune school, its western-oriented rival. In 1903, supported by the Hindu community and sponsored by wealthy landowners, such as the Maharaja of Darbhanga and the Maharaja of Burdwan, the school bought its own Calcutta premises on 69 Sukeas Street. The school catered for girls from high-caste Hindu families. Nonetheless, it was a milestone on the way towards introducing school education for middle- and lower middle-class girls because it made female education acceptable by basing it on the preservation of Hindu traditions and knowledge. By 1915, however, the Calcutta school was in financial difficulties because wealthy Hindus no longer subscribed to its funding. By then, more secular female education was gaining popularity in Calcutta while in the mufassal orthodox education was still in demand. In Mymensingh and Faridpur, mahakali pathsalas flourished with hundreds of pupils until well into the 1920s.[43]

Sister Nivedita's school in Bagh Bazar was for girls from poorer families. The school was inspired by Swami Vivekananda who intended to 'start a school which would combine in it all that was best in Eastern and Western culture'.[44] Sister Nivedita, then Margaret Noble, met Vivekananda in London in 1895 when he was touring Europe to preach the word of the Bengali ascetic,

Ramkrishna. Vivekananda opposed social reform in India as practised by the Brahmo Samaj. Instead, he propagated the moral
rejuvenation of Hindu society in order to improve the material
conditions of the country. In doing so he redefined the Hindu
meaning of the renunciation of material life. He did not believe in
giving up worldly pursuits alone, but was rather committed to a
life of community service.[45]

Sister Nivedita was converted to Vivekananda's cause and in
1898 went to Calcutta as his disciple. She lived like an ordinary
Hindu woman in the poor central districts, where she learnt
Bengali and came to understand Hindu culture. Her idea was to
start an educational movement for women in support of
Vivekananda's wider aims for the moral and material rejuvenation of India. She rented a small house in Bosepara Lane and, after
overcoming prejudices against her as a foreign woman, she
opened a kindergarten and a school for young girls. In 1902 she
started another school for older girls and women, the Ramkrishna
Balika Bidyalaya. On the first day sixty women in purdah attended, who were from middle class families.[46] She encouraged
child widows to attend and clashed with the orthodox community
on this issue.

Despite opposition, her school flourished. She was supported
by another European, Sister Christina, and the free services of the
Brahmo teacher, Labonyaprabha Bose. The curriculum comprised
reading, writing, sewing and discourses on the lives of religious
leaders. In time, advanced students were employed as teachers
and received a monthly allowance; amongst them were widows,
who managed to escape the oppressive life of widowhood. An
unmarried woman, Srimati Sudhira, dedicated her life entirely to
the school, and giving up the idea of marriage, became Sister
Nivedita's closest helper and later the principal of the school.[47]

The purpose of the school was to provide modern education 'in
the context of Indian culture, without making it academic'.[48] The
school was improved through the addition of a teacher's training
class. Here, Bengali, history, grammar, arithmetic, geography,
English, Sanskrit, geometry, brush-work, needlework and kindergarten teaching methods were taught.[49] As the curriculum became
more varied, it became more difficult to safeguard the Hindu
character of the school. Sister Nivedita became more and more
concerned about the spiritual discipline of her students. In 1914,

as a consequence, Sister Sudhira founded the Saradweswari Asram school.[50] The school continued to thrive because of its proximity to the Ramkrishna Mission and the reputation of Sister Nivedita.[51] However, in the early 1900s, as girls' schools were founded in increasing numbers, the Ramkrishna Balika Bidyalaya lost its unique status.

The Swadeshi Period

During the Swadeshi period female education became linked for the first time with politics in India. Although most Swadeshi leaders were unconcerned in general with participation in the movement, there were some activities such as rakhi bandhan and arandhan which required female support.[52] In the press and, most importantly, by Mukhunda Das' jatra performances, women were called on to boycott foreign goods including British-made hair ribbons and glass bangles. Moreover, during the revolutionary phase of the movement help from women was essential for hiding men on the run from the police.[53]

This sort of political mobilization had a limited impact on the spread of female education in Bengal. Although nationalists were made aware of the advantages of female political participation and considered women's education a necessary prerequisite, the National Education Movement during the Swadeshi period was directed solely at the education of males. Two independent attempts to found national girls' schools in Mymensingh and Rajshahi turned out to be failures.[54] In 1908 Tagore, by then the leading literary figure in Bengal, tried to include girl students in his educational asram in Santiniketan, but abandoned his plan of co-education after a girl's suicide attracted unwelcome publicity.[55]

The policies of Swadeshi drew middle-class women gradually into the struggle for independence. Women contributed money or special skills for relief work or the spread of female education. Until then middle-class women, if concerned at all, had concentrated on raising the level of political consciousness amongst members of their immediate circle. Now they directed their attention towards other women in Bengal. This trend was reinforced once nationalist ideology focused on the economic effects of British rule, notably the gradual impoverishment of lower middle-class families.[56]

Economic hardship encouraged calls for the education of widows. The education of middle-class widows, it was hoped by nationalists, would make them economically independent of their families, but at the turn of the century the idea was still ahead of its time and had a limited impact. Nonetheless, it was easier for middle-class women to bridge the status gap with widows than to bridge the class gap with women from poorer families. Widows were an easy educational target, because they were less restricted than wives by their mothers-in-law. Thus, during the Swadeshi period women adopted a new and organized approach to reforming the hardships of middle-class Hindu widows.[57]

Existing groups like the Sakhi Samiti, founded in 1886, were reorganized with a stronger emphasis on education and help for widows. Originally the Sakhi Samiti had been established 'so that women of respectable families should have the opportunity of mixing with each other and devoting themselves to the cause of social welfare'.[58] Then the idea was to organize zenana education and to support widows and orphans. The Samiti financed two girls at the Bethune School and two widows at the Baranagore Bidabha Asram which had been established by Sasipada Banerjee in the same year. As the organization suffered from a constant lack of funds, its members arranged annual exhibitions with sales of women's handicrafts in Bethune College. The zenana education programme, however, failed because the former pupils did not fulfil their obligations to teach as many years in the organization as they had been taught.[59]

By the time of the Swadeshi movement it was apparent that the ailing Sakhi Samiti was in need of new direction. In 1906 it was restarted by Hiranmoyi Debi, daughter of the original founder, Svarnakumari Debi. She opened the Mahila Bidabha Asram, a widows' home which, in true Swadeshi spirit, concentrated on industrial education. By 1909 the Asram had 30 members and 50 dayscholars, and a larger building was needed to take in the many widows who had applied for admission. From 12 to 3 p.m., 'the time on which men have no claim, which is women's own for wasting away or spending in self-improvement', classes were held in spinning and weaving, making stockings and vests, lace-making, tailoring, painting, modelling, music, singing and other subjects. Although this initiative was supported by many Brahmo and English women it was by no means generally accepted by

Bengali middle-class society. Most families still insisted on keeping their widows at home, either out of concern for their status or because they did not want to dispense with widows' work in the house.[60]

On the initiative of Sarala Debi, the younger sister of Hiranmoyi Debi, female education was taken up, in the face of male opposition, at the All-India Ladies' Conference (an offspring of the Indian National Social Conference), which was held at the Allahabad Congress session in December 1910. The Ladies' Conference decided on the foundation of the Bharat Stri Mahamandal, which was to set up provincial organizations with funds and teachers for zenana education. Zenana education was an old idea. What was new was its organization on an all-India basis. New, too, was the commitment of Krishnabhabini Das, a widow, to the Bengal branch. Her husband and daughter had died within a year of the family's return from Cambridge, where her husband had worked as a lecturer for fourteen years. She put on a home-spun sari and walked bare-foot from door to door to convince the *purdanashins* of the value of zenana education.[61]

Teachers at the Mahamandal taught a well-planned curriculum containing Bengali, history, English, geography, arithmetic, sewing, handwork, music and singing at private houses or the three centres in north, south and central Calcutta. There were fixed time-tables and properly organized examinations. By June 1911, 50 women from 30 families were taught by nine teachers; a year later the figure had more than doubled. Ever-growing demand, however, could not be satisfied because the costs of transporting the purdah teachers were too high and had already pushed the Mahamandal into heavy debt.[62] It was the degree of organization, the backing of Sarala Debi and the intensity with which Krishnabhabini Das fulfilled her duty that made the Mahamandal more efficient and long-lived than previous attempts at zenana education. But the future belonged to female school education, even though the orthodox sections of Hindu society, particularly in Calcutta, still insisted on purdah and home education.

Compared to well-organized zenana education and industrial training for widows (which only became accepted in the 1920s), school education for girls became extremely popular after 1900. The number of day schools for girls all over Bengal trebled between 1901 and 1911.[63] A husband's desire for an educated wife

was not without influence on this development. But when formal
education for girls is seen in comparison with adult and widow
education it becomes clear that it was more than just a female
response to a male stimulus.

While in 1902 less than 2 per cent of all girls of school-going age
were at school, by 1927 the ratio had increased to 7.5 per cent. The
sheer numbers were more impressive. In 1901 almost 50,000 girls
attended a school, and three decades later, in 1931, the number
had reached 450,000.[64] The growth in the number of girls attending
primary schools was most dramatic, but a smaller proportion
went on to higher schooling. In 1907 there were 7 high schools for
girls out of which only Bethune School was managed by the
government. Of the remainder, one in Calcutta and another in
Bankipur, were privately organized, while the others were run by
missionaries. By 1930 there were 36 girls' high schools in the
province, the most renowned being Bethune School, the Brahmo
Girls' School and Victoria College in Calcutta and Eden High
School in Dhaka. But female higher education remained the
preserve of a few—only 15,000 in 1931. Although the number of
girls attending high school trebled during each decade between
1901 and 1931, only 394 girls passed the matriculation examination in 1932.[65]

If comparative literacy between men and women is taken as an
index of education, then female education took major strides in
this period. Female, as compared to male literacy improved, although it still lagged far behind. In 1891 there were only 5 literate
women to every 100 literate men, but by 1931 this ratio had grown
to 18:100. More Hindus were literate than Muslims, but the
regional differences were more interesting. In Calcutta female
literacy was more widespread than anywhere else and in the
whole of the Presidency Division there was one literate woman
for every four men. The ratio between male and female literacy
was also relatively high in the Dhaka division, namely one in five.
In Calcutta and Dhaka western education and social reform had
left a mark. In Calcutta the western and social reformist impact
was particularly strong, but in Dhaka the spread of female literacy
was partly based on the cultural norms of the Baidya caste; by 1930
among the Baidyas over 75 per cent of the men and almost 50 per
cent of all women were literate. Next in female literacy rankings,

but in considerably lower numbers, came Brahmans, Indian Christians and Kayasthas.[66]

The spread of female literacy was not unique to Bengal. By the turn of the century the percentage of literate women in the Bombay and Madras provinces was considerably higher than in Bengal. Twenty years later there were as many literate women in Bengal as in Madras, but the percentage of literate women in Bombay was still higher. Compared to the provinces west of Bengal, however, the Bengali achievements were most impressive. The percentage of literate women in Bihar and Orissa and, particularly, in the Punjab and the United Provinces was considerably lower. However, the overall perspective was still bleak. The female literacy rate for Bengal only grew from 1.8 to 2.8 per cent between 1921 and 1931.[67]

Throughout the nineteenth century school education for boys in Bengal had been based on the private initiatives of members of the bhadralok, who used the government's grants-in-aid policy to set up schools and high schools in villages and district towns. After the turn of the century a similar initiative was taken for the education of women. By 1922, 99 per cent of all girls' schools were privately managed with growing, but never sufficient financial support from the government.[68]

Private initiative resulted in the establishment of the Maharani Girls' School in Darjeeling. When Hemlata Debi, who had grown up and gone to school in Calcutta, moved to Darjeeling with her husband, she found that, apart from the American School, there was no school for her daughters. The British school there would not accept Indian girls. The numerous Bengali middle-class girls—daughters of clerks, station masters, teachers and postmasters—spent their time at home while their brothers went to school. Consequently, in September 1908, Hemlata Debi started the Maharani School in Darjeeling. It was a free day school financed by the daughters of Keshub Chandra Sen, the Maharani of Cooch Behar and the Maharani of Majurbanj, who spent their summers in Bengali, middle-class fashion in the hills.[69]

Hemlata Debi, the daughter of the Sadharan Brahmo leader, Sibnath Sastri, opened her school with only 7 pupils, including her own children. To attract more pupils she went from house to house and tried to convince middle-class families of the need for female education. It was not a hard task, because the social atmosphere in Darjeeling was more liberal than in Calcutta. Moreover, the local residents were used to the sight of educated Bengali and European women moving freely around during their summer holidays in the hills. Between 1908 and 1910 the enrolment figure grew to 77, including 9 boarders at the 'high class Home School' which was opened in 1910 and equipped with several trained women teachers. Pupils came as a result of the constant efforts of the founder principal, who asked her friends in the plains to send their daughters—even Nepalese, Sikkimese, Bhutanese and Tibetan aristocratic girls were sent—first as pupils and then as teachers.[70]

Hemlata Debi was a Sadharan Brahmo, but her school was neither distinctly Brahmo nor Hindu. What was attractive for lower middle-class families, from whom the majority of the day-pupils came, was her common sense and understanding of the practical problems which arose from a girl attending school. Lessons began at half past ten in the morning, so that the girls had ample time for working in the household, for praying and bathing. Hemlata neither insisted on plaited hair, which posed a problem for a Hindu girl who wet her hair each morning, nor on a white school uniform which would have been a financial burden on most families. These issues might seem minor, but in orthodox families practical problems often impeded female education more than objections in principle.[71]

Hemlata Sarkar's pragmatic approach to female education was representative of new developments at the beginning of the twentieth century. Female schooling became a means of improving the material and social conditions of women without coming into conflict with Hindu orthodoxy. Schooling was also encouraged as a protection for middle-class girls against the worst consequences of widowhood, as a widow could contribute to her family's household budget through a teacher's salary.[72]

Government support for female education in Bengal took various forms. In Rangpur, for instance, a district with an extremely low female literacy rate, a prototype of a primary school for 80 girls was developed and then copied in a number of towns and larger villages. Between 1913 and 1917 expenditure on female education rose from Rs 6000 to over Rs 16,000, which was met out of the Rangpur district fund. On an average, however, in 1931 an aided school in Bengal received only Rs 33 to Rs 38 per year from

district boards, union boards or municipalities which was not
sufficient to run the schools satisfactorily. About 100 model
primary and peasant girls' schools were well-managed and well-
maintained by the provincial government but were only a small
improvement in the sphere of female education.[73] Middle English
schools were founded parallel to the middle vernacular schools,
but the latter lost popularity during the 1920s, as female higher
education without English came to be regarded as a waste of time
and money. Existing schools, like those which had originated
through Brahmo initiatives in the late nineteenth century, received
increased or special grants for building or extending schools.
Scholarships and prize money to individual girls served as an
additional encouragement. Prize distributions became important
social events in district towns; local zenana ladies attended
together with the wives of district officials. In addition, home
education was sponsored for purdah girls. Even with a scholarship they did not have to attend classes, but could keep the money
as a prize if they sat for examinations at the end of the year. In
Dhaka, Bogra, Noakhali, Comilla and Chittagong, for instance,
home tutors were financed through public money.[74]

Aspects of the Curricula

The syllabus taught at primary schools was 'female' in orientation.
Science was only included in high school and even there only to
a limited extent. But hygiene, needlework, household management and child rearing comprised the core of the curriculum.[75]
Formal education reinforced gender relations; in some ways by
professionalizing female duties education supported the idea of
the complementarity of the sexes, thus liberating women from
subordination without providing for self-discovery. Female self-
realization was channelled into areas which were not threatening
to men.

While Hemlata Debi was planning her school in the early 1900s,
she published an article on education in *Bharat Mahila*, a women's
journal. She argued that two distinct types of female education
were needed: basic schooling comprising Bengali, mathematics,
geography, Indian history, hygiene, everyday science, art and
music; and higher education for those who were not affected by
child marriage, consisting of additional subjects such as English,

higher mathematics, world history, science, philosophy and Sanskrit. The basic thrust of her argument was that educated women were better mothers and wives. She used John Stuart Mill as an intellectual authority on the double burden of working women, and the conclusion she drew was that women should not take wage employment. The only women for whom she suggested education as a preparation for work outside the home were widows; she wanted to prevent them from either becoming maid-servants or financial burdens to their families.[76]

At high schools the curriculum prepared girls for the matriculation examination. However, due to early marriage only about a third of high school students reached the higher classes and in 1932, for instance, only two thirds of those who wrote the examinations actually passed.[77] British educational administrators suggested a revised curriculum which would be 'more in accordance with the needs of the pupils'. In the years before the First World War, Miss Brooks, the school inspectress, put forward a curriculum including 'in addition to the ordinary subjects of a secondary school, hygiene, nursing, needle-work, cookery and domestic work'. Only one or two mission schools, in her plans, should prepare girls for matriculation examinations.[78] These plans were never implemented because they met with strong Bengali protest.

Bengalis rejected the idea that academic qualifications should be restricted to mission schools, symbols of cultural alienation, while respectable Bengali Hindu girls were to learn 'refined housewifery'. British educational administrators explained the reaction in a different way. They referred to 'the dominance of examinations' in Bengal which to them was another case of the Bengali attempt to succeed on British terms without, however, giving up traditional cultural practices, such as early marriage. But in the 1920s Bengalis were quite prepared to change the curricula of girls' schools and to introduce folk art, such as Bengali drawing and singing. Only now the reforms were part of the process of recreating Bengali cultural identity rather than a colonial measure which would have favoured foreign (missionary) schools.[79]

Two innovations in the female syllabus deserve special attention, namely singing and dancing. Both extended the sphere of female respectability and self-expression without trespassing into the male world of jobs, money and competition. Inspired by kindergarten didactics, Sister Nivedita was the first to redefine education in this way—by including playing music in the lower, and modelling and painting in the higher standards.[80] The syllabus ·of the Maharani Girls' School also included music. But Rabindranath Tagore helped to incorporate music and dancing into the school curriculum to a greater extent. When the Santiniketan school was started in 1901, Tagore aimed to create, in the spirit of the Swadeshi movement, a school which was close to Bengali life and culture. As pupils become acquainted with life in the neighbouring village, Surul, they were instructed in Bengali traditions. Music, dance, drama, drawing and crafts were taught, not as imitative skills, but as creative arts. Although girls were excluded from the school—apart from the daughters of teachers— Tagore's artistic and educational concepts were always meant for both sexes and influenced female education in Bengal, even before girls were formally admitted to his school in 1922. Until then singing had been a skill confined to courtesans, but Tagore turned it into a patriotic art form which could be performed by men and women. By the 1920s men were looking for wives who were educated and could sing Rabindra Sangit.[81]

Dance education for girls in Santiniketan had the same creative function as music, but it touched on a cultural taboo in Bengali society which was even more sensitive than singing. Performing on stage was only semi-respectable, even for men. Actresses were always seen as prostitutes. For this reason dance was not taught as a subject in Santiniketan. However, Tagore would sing and ask his pupils to dance spontaneously, interpreting the meaning of his words. He was not content with beautiful steps and graceful arm movements, but encouraged a dramatic interpretation. In the 1920s, after seeing girls dancing in the *rajbari* in Manipur, Tagore arranged dance lessons at his school. Dance, like the art of alpana, was performed in Santiniketan as a combination of different elements which allowed the artist to develop his or her creativity within strict rules.[82] The first success at the school was a private dance interpretation of Tagore's poem *Katha-Kahini*. Then he planned a public dance performance in Calcutta of *Natir Puja*. On the poet's birthday, 27 January 1927, Gouri Bhanja, a teenage girl, danced the female solo part of the drama. Tagore, who was concerned about Gouri's honour and future marriage prospects, took a role in the play to underline its acceptability. Gouri's dance performance was another step in widening the sphere of female respectability and creativity. Other schools imitated the performance, but only in front of women.[83] With paid employment still beyond the reach of most middle-class women, female education became more sophisticated in what was regarded as typically female and cultural skills.

New Frontiers: Women in White Collar Jobs and the Expansion of Higher Education

Those women of European, Eurasian or Bengali origin, however, who sought white-collar jobs or who went to university in Bengal were confronted with male racist and sexist reactions. The only exception was the attitude of the Brahmo community whose acceptance of female education did not end at the doors of the Bethune or Diocesan Colleges. Although they were a numerically small group, they comprised the large majority of female college students in Calcutta until the 1920s. Borthwick has analysed the careers of some of these women and concluded that they were accepted as long as they gave up employment before marriage. Moreover, their social acceptance depended on the fact that they catered for other women, as teachers and doctors, and did not compete with men.[84]

In the Hindu community a comparable development started only in the 1920s, motivated, however, not by support for the idea of female emancipation, as in the Brahmo community, but mainly by economic considerations. Employment of middle-class women became acceptable as a means of easing the burden, particularly of widows, on the family budget. Education would enable a widow to teach at a girls' school rather than to make lace and jellies in a women's co-operative. A genuine hostility, however, remained against women's employment as soon as the post carried authority and demanded respect from men.

As gender relations and culturally-specific practices were situated in the context of colonial superiority and native subordination, so the employment of British and Bengali women professionals gave rise to racial and political antagonism. The British Indian government accepted responsibility for British professional women who came to India looking for employment which was not available in England. Taking into account how important it was to maintain the white woman's superiority in British India, a situation in which white and Indian women competed for jobs was prone to conflict.'

Seen in bare numbers women in white collar jobs were an insignificant group in the labour market. During the first three decades of the twentieth century the number of women teachers at schools and colleges grew from about 1000 to over 5000. Women taught almost exclusively at girls' schools and colleges. During the same period the number of male teachers increased almost threefold to 79,000. The same disproportion applied to women doctors. In 1931 there were 1500 women doctors compared to 61,000 men doctors.[85]

The target of Bengali criticism was not Bengali women teachers, or the very few Bengali women who became doctors, but the white and Eurasian professional women who were seen as agents of imperialism. There were numerous Eurasian female clerks in post, telegraph and railway offices. Education in mission schools had liberated Eurasian women from manual labour. In 1905 there were said to be as many as 60,000 female Eurasian clerks in the whole of British India.[86] This figure, however, seems to be exaggerated, at least in Bengal. In 1921 and 1931, respectively, there were only 255 and 143 women clerks employed in Calcutta.[87] As Eurasian men monopolized jobs in the railways and in post offices, their wives and relatives did much of the secretarial work. But they were employed in white collar jobs which Indian men could have done as well. Eurasians occupied a special niche in colonial India and their position was bolstered by the Indian government. In the 1920s, for instance, to safeguard a Eurasian woman employee's respectability, a Eurasian female clerk's starting salary was as much as Rs 120, whereas a man's salary was between 10 and 20 per cent lower.[88]

Despite the growing number of female teachers, girls' schools and colleges were predominantly staffed by men. This was a major obstacle to the schooling of married and post-puberty girls. During the 1890s in the Chittagong division only 42 out of 492 girls' schools 'were under female teachers'. At Bethune College, 30 years later, there was only one woman lecturer on a staff of seven. In the mid-1920s primary education for girls was still 'regarded as a convenient nursery for young children rather than as an educational institution'. Indeed, many so-called girls' schools were classes, which a half-time *pandit* taught in the afternoon, without books or other materials, after he had finished the boys' instruction. Still in 1932 'only about one in four of even the girls' primary schools has a woman teacher'. Consequently, school inspectresses argued that teachers' training schools and colleges were desperately needed to improve the situation.[89]

Before 1930 there was not much progress made in furthering higher female education. At the turn of the century, Calcutta University issued new instructions in a bid to increase the number of women graduates. Women who had passed the matriculation examination could be 'admitted to the intermediate examination and to the B.A. examination' without studying in an affiliated college if they presented a certificate proving their 'good conduct' and 'diligent and regular study'. Only the science subjects, which included practical courses, were exempted from this regulation. Despite such concessions, it was only in the mid-1920s that the long-standing 'record of Brahmo majority' in Bethune College was broken and Hindu women outnumbered any other single community. But in 1927 there were still only 384 women who attended college in Bengal.[90]

Training schools met with more hostility than the Bethune and Diocesan Colleges. Whereas the latter were seen as isolated institutes for Brahmo and Christian girls, and later as finishing schools for desirable brides, teachers' training clearly led to paid employment for women. Consequently, in 1906 when the government proposed the opening of two female teachers' training colleges for secondary work, neither did the management of Bethune College nor did the Calcutta public show much enthusiasm. Instead, a college was opened in Bankipur in Bihar. The Maharani of Bettiah provided a building with a compound and Syed Badshah Nawab Razvi of Patna made a permanent annual donation of Rs 7500.[91]

Inspired by the spread of nationalist sentiments during the Swadeshi period, the Bengali Hindu and Brahmo press criticized the plan as a waste of money. It was, they argued, only intended to provide jobs for white women and to familiarize Bengali girls with 'vitiated English manners'.[92] Moreover, government interference with higher female education was objected to because there was no demand from within the Hindu community for such institutions. 'Hindus will never allow their young women to attend schools and colleges', wrote the Asansol newspaper *Ratnakar*, predicting educational stagnation—middle-class girls' school education apart—which was to last for the next two decades.[93]

Women teachers were assumed to be, by nature, best qualified to teach the lower classes in primary schools. They were, however, even more important in secondary schools, because most parents took their daughters out of school once they had reached puberty—unless there was a Hindu woman teacher. Most existing training classes for junior teachers were run by missionaries and thus not attended by Hindu women. The only classes which were likely to attract Hindu women were the ones attached to the Eden High School at Dhaka and the Calcutta Hindu Widows' training class at Ballyganj. Both were government institutions and had, in 1917, 22 and 16 pupils, respectively. In the same year, there were seven missionary training classes with a total of 95 pupils. The government repeatedly delayed its plans for opening a senior training college, at first because of lack of Bengali response, and later, during the First World War, because of lack of funds. Finally, from 1917 onwards, at Diocesan College and Loreto House, women were trained to teach the higher classes of secondary schools. In the first five years 42 women passed the respective examinations for the qualifications of B.T. and L.T.[94]

There were objections to non-Bengali women appointed as headmistresses or school inspectresses. Their racial and religious backgrounds were scrutinized and criticized, although there were few well-qualified Bengali women. The Brahmo paper *Sanjibani* opposed any non-Bengali appointment and confined educational employment to Bengalis. In 1914, for example, it supported a campaign against the Parsi lady superintendent, Mrs Merwanji, of the Dhaka Eden Female School. Mrs Merwanji, together with her apparent supporter, Cornelia Sorabji, was accused of following a European lifestyle, being a member of a European club and having 'no acquaintance with the habits and manners of Bengali girls'.[95]

There was also a deep-seated antipathy against women in positions that involved social contact with Bengali men. In 1897 the acceptance of two Bengali women to the first year class of Presidency College aroused a storm of criticism, as did Miss

Regina Guha's appointment as English Professor at Carmichael College in Rangpur twenty years later.[96] The situation was resented even more by men in the case of European women, particularly if well-qualified Bengali women could have held the posts as well. For instance, from November 1907 two European women held the post of Inspectress of Schools, one for the Bengali-speaking divisions and European Female Education, and the other in charge of the Hindu-speaking divisions. They then had two assistants, so-called 'native-speakers'. Between 1910 and 1920, new job opportunities for Bengali women were created by increasing the number of assistants to 12, but the top ranks remained closed to them and women received smaller salaries than men in the same jobs.[97]

Most salaries were so low that women teachers usually lived with their families. After the turn of the century, the monthly salary was about Rs.8 to Rs 13, compared to Rs 47 in Bombay, Rs 25 in the Punjab and Rs 15 in Madras.[98] Thus, while government reviews of public instruction lamented Bengali hostility to female teachers' training, the low salaries the Bengal Government offered did little to act as an incentive. On the contrary they reinforced existing prejudices regarding the dubious morals of working women. The government did, however, initiate improvements at the upper end of the employment scale by increasing travel allowances and appointing female attendants. This, in fact, just gave added advantages to privileged, often European, school inspectresses and mistresses.[99]

New Frontiers: Village Schools and Industrial Training in the 1920s

As in the case of birthing reforms, the 1920s witnessed the success of middle-class women's educational initiatives in the name of nationalism. Schools and female adult education centres at the village level were established and many of the prejudices which state-induced institutions had provoked were overcome. Gandhi's programme of village reconstruction and Tagore's Sriniketan village project made village work popular and set the trend for social work from the 1920s onwards.[100] The Nari Siksha Samiti, founded in 1919, and the Saroj Nalini Dutt Memorial Association (SNDMA), founded in 1925, were the two leading organizations in the field. In addition, both groups worked for the improvement of post-natal care and midwifery (see chapter 4). The Siksha Samiti concentrated on primary education, village schools, female teachers' training and the publication of textbooks, whereas the SNDMA concentrated primarily on industrial training for women, in particular widows, and health education in the villages.[101]

In the beginning the Nari Siksha Samiti opened several primary schools in Calcutta but soon restricted itself to setting up village schools. In 1921 eight schools were founded in Hooghly and Howrah, the districts neighbouring Calcutta; in 1924, 14 new village schools were established in the Dhaka, Faridpur and Pabna districts in eastern Bengal. By the late 1940s the number of schools had grown to 59. The Samiti employed a village school organizer and a lady superintendent, who co-ordinated the working of the schools during the initial period. Once the schools began running smoothly a local committee took over and the Nari Siksha Samiti could open new schools.

In 1922, 650 female students attended the Siksha Samiti's schools. As the lack of female teachers was a constant problem for the Samiti, in the early 1920s, the Vidyasagar Bhani Bhawan was started for training widows· as primary school teachers. The widows were taught at the Bhawan up till Class VI, and then at the Brahmo Girls' School Teachers' Training Department until, in 1935, a teachers' training institute was added to the Bhawan. The women who had promoted the organization of the Nari Siksha Samiti—Abala Bose and her sister Mrs P.K. Ray—were, in 1927, also among the founders of the Bengal Women's Education League. The League aimed at influencing the provincial government in favour of female education.[102]

The educational work of the SNDMA covered two aspects: industrial and formal education for village women, and industrial training for widows and other deprived women in Calcutta. The work outside Calcutta was based on the Gandhian concept of village reconstruction in connection with women's emancipation. 'No village improvement work', the 1925 SNDMA Report announced programmatically, 'whether in the sphere of education, sanitation or economic uplift can be satisfactorily effected without the active co-operation of the women of the country.'[103]

Apart from health education the mufassal samitis encouraged women's co-operatives and primary education. Industrial training was welcomed by poorer village women who joined the samitis in increasing numbers, because they hoped to supplement their meagre household budgets with their incomes from sewing, cutting, knitting, weaving, spinning, and jelly and chutney making. But the middle-class women who ran the samitis were just as concerned with female education; they hoped to postpone the marriage of girls until they had at least studied up to the age of 13 or 14. Thus they opened a large number of primary schools, for instance in Perojpur, Goila, Baraset, Barisal, Bally, Hooghly, Chandpur, Natore, Satsang, Labpur, Bantara and Dhaka.[104]

Despite such educational efforts maternity care was the main concern in the districts. But in Calcutta the Industrial School was the biggest success. In December 1925 Guru Saday Dutt opened the school at 45 Beniatola Lane in co-operation with the Singer Sewing Machine Company. When the initiative became public, Dutt received thousands of letters from women or their guardians asking for admission. Pupils usually stayed for six months during which they paid a small tuition fee and the fare for the school bus. By 1926 the Bengal government had given a one-off grant of over Rs 4000 for a motor rather than a horse-drawn bus, and regularly supported the school with Rs 200 per month.[105]

The idea of the school was to provide women with the skills they needed to earn money through cottage industry-style work at home or to educate women to go to village samitis and work there as instructors. Under Kumudini Basu as the school's secretary the girls and women were taught sewing, cutting, embroidery, lace making, carpet weaving, basket making, cotton weaving, silk and jute spinning as well as reading and writing. In the first six months the school was attended by 37 widows, 51 wives and 17 unmarried girls, all above the age of 12 years. By 1928 the school had 200 women on its books and by then 400 students and 25 instructors had graduated from the school.[106]

Conclusion

By 1930, encouraged by Hindu Revivalism, Swadeshi self-confidence and the nationalist desire for social progress, the numbers of literate and school-educated women had increased significantly since the days when bratas were the most formalized element of female education. During the nineteenth century only women from Brahmo or westernized Hindu families had been formally educated, but after 1900 the orthodox Hindu middle class gradually came to accept female education. The vast majority of women and men, however, still had little or no access to any formal education.

Until 1930 high-caste middle-class women, if 'gainfully employed' at all, predominantly worked in caring sectors like teaching and, to a limited extent, in medicine. Women teachers competed for the same posts as Bengali men in only a few cases. Despite middle-class women working outside the household, female 'otherness' and the notion of women's domestic predisposition remained unchallenged in the dominant ideology. Only the middle-class and high-caste widows who had been the most exploited and most miserable among Hindu high-caste women, profited clearly: their education and employment outside the home was accepted even by orthodox 'public opinion'.[107]

School and college-leaving women who entered the labour market faced much tougher opposition than those who used their education solely to look after their families more skilfully. Despite limited numbers during the 1920s educated and professional women as well as female white-collar workers were felt by some men to be a threat to Hindu culture—and male dominance. Criticism against comprehensive female education was rarely clearly expressed, but the challenge to male domination was a clear motive behind women's use of Swadeshi terminology. 'Self-determination', it was argued, 'is the greatest message of modern times and Indian men who have so long played the overlord in all matters relating to women must no longer arrogate rights which do not belong to them.'[108]

Following the same line of argument progressive Bengalis called for more village primary schools so that education could be extended to the rural population. Co-education was demanded in those districts where there was as yet no girls' high school.[109] More cautious supporters of female education feared a cultural backlash if education progressed too fast. Using Swadeshi ideology they warned of cultural alienation in the wake of westernized female education. Instead of mathematics, science and English, girls should receive, they believed, instruction in Bengali on hygiene, domestic science, music, painting and sculpture.[110] The ideology of Swadeshi was flexible enough to be used both in support of and in opposition to female education.

The debate on school curricula showed that the spread of female education had only scratched the surface of the Bengali gender hierarchy. Rural and urban working-class women were to realize that female education was of no concern in their struggle for survival in the agrarian, bazaar or organized industrial economy.

NOTES

[1] Such a study would be beyond the scope of this book. For a comparison, see Michelle Maskiell, *Women Between Cultures: The Lives of Kinnaird College Alumnae in British India*, Syracuse, New York, 1984.

[2] D. Kopf, *British Orientalism and the Bengal Renaissance. The Dynamics of Indian Modernization 1773–1835*, Berkeley and Los Angeles, 1969; M.A. Laird, *Missionaries and Education in Bengal (1793–1837)*, London, 1972; S. Nurullah and J.P. Naik, *A History of Education in India during the British Period*, London, 1951; B.T. McCully, *English Education and the Origin of Indian Nationalism*, New York, 1940; B.K. Boman-Behram, *Educational Controversies in India. The Cultural Conquest of India under British Imperialism*, Bombay, 1943; A. Basu, *The Growth of Education and Political...*; J.C. Bagal, *Women's Education in Eastern India—The First Phase (Mainly Based on Contemporary Records)*, Calcutta, 1956; M. Borthwick, *The Changing Role of Women in Bengal 1849–1905*, N.J., 1984, pp.60–108.

[3] H. and U. Mukherjee, *A Phase of The Swadeshi Movement (National Education) 1905-1910*, Calcutta, 1953; D. Kumar, 'Science Education, Imperial Perceptions and Indian Response, 1860–1900', unpublished paper at the conference of the German Historical Institute, London, Berlin, June 1989.

[4] For a good summary, see B. Southard, 'Bengal Women's Education League: Pressure Group and Professional Association', *Modern Asian Studies*, 18, 1984, pp.56–9.

[5] Borthwick, 1984, p.59.

[6] Ibid., p.68.

[7] Ibid., p.61; Girijaprasanna Rayachaudhuri, *Griha Laksmi*, Calcutta, 1887, p.13.

[8] Banganari, *Agami*, Calcutta, 1926, pp.8–10.

[9] Interview with Phulrenu Chanda, Calcutta, 3 February 1985; interview with Amiya Sen, Calcutta, 9 February 1985; interview with Abha Mukherjee, Calcutta, 7 February 1985.

[10] E.M. Gupta, *Brata and Alpana in Bengalen*, Wiesbaden, 1983; interview with Radharani Basu, Calcutta, 7 March 1985; 'Purbabange Meyeli Brata', *Prabasi*, 1311, pp.516–20.

[11] Interview with Amiya Sen.

[12] S. Mazumdar (ed. G. Forbes), *A Pattern of Life. The Memoirs of an Indian Woman*, Columbia, 1977, pp.33–4.

[13] Ibid., p.34.

[14] Ibid., p.32; during the sib puja season girls came late to Sister Nivedita's school where the discipline was less strict than at a convent school (interview with Radharani Basu, Calcutta, 7 March 1985).

[15] 'Purbabange Meyeli Brata', *Prabasi*, 1311, pp.516–20.

[16] Gupta, 1983, p.17; interview with Subarnaprabha Baksi, Calcutta, 3 February 1985.

[17] Gupta, 1983, p.22; Borthwick, 1984, p.14.

[18] Gupta, 1983, p.8; 'Purbabange Meyeli Brata', *Prabasi*, 1311, pp.516–20.

[19] Forbes (Mazumdar), 1977, p.36.

[20] Gupta, 1983, pp.4–10.

[21] G. Forbes, 'Political Mobilization of Women in India Through Religion: Bengal, 1905–1947', unpublished paper given at *Conversation in the Discipline: Woman in Religious Traditions, SUNY College at Cortland, October 14–15, 1977*; Borthwick, 1984, pp.352; S. Sarkar, *The Swadeshi Movement in Bengal 1903–1908*, New Delhi, 1973, pp.287–8. See also chapter 1 in this book.

[22] Interviews, cited above. The decline of brata education due to western education was regarded as unfortunate. Rajanikanta Bidhyabinod, 'Meyeli Barbrata', *Bharat Mahila*, 5, 1910, pp.86–9; Probodh Chandra Bagchi, 'Female Folk-Rites in Bengal: The Suvachani-Vrata Puja', *Man in India*, 1922, pp.52–7.

[23] Borthwick, 1984, pp.73, 85, 90–5; J.C. Bagal, 'History of the Bethune School & College', in K. Nag (ed.), *Bethune School and College Centenary Volume 1849–1949*, Calcutta, 1949, p.12.

[24] Borthwick, 1984, p.60.

[25] Ibid. p.86; COI, 1931, VI, 1, p.340.

[26] Borthwick, 1984, pp.68–72; European women missionaries and zenana teachers in Bengal were very outspoken about their proselytizing intentions; see 'Report of Miss Muller's Work', *The Twenty-Third Annual Report of the Indian Female Normal School and Instruction Society*, Birmingham, 1875, pp.16–26. M.A. Sherring, *The History of Protestant Missions in India from their Commencement in 1706 to 1881*, London, 1884, pp.107 and 141, states that in 1881 there were 4150 female scholars (supposedly under school instruction) and 1228 zenana pupils in Calcutta. For the whole of Bengal missionaries claimed to have 2917 female scholars as compared to 9737 male scholars. Although the majority of these pupils were probably sons and daughters of Christian converts the figures still seem to be very high.

[27] Pramilabala Devi, 'Amader Mahila Karmi', *Bangalaksmi*, 1335–36, pp.621–3; Stri Hariher Seth, 'Svargiya Krisnabhabini', ibid., pp.376–8; 'Radharani Sanyal', *Bangalaksmi*, 1334–35, pp.776–8; 'Hemangini Sen', ibid., p.615–8.

[28] Interview with Amiya Sen; didactic novels in dialogue form were written, articulating the need for female education in order to facilitate conjugal communication. Girijaprasanna Rayachaudhuri, *Griha Laksmi*, Calcutta, 1887, 14, illustrates the mother-in-law problem; Yadunath Chakravarti, *Kayekkhani Patra*, Calcutta, 1902, pp.4–5.

[29] Interview with Radharani Basu, Calcutta, 7 March 1985.

[30] Baradakanta Majumdar, *Naritattva*, Calcutta, 1889, pp.31–5; Yadunath Chakravarti, *Kayekkhani Patra*, Calcutta, 1902, p.14; Dineshcandra Sen, *Grihasri*, Calcutta, 1915, p.23.

[31] 'Hemangini Sen', *Bangalaksmi*, 1334–35, pp.615–8.

[32] Interview with Amiya Sen.

[33] Susantakumar Ghose (ed.), *Nari-ratna*, Calcutta, 1919, pp.633–42.

[34] Bipin Mohan Sehanobis, 'Strisiksa Pranali Sambandhe Kayekti Katha', *Prabasi*, 1323, 1, pp.199–200.

[35] Numerous articles in women's journals attacked this position: Satadalbasini Biswas, 'Narisaktir Apacay', *Bharat Mahila*, 1911, pp.100–3; 'Strisiksa Sambandhe Du-ekti Katha', ibid., 1912, pp.94–5; Hriday Krisna De, 'Strisiksar Antaray', ibid., 1912, pp.331–6; Banganari, *Agami*, Calcutta, 1926, pp.145–52.

[36] Interview with Amiya Sen; Borthwick, 1984, pp.5–6.

[37] Prabhavati Devi Saraswati, *Amal-prasun*, Calcutta, 1900.

[38] Borthwick, 1984, pp.80–6, 359.

[39] Lotika Ghose, 'Social and Educational Movements for Women and by Women', in K. Nag (ed.), Bethune School and College Centenary Volume 1949, pp.144–5; Government of Bengal (GOB), *Progress of Education in Bengal 1902–03 to 1906–07. Third Quinquennial Review*, Calcutta, 1907, p.121; GOB, *Progress of Education in Bengal 1907–08 to 1911–12. Fourth Quinquennial Review*, Calcutta, 1913, p.117.

[40] Ghose, 1949, p.145; *Indian Ladies Magazine*, 5, 1905–06, pp.305, 451.

[41] Ghose, 1949, pp.145–6; GOB, *Education 1907–08 to 1911–12*, p.117.

[42] *Indian Ladies Magazine*, 1905–06, p.305; Borthwick, 1984, p.100.

[43] Ibid., pp.100–1; Ghose, 1949, pp.145–6; GOB, *Progress of Education in Bengal 1912–13 to 1916–17. Fifth Quinquennial Review*, Calcutta, 1918, p.111; GOB, *Progress of Education in Bengal 1917–18 to 1921–22; Sixth Quinquennial Review*, Calcutta, 1923, p.66; GOB, *Seventh Quinquennial Review on the Progress of Education in Bengal for the Years 1922–23 to 1926–27*, Calcutta, 1928, p.69.

[44] Ghose, 1949, p.146.

[45] C.H. Heimsath, *Indian Nationalism and Hindu Social Reform*, Princeton, 1964, p.333; C. Isherwood, *Ramakrishna and his Disciples*, London, 1965, pp.324ff; H.W. French, *The Swan's White Waters*, London, 1974, pp.152–5.

[46] Ghose, 1949, p.146; Yogesh Chandra Dasgupta, 'Bagani Nivedita', *Bharat Mahila*, 1912, pp.142–4.

[47] Ghose, 1949, p.146; Sankari Prasad Basu, *Amader Nivedita*, Calcutta, n.d., pp.48, 68–9; Saralabala Das, 'Nivedita', *Prabasi*, 1319, pp.102–12.

[48] Ghose, 1949, p.147.

[49] Ibid.

[50] Ibid.

[51] Myths surround her involvement with the nationalist movement during the Swadeshi period. See, for instance, Kamala Das Gupta, *Svadhinata-Sangrame Banglar Nari*, Calcutta, 1963, pp.10–4; for a critical account, S. Sarkar, 1973, pp.29, 105, 118, 162, 284, 470–6, 484–5, 498–500.

[52] Forbes, 1979; S. Sarkar, 1973, pp.287–8.

[53] Borthwick, 1984, pp.351–2; West Bengal State Archives (WBSA), *Towards Freedom Files (TFF)*, Paper No 47, p.17, No 63, pp.7–8; Das Gupta, 1963, pp.20, 36–41.

[54] S. Sarkar, 1973, pp.173, 181.

[55] Uma Das Gupta, *Santiniketan and Sriniketan*, Visva-Bharati, Calcutta, 1983, p.17; personal information by the author.

[56] Borthwick, 1984, pp.286, 288–92, 300. Women helped finance National Schools (WSBA, *TFF*, No 58, 23; Saratkumari Caudhurani, 'Narisiksa o Mahila

Silpasram', *Bharati*, 1320, pp.1190–3; Stri Hariher Seth, 'Swargiya Krishnabhabini', *Banga Laksmi*, 1334–5, pp.376–8). The most outstanding example of female participation was Sarala Devi who organized numerous samitis, clubs and Swadeshi shops; moreover she travelled through Bengal to convince people of the anti-partition struggle and the Swadeshi campaign; Borthwick, 1984, pp.349–56; S. Sarkar, 1973, pp.288, 304–5, 353, 360, 397–8, 470–6; WBSA, *TFF*, No 58, 2, No 63, pp.29–30.

[57] Hemlata Sarkar, 'Narijati Siksa', *Bharat Mahila*, 1908, p.51; Nepal Chandra Ray, 'Bharater Strisiksar Phal', *Bharati*, 1297, pp.336–40; 'Narisiksa Samitir Karjaksetra Bistar', *Prabasi*, 1329, 1, pp.153–4; Ghose, 1949, pp.148–54; X, 'Project for a Hindu Girls' School', *Modern Review*, 1912, pp.632–4.

[58] Ghose, 1949, pp.148.

[59] Borthwick, 1984, pp.285–6; Nepal Chandra Ray, 'Bharater Strisiksar Phal', *Bharati*, 1297, pp.336–40; Ghose, 1949, p.148.

[60] Ghose, 1949, pp.148–50; interview with Kalyani Mallik, Calcutta, 30 January 1985. The Sikshasadan which was founded in 1930 chose the same time for zenana education. Sarala Debi Chaudhuri, 'Calcutta Activities of Bharat Stree Mahamandal', *Modern Review*, 1931, p.615.

[61] Ghose, 1949, pp.150–1.

[62] Ibid.; Sarala Debi, 'A Women's Movement', *Modern Review*, 1911, p.344; Sarala Debi Chaudhurani, 1931, p.615.

[63] COI, 1911, v, 1, p.366.

[64] Ibid.; COI, 1931, v, 1, p.343; 'Education of Girls in Bengal', *Modern Review*, 1927, pp.603–4; GOB, *Education 1902–03 to 1906–07*, p.111; GOB, *Education 1907–08 to 1911–12*, p.107.

[65] COI, 1931, v, 1, p.343; GOB, *Education 1902–03 to 1906–07*, pp.114–5; GOB, *Education 1907–08 to 1911–12*, p.110; GOB, *Eighth Quinquennial Review on the Progress of Education in Bengal*, for the years 1927–32, Calcutta, 1933, p.71.

[66] COI, 1931, v, 1, pp.325, 327.

[67] COI, 1921, v, 1, Calcutta, 1923, p.286; Southard, 1984, p.58.

[68] GOB, *Education 1912–13 to 1916–17*, p.103; GOB, *Education 1917–18 to 1921–22*, p.63; GOB, *Education 1927–32*, p.72.

[69] S. Sarkar, 1973, p.149; Suniti Debi, 'Oh, Calcutta', *Eve's Weekly*, October 24–31, 1981, pp.52–8; interview with Bina Bose and Mira Sanyal, Calcutta, 24 February 1985.

[70] Ibid.; Suniti Debi, 1981; *Indian Ladies' Magazine*, 9, 1909–10, p.394.

[71] Interview with Bina Bose and Mira Sanyal, Calcutta, 24 February 1985; wet hair was a problem for many Bengali girls who had to attend English schools with plaits, see Forbes (Mazumdar), 1977, p.48.

[72] Hemlata Sarkar, 'Narijati Siksa', *Bharat Mahila*, 1908, pp.49–53.

[73] J.N. Gupta, *Rangpur Today*, Shampukur, 1918, pp.103–4; GOB, *Education 1902–03 to 1906–07*, p.117; GOB, *Education 1907–08 to 1911–12*, p.116.

[74] COI, 1931, v, 1, p.343; *Indian Ladies Magazine*, 4, 1904–05, pp.92, 386–7; Sri-Chakraborti, 'Purbba Benga Assame Strisiksa', *Bharat Mahila*, 1912, pp.124–6.

[75] Ibid.; Sarala Ray, 'Notes on Female Education' (1909), Sarala Ray Centenary Committee, *Sarala Ray Centenary Volume*, Calcutta, 1961, pp.7–23; Hemalata Sarkar, 'Narijati Siksa', *Bharat Mahila*, 1908, pp.49–53.

[76] Ibid.

[77] GOB, *Education 1927–32*, p.71.

[78] GOB, *Education 1912–13 to 1916–17*, pp.100–1; GOB, *Education 1922–23 to 1926–27*, pp.65–6.

[79] Ibid.

[80] Ghose, 1949, p.147; Hemala Sarkar organized music lessons in her school, *Indian Ladies Magazine*, 10, 1910–11, p.173.

[81] Uma Das Gupta, 1983, pp.9, 12, 24–5; interview with Abha Mukherjee, Calcutta, 7 February 1985.

[82] Gupta, 1983, p.57–137; Alpana Raychaudhuri, 'Natir Puja. Interview with Gauri Bhanja', *Visva-Bharati News*, January 1978, pp.176–8.

[83] A. Raychaudhuri, 1978; *Bangalaksmi*, 1335–6, p.76.

[84] M. Borthwick, 1984, pp.330, 334–6. In order to keep women feminine, female higher education did not cover science, mathematics and botany until Bethune College introduced the two latter subjects in the early 1920s. GOB, *Progress of Education in Bengal 1917–18 to 1921–22, Sixth Quinquennial Review*, Calcutta, 1923, p.61; 'Notes: A Women's College', *Modern Review*, August 1912, p.217. The Calcutta University Commission Report, 1917–19, expressed conservative attitudes to female higher education and was criticized for its bias, GOB, *Education 1917–18 to 1921–22*, p.59; Prasanna Kumar Samadhar, 'Hindu Samaje Naristhan o Siksa', *Prabasi*, 1327, 2, pp.109–11. Sexual segregation among non-manual women workers in Britain was different, but comparable, J. Lewis, *Women in England 1870–1950: Sexual Divisions and Social Change*, Brighton, 1984, pp.193–200. To a certain extent, access to the professions was more restricted than in Bengal where gender ideology as implemented in the family and lack of education worked as an earlier barrier against women's professional aspirations.

[85] See chapter 4. The figures of registered medical practitioners, including oculists, dentists, veterinary surgeons, in 1901, were 1002, and of teachers or professors 1156. In subsequent years the equivalent totals were: 1911, 937 and 1836; 1921, 1036 and 2593; and 1931, 1538 and 5225. The figures are very dubious in what they refer to. Only the trend can be accepted. Between 1890 and 1910 only one Bengali woman finished her studies at the Calcutta Medical College, G. Murshid, *Reluctant Debutante*, Rajshahi, 1983, 102. In 1912, medical colleges all over India had female students mainly from the European, Eurasian and Indian Christian communities. There were very few Hindus. National Archives of India (NAI), GOI, Home Dep./Medical Branch, Deposit, July 1912, 1.

[86] Borthwick, 1984, p.1.

[87] COI, 1931, VI, 1, p.58. .

[88] Borthwick, 1984, p.330–1. For a contemporary account of the problems of Eurasian women, see M.H. Tabor, 'Eurasian Women in India', *The Englishwoman*, 10, 1911, pp.24–32. For the development of British prejudices against Eurasian men, see K. Ballhatchet, *Race, Sex and Class under the Raj*, London, 1980, pp.96–111. See also M. Zimmeck, 'Jobs for the Girls: the Expansion of Clerical Work for Women, 1850–1914', A.V. John (ed.), *Unequal Opportunities, Women's Employment in England, 1800–1918*, Oxford, 1986, pp.153–77 for the situation of woman clerks in England. For woman clerks in Bengal, see *Bangabasi*, 4 October 1922; NAI, *RNNB*, 11 November 1922; NAI, GOI, Home/Ests., 370/1929.

[89] GOB, *Review of Education in Bengal (1892–93 to 1896–97). Being the First Quinquennial Report*, Calcutta, 1897, p.129; GOB, *Progress of Education in Bengal 1912–13 to 1916–17, Fifth Quinquennial Review*, Calcutta, 1918, pp.96, 104; GOB,

Seventh Quinquennial Review on the Progress of Education in Bengal. For the Years 1922–23 to 1926–27, Calcutta, 1928, p.61; GOB, *Eighth Quinquennial Review on the Progress of Education in Bengal. For the Years 1927–32*, Calcutta, 1933, p.69.

[90] GOB, *Progress of Education in Bengal, 1902–03 to 1906–07, Third Quinquennial Review*, Calcutta, 1907, p.112; GOB, *Education 1922–23 to 1926–27*, p.61; Southard, 1984, p.58.

[91] India Office Library and Records (IOLR), Home Dep./Education Branch, July–October 1907, No. 95–96, pp.1375–82; *Sanjibani*, 5 April 1906 and 3 May 1906, IOLR, L/R/5/32, *Report on Native Newspapers Bengal (RNNB)*, 14 April 1906 and 12 May 1906.

[92] *Khulnabasi*, 4 April 1906, *RNNB*, 21 April 1906; *Sanjibani*, 5 April 1906, *RNNB*, 14 April 1906; *Sri Sri Vishnu Priya-o-Ananda Bazar Patrika*, 26 April 1906, *RNNB*, 5 May 1906 (IOLR L/R/5/32).

[93] *Ratnakar*, 28 April 1906, IOLR L/R/5/32, *RNNB*, 12 May 1906. In 1931–32 when the government report on education regretted the continuing lack of women in the teaching profession, only 98 women took an arts degree from Calcutta University. GOB, *Education 1927–32*, p.62.

[94] GOB, *Education 1912–13 to 1916–17*, p.70; GOB, *Progress of Education in Bengal 1917–18 to 1921–22, Sixth Quinquennial Review*, Calcutta, 1923, pp.45–6.

[95] *Sanjibani*, 15 January 1914, IOLR L/R/5/41, *RNNB*, 24 January 1914.

[96] Borthwick, 1984, pp.101, 309, 314; *Nababanga*, 26 December 1916, West Bengal State Archives (WSBA), *RNNB*, 13 January 1917.

[97] The nomination of Miss Wright, Principal of Bethune College, as Fellow of Calcutta University in 1922, for instance, was criticized for such reasons, *Sanjibani*, 9 March 1922, NAI, *RNNB*, 18 March 1922. 'Inspectress of Schools in Bengal', *Modern Review*, October 1929, p.468; GOB, *Progress of Education in Bengal 1907–08 to 1911–12. Fourth Quinquennial Review*, Calcutta, 1913, p.107; GOB, *Education 1912–13 to 1916–17*, p.94; GOB, *Education 1917–18 to 1921–22*, p.60.

[98] H. Gray, 'Education', A.R. Caton (ed.), *The Key of Progress*, London, 1930, p.15.

[99] GOB, *Education 1912–13 to 1916–17*, p.95.

[100] Dhirendranath Bhattarcharya, 'Meyeder Katha', *Bangalaksmi*, pp.896–8; Das Gupta, 1983, pp.21–4.

[101] Ghose, 1949, pp.151–2; 'Narisiksasamitir Karjaksetra Bistar', *Prabasi*, 1329, 1, pp.153–4; Saroj Nalini Dutt Memorial Association for Women's Work in Bengal, *Annual Report of the SNDMA, from the year 1925 to 1931*, Calcutta, n.d. (*SNDMA Report*), Report 1925, p.2.

[102] Ghose, 1949, p.152; Southard, 1984.

[103] *SNDMA Report*, 1925, p.9.

[104] Ibid., pp.2, 7; *SNDMA Report*, 1926, 36; *SNDMA Report*, 1927, p.32; *SNDMA Report*, 1930, pp.18–9.

[105] Ghose, 1949, p.154; *SNDMA Report*, 1925, 1, p.3; *SNDMA Report*, 1926, 35, pp.16, 41.

[106] *SNDMA Report*, 1926, 16; *SNDMA Report*, 1928, 1; *SNDMA Report*, 1929, p.4.

[107] A Bengali, summarizing the opinion of the orthodox and progressive majority, wrote: 'We feel that there is want in the country of women teachers, women doctors and women nurses and to a limited extent we are prepared to admit a certain number of widows of mature age to take to such professions for the benefit of womankind in general, but their number must be limited. But we are

opposed to a general participation of women in professional careers or in public affairs.' COI, 1931, v, 1, p.401. For Indian women's chances in professional careers in recent times, see P. Caplan, *Class and Gender in India*, London, 1985, pp.84–101; U. Sharma, *Women's Work, Class, and the Urban Household*, London, 1986, pp.119ff; J. Liddle and R. Joshi, *Daughters of Independence*, London, 1986, pp.124–41.

[108] 'The Ideal of Female Education in India', *Modern Review*, 1918, p.613.

[109] 'Co-education in Bengal Schools', *Modern Review*, 1928, p.512; 'Women's Education in Bengal', ibid., 1929, p.118; Dhirendranath Bhattarcharya, 'Meyeder Katha', *Bangalaksmi*, 1334–35, pp.896–8. India Office Library and Records, L/R/5/23, *Bikrampur*, 23 April 1927, *Report on Native Newspapers, Bengal*, 1 May 1927. The paper accused the government of neglecting girls' schools. It argued that girls' schools never received more than a grant of Rs 5 ot 6 per pupil per year while Rs 20 to 40 should have been the minimum.

[110] X, 'Project for a Hindu Girls' School', *Modern Review*, 1912, pp.632–4; 'A Proposal for Women's Higher Education in Bengal', ibid., 1922, p.268; 'Bengal Women's Education Conference', ibid., 1929, p.396.

6

WOMEN'S WORK IN THE BENGAL ECONOMY

It is no longer contested that terms such as labour and waged labour have a specific meaning in the analysis of women's past because they cover but a part of a women's daily duties. Women's reproductive role meant that many women shouldered the double burden of working inside and outside the house.[1] Accordingly, when the agricultural and bazaar economy was restructured between 1890 and 1930, it was clear that women's work was not just a matter of the market, but of gender-specific definitions of status and honour.[2] Although these differed from middle-class definitions of purdah, they nevertheless assumed that a woman should be constantly supervised by the men or elder women of her family. This was in many cases merely a justification for excluding women from better-paid jobs or for not paying male wages. As this was a world-wide development, purdah seen in relation to class was not as unique as many western observers have suggested.

More importantly, while purdah-related values came naturally to artisan or peasant women working with their husbands, such values became a significant obstacle once these women had to choose between work among strangers. or unemployment. Women in larger economic units, particularly in jute mills, worked without their families and among strangers. As we shall see, their male colleagues and superiors treated them as if they had broken the purdah-related code of conduct. Most of their colleagues did not show any solidarity towards jute mill women, which left them at the mercy of Indian foremen, *sardars*, and European managers and led to their increasing marginalization in the jute labour force. Here the pre-eminence of cultural stereotypes was as striking as in the organization of jute labour as a whole, as Dipesh Chakrabarty argues most convincingly in his *Rethinking Working-Class History*.[3]

Compared with India as a whole or with neighbouring provinces, the ratio of women to men at work, that is in wage employment or self-employed, was extremely low in Bengal. While there was an average of 5 working women to every 10 working men in the whole of India, there were fewer than 2 working women to every 10 working men in Bengal. In 1911 and 1921, out of a female population of 22.1 million and 22.5 million, respectively, only 10 per cent appeared as wage-earners in the census. In 1931, by which time the female population had increased by 1.5 million, the proportion of women in the labour market was down to 8.3 per cent, which was an absolute decrease in the number of women at work.[4] Reasons for this decrease are hard to trace because of the lack of detailed information on women workers. The information gap reflects deep-rooted British and Bengali attitudes to women who, as we have seen in the previous chapters, were defined by their reproductive functions and the roles they played within the family. Male hostility to women's work outside the house was based on restrictive definitions of womanhood in the dominant patriarchal ideology of Bengal. Yet how far were gender relations and gender ideology redefined by the major economic changes, such as depeasantization, the restructuring of traditional crafts and the escalating costs of living, which affected female employment in the province during our period?[5] The re-definition was complex: an appeal was made to British and Bengali gender ideologies alike in a variety of contexts.

Women Workers on the Land, in Domestic Service, Trades and Crafts

Tracing sources documenting women's presence in the peasant and the bazaar economies is a considerable task.[6] The difficulties do not stem from the absence of women earning wages during the period 1890 to 1930, but from the lack of attention paid to these women by British and Bengali male observers. Only a relatively small number of women was returned by census enumerators as 'gainfully employed', because women's work was seen as the property of male relatives, in particular of husbands.[7] Moreover, in contrast to jute, tea and coal, the so-called organized sector, the rural and urban economy was not subject to the regulations of the Factory Acts, which required annual reports containing at least some information.

Census findings and reports on selected villages or cottage industries are all the documentary evidence I have of the contributions of women to family economies. Census officials were motivated by the idea of statistical completeness and usually included women's non-domestic work in their accounts unless they were, as in 1891, otherwise instructed. They restricted their descriptive accounts, however, to women working in crafts and trades, ignoring the majority of women who worked on the land. Women's agricultural labour was often equal in time and energy to their male relatives' work, but officials and observers regarded women as helpmates or assistants and did not recognize the double burden they carried in working with their husbands and shouldering domestic work.[8]

Agriculture was the largest single employment sector for women. The number or percentage of women who 'earned' a living in agriculture is, however, difficult to determine as the categories of enumeration changed from census to census. Figures compiled from various estimates suggest, however, that 40 to 50 per cent of all women in paid employment (that is, 4 to 5 per cent of all Bengali women) depended on the agricultural sector for a wage in kind or cash.[9]

As the proportion of employed women was low compared to Bihar and Orissa, the neighbouring provinces, it is no surprise that women were stereotyped as housewives. The contemporary sociologist, Radhakamal Mukherjee, completely ignored the innumerable female agricultural labourers, whose numbers had grown sharply after the turn of the century.[10] Describing the families of 'agriculturists' in 1912, he contrasted Bengali women with Bihari women:

In Bengal, however, the woman leads a more secluded life seldom taking an active share in outdoor work and the seclusion is greater as the family is richer or the caste higher... Agriculturists' wives will on no account come to the fields in which their husbands work, the breakfast being brought by infant girls or old females, usually the mother. As a rule females do not work in the fields, except the very old or very young, who are sometimes deputed to tend cattle in plots adjoining to homesteads.

But the women may be sometimes seen employed in threshing out the grains, winnowing or stacking the hay.[11]

Here, two of Mukherjee's observations are important for our understanding of Bengali gender ideology and women's position in the agricultural economy. First of all, he equated seclusion with non-employment and leisure. In fact, he believed that women maintained their femininity by being confined to the household. Thus, exhausting work such as threshing paddy—as essential to the families' survival as male work in the fields—was devalued for the simple reason that it was done at home. Secondly, Mukherjee noted that some outdoor work was age-specific. It was precisely the young and the old who worked in the fields. Young girls had yet to fulfil their primary role in biological and social reproduction, while old women had completed theirs. Although the household depended on the joint labour of men and women, women's work was not valued in Mukherjee's view:

She cooks the food and makes all necessary preparations for that process. She has also to grind the wheat or the pulses in the janta or husks the rice with dhenki and if she has any leisure, she spins cotton or silk threads or twists the san, coconut, jute…into ropes.[12]

In a footnote, Mukherjee added further details on a woman's 'leisurely hours':

The spinning hours are those which a woman snatches from her other labours at home; an hour after the mid-day and the night meal is the most usual time in which she plies her wheels. Sometimes she works at it in the dark before day dawn, guided by the dexterity of her fingers. In the course of two months her savings in thread after exchanging with the trader suffice for a piece of cloth for herself or her husband, for which she pays the weaver at the rate of two pies per cubit, either in cash or in dhan, the length of the cloth being 7 or 8 cubits.[13]

Activities which counted as work when they were done by men became 'leisure' activities when they were done by women, even if crafts, such as spinning, were included which produced marketable goods or useful household products.

The evidence suggests that women bore the brunt of poverty when economic conditions on the land deteriorated. In the 1880s already, 'the basic tendencies of agrarian change in colonial Bengal were clearly visible' and this included—apart from 'the fragmentation of estates, subinfeudation' and 'rackrenting'—a differentiation within the peasantry.[14] After the turn of the century, and particularly so after the First World War, the agrarian economy went through a serious crisis. It was at this time that peasant women faced the full impact of gender ideology which pigeon-holed women's work as domestic labour or leisure and which valued women as secluded beings.

During the 1920s, deepening rural class formation led to an estimated three million peasant families losing their land. The process was a complex one, and it is impossible to analyse it in detail here. Suffice it to say that the crisis for peasant families was the outcome of increasing rural indebtedness, rising prices, the commercialization of the rice trade, changing forms of rent collection and, in the long run, a decrease of arable land due to British-planned railway construction and other public works.[15] The crisis did not affect all regions equally but struck the Hindu heartland in the western districts most severely. There, due to a high rate of land transfers, 'the number of landless labourers was also much higher...than elsewhere in Bengal; the employment of their labour entailed, in most cases, various degrees of bondage or dependence on the landlord'.[16]

What happened to the women of the estimated three million peasants who had lost their land during the 1920s?[17] The material foundations of many of their traditional tasks disappeared once their families were landless. Mahishya and Namasudra women in Narkila village, Sylhet District, for instance, earned around Rs 20 each year through vegetable farming. Men fenced and ploughed a plot of land near their houses and the women of the family grew aubergines, chillies, tobacco, pumpkins and potatoes. Chillies and tobacco were dried and usually provided a year's supply. The other vegetables were partly for home consumption and partly for the market.[18] While vegetable gardening provided a seasonable income only, there were other important female activities.

Rice-husking with dhenkis—more lucrative than spinning—was a major female contribution to a family's income. During famines rice-husking provided relief work for starving women.[19] Developments in this informal and exclusively female economic sector were representative of the declining opportunities faced by impoverished peasant women. In the twenty years after 1911, the number of women involved in the occupation declined by half from 270,000 to 136,000.[20] The reasons are not hard to find. The rice-husking sector was affected by the introduction of mechanized village huskers and the opening of rice mills in the early 1920s. As a result rice-husking became more profitable and attracted men from a growing number of landless families.

Mechanized huskers were encouraged in an attempt to revitalize the cottage industry. In 1928 the Government of Bengal published S. C. Mitter's analysis of recent innovations in the sector. Of general importance was his claim that the new husker was 40 per cent more efficient than husking with dhenkis.[21] Not once did he mention the fact that men had never worked in rice-husking before. All that counted for Mitter was that a man was now able to support himself and his family by husking rice. Women working with dhenkis were the casualties of mechanization.

Simultaneously with the mechanization of rice-husking at the village level, rice was now being husked in newly-opened mills. Between 1921 and 1927 the number of rice mills in Bengal doubled to more than 350. Each mill, employing between 40 and 500 men, displaced women home-workers. Working in the mills was socially acceptable only for men and for scheduled caste or adivasi women, but not for Hindu village women.[22]

The developments in mechanized rice-husking were most significant for the trend they set. In 1927 'this ancient cottage industry' was still said to give 'occupation to innumerable poor and destitute women'. Moreover, it was the only occupation which was managed by women.[23] But there was one important new distinction that mechanization introduced. 'Mill rice is mostly exported', wrote one official, 'but "dhenki" rice is generally used for local consumption.'[24] The export of rice, which promised higher returns in the long run, was monopolized by men.

While nearly a third of dispossessed peasants became landless labourers during the 1920s, fieldwork was only an option for Hindu women in the worst of all cases. In accordance with the ideal of purdah, fieldwork was regarded as inappropriate for women in Bengal. Still, in 1921, almost 17 per cent of agricultural labourers were women, but in 1931 their share was down to less than 10 per cent.[25]

One sector of female employment that expanded rapidly was domestic service. Between 1921 and 1931 the number of women domestic servants increased by 300 per cent to over 450,000. In the 1931 census more than half of them were listed as 'working dependants' in the Burdwan division in the west of the province where 'depeasantization' was most advanced.[26] It is, however, unlikely that these women were helping wealthy peasants or landowners with strictly domestic tasks. They were probably employed in work done in the house, but directly related to the agrarian sector, such as processing grains or vegetable gardening. This seems the only viable explanation for the increase in the number of female domestic servants in Burdwan division in the 1920s.

Nevertheless, what is important is that at an all-Bengal level a growing number of women lost status by working outside their families' control.[27] Before the 1920s a greater proportion of women domestic servants came from Nepal and Orissa or from among Bengali widows. Now for the first time married Bengali women— many of them wives of landless labourers—were employed as servants. On special occasions in the employers' families, the husbands would travel to Calcutta to help with the additional work in the household.[28]

In Calcutta women had to cope with male competition in domestic service. In the 1920s the number of maid servants decreased by over 25 per cent from over 19,000 to less than 15,000 while the number of male employees grew from 55,000 to 83,000. Big cities had always been regarded as dangerous for women. Thus, men migrated by themselves and families preferred to employ men as cleaners, watchmen and cooks. Women were employed mainly as zenana attendants and by less well-off middle-class families who could not afford to pay men to cook and clean. These families were affected by the rising cost of living during the 1920s, and they cut down on the number of servants they employed when moving to smaller flats or subdividing their houses.[29]

The changing economic circumstances and social aspirations of middle-class women affected the employment opportunities of another group of women: ayahs, barber women, matchmakers flower and bangle sellers—all of whom were loosely attached to the urban bazaar economy. Due to the relaxation of purdah among middle-class women, the ayah as an ever-present child-minder in the house became more important than before, as did the cook who relieved middle-class women of the time-consuming process of cooking. In contrast, barber women, matchmakers, flower and bangle sellers gradually lost their clients. Traditionally, a barber woman, *naptini*, visited a middle-class family twice a week or even more often to paint the *alta*, the artistic henna decoration on the hands and feet. As in the case of the other women in the urban service sector, her importance was not only due to the visible service she fulfilled, but also because of her function as an intermediary between secluded purdah women and the outside world. With the decline of purdah she became less important in this regard. Moreover, as middle-class wives took over wider responsibilities as housewives, there was less time and need for the services and entertainment provided by the barber women. This more or less applied to the matchmaker and the bangle woman. As the division between the public and the private became less strict for middle-class women, women in the service sector who had catered to them became gradually redundant.[30]

Women in the traditional craft sector were as adversely affected by the economic changes of the 1920s as peasant women. Traditional crafts had suffered as a result of Bengal's integration into the imperial economy. During the second half of the nineteenth century 'deindustrialization' of the countryside, caused partly by British imports and partly by the mechanization of manual crafts, made craftworkers redundant and increased the pressure on the land.[31]

Women's participation had been more widely integrated and accepted in craft production and distribution than in the agricultural sector. In fact, it seems that artisan women were worse affected by deindustrialization than were men. Throughout our period the ratio of women workers to men in the craft sector declined. Between 1901 and 1931 the number of women working in pottery declined by 50 per cent, but the number of men declined by less than 30 per cent. Whereas the number of men producing baskets, mats and leaf bowls remained more or less constant, in 1931 there were 50 per cent less women working in this craft than in 1901. Similarly, in 1901, women dominated the fuel trade, mainly of cow dung cakes formed and dried by the women themselves, but by 1931, their number had shrunk to a third that of the men involved.[32]

The causes of the radical changes in the sexual composition of the workforce varied from craft to craft. In the pottery sector the number of women had always been low, and a further decline was

restricted to the wives of potters who lost their work. In the fuel
trade the gradual shift from cow dung to coal led to male takeover
of the trade. Finally, women who made leaf bowls were unable to
compete against the increasing foreign imports of hardware and
glassware which were preferred by middle-class consumers.[33]
Whatever other reasons there were, including changing clas-
sificatory categories of census enumerators, the overall picture of
an increasing number of women being pushed out of traditional
crafts and trades is clear.

Declining employment in crafts trapped women between the
compulsion of the labour market and the rigidity of gender ideology. Women could not switch to another craft or employment
sector without suffering a loss of respectability. 'Only the lowest
social grade of woman goes out and earns her living independently', Radhakamal Mukherjee stated in 1912. In 'an artisan's
family', wrote Mukherjee

the woman can assist in the husband's work more materially. The
weaver's wife cleans the thread and arranges the warp and woof. The
oil-presser's wife manages the bullocks and runs the ghani when the Kalu
is working in the fields. The silk rearer's wife diligently and carefully
feeds the cocoons. The tailor's wife uses the sewing machine when there
is hard work for the family. The laundress herself washes the clothes in a
tank. The banglemaker's wife makes the slow fire and rolls the lack rods
into thin pencils. The Muchi's wife helps her husband in the collection of
hides and skins. The Dom woman weaves the baskets. The potter's wife
collects and prepares the clay.[34]

Mukherjee's description of the sexual division of labour after the
turn of the century linked women's work closely to the work of
their husbands. The female sphere of economic and social activities in artisan families was less restricted than that of peasant
women; the artisan's sphere of work was not as clearly distinct
from the domestic sphere as were the fields from the home.
Accordingly, male and female tasks were not as differentiated as
among peasants.

However, confronted with 'deindustrialization' artisan
women's traditional integration into the process of production
and distribution was of only limited help in the search for alternative work. In fact, the outright equation of economically active
artisan women with artisan wives was already the effect of
'deindustrialization'. Such a classification ignored the economic

activities of a large number of unattached women and widows, and the decline of former female economic strongholds, such as rice-husking and silkworm rearing.[35]

Bengali women working in the agrarian, service and crafts sector were more adversely affected than their male relatives by the economic crises of the 1920s. On the one hand, the reasons for their economic displacement were closely linked with the pre-colonial undervaluation of women's economic contributions, as in the case of peasant women. On the other hand, traditional notions of femininity clashed with the working conditions in capitalist industrial units, such as rice mills where people of different sexes and castes mixed freely. Moreover, the long working hours and the strict separation between the place of work and the household were insurmountable problems for women with small children. Thus, purdah-related gender ideology which was hostile to independent female work outside the household was reinforced by the requirements of a working day in a capitalist unit where the norms were shaped according to the daily routine of the men.

Women in the service and crafts sectors moved around freely in villages, towns and cities supplying other, more secluded, women with services, artisanal products and news. In their case, it seems, the road to marginalization was paved by the increasing penetration into Bengal's economy of commodities manufactured abroad or in Indian factories, and the changing social outlook of middle-class women. Women in the traditional urban service sector paid the price for the increasing social space middle-class women gained through education, the erosion of purdah and paid or unpaid activities, mainly as social workers and teachers.

Women in Mills, Mines and Plantations

Bengal was the most industrialized province in India at the turn of the century, but industries were still scattered islands in a sea of agriculture. The jute mills in and near Calcutta, coal-mines near the Bihar border, and tea plantations in Darjeeling employed only a miniscule number of people compared to agriculture and the labyrinthine bazaar economy of the cities.[36] But historians have largely concentrated on the growth of the large economic units because of the wealth of evidence in official reports and its export importance.[37] These reports have largely dealt with men at work and it comes as a surprise to discover that one out of every three workers was a woman.[38]

While the high proportion of women workers in the labour force of these companies is not reflected in historiography, it does come through in relevant source material.[39] For a number of reasons sources on women's work in mills, mines and plantations are richer than on women in other areas of production. In jute mills, for instance, women were employed as individual wage-earners according to their terms of employment and were thus entered in the statistics. In coal-mines and tea plantations women were a vital part of the labour force and accordingly gained recognition. The most prolific source material on women in these economic branches, however, exists for reasons which are only indirectly related to the conditions of women working in the industries: jute, tea and coal companies were competing in the world market and foreign, in particular British, competitors closely watched the terms of employment and conditions of work in Bengal to identify exploitation which increased the margins on goods produced in Bengal. Moreover, concern for public health in the 1920s, especially as regards maternity and childbirth, directed even more attention to women's work in factories, plantations and mines. British women doctors in India who were unemployed after the First World War identified this niche in the market and obtained state funding for various survey projects.

There were proportionally more women employees in mills, mines and plantations than in the traditional economic sector, that is in the rural and bazaar economy. But compared to other provinces the pattern of employment in the large companies was similar to Bengal as a whole. The ratio of women to men was considerably lower than in Bombay, the next biggest industrial centre, or in the neighbouring provinces of Bihar and Orissa.[40] The most common explanation for this ratio is that Bengali cultural values combined with the relative wealth of the province inhibited the growth of a female labour force working outside the home.[41] This certainly helps to explain the small and declining proportion of Bengali women in large economic units. However, the majority of women—the absolute number was higher than elsewhere in India—came from outside Bengal or from adivasi areas where female wage labour was more widespread.

Migration

While the search for a decisive reason for labour migration by men and women has been abandoned, we can assume that developments within the family were more important for female than for male migration.[42] Most women left their home villages, like men, because of poverty; but whereas men often migrated as a strategy of familial survival in their villages, women usually left only when there was no further hope of subsistence at home. Impoverishment resulted from two different developments: first, as in the case of men, from economic changes such as the declining productivity of the land; and second, as regards women, from marginalization in the patriarchal family due to barrenness, desertion or widowhood. In both cases women experienced either partial or total separation from the means of production.[43] Thus, as Sharon Stichter has argued for the African case, women who migrated did so not only for development in the area of production, but also because their position in the patriarchal family was crumbling. Nevertheless, despite their single status women had to cope with the ignominy of being subordinate to men, a position that stemmed from their being identified with the domestic sphere, which was used to justify male prerogative over women and undervalue women's contribution in the labour market, either by paying them lower wages for the same work or by excluding them from certain areas of production.

Incorporation into the new sector was a gradual process and not a sudden event. Moreover, it is questionable if the Indian labour force ever experienced a complete integration into the capitalist sector of the economy. The survival of village patterns of authority and control suggests a partial break with the past. A case in point, we shall see, is the role of the sardars, foremen, whose handling of labour recruitment and payment of wages was partly informed by their status in the rural economy from where they recruited the migrants. In the case of women, sexual abuse, or the threat of abuse, worked as an additional source of the foremen's power. The mode of sexual oppression was to a considerable degree influenced by the extent to which women conformed or broke with purdah-related values, such as modesty, gender segregation and attachment to the men of their consanguine or affine families. In addition there were clear links between women workers in each sector of employment, their economic exploitation and the extent of sexual oppression with which they were confronted. For working women the meaning of purdah depended on gender as much as on class.

The rapid growth of tea gardens, collieries and jute mills after the 1860s was dependent on a steady increase in the migrant labour of men and women, mainly from Bihar, Orissa and UP.[44] While whole families migrated, men and women also went to Bengal without their families, although we do not know their exact proportion vis á vis the total organized industrial workforce. The presence of women, both single and married, depended on the nature of the production processes in plantations, collieries and mills and on the housing conditions which the companies provided in order to attract or discourage women workers. Women were mostly concentrated in the plantations and collieries. Between 1890 and 1930 more than half the workers in the Darjeeling and Jalpaiguri tea gardens were women; in the Raniganj coalfields the proportion of women was only slightly smaller. In the jute mills, in contrast, women comprised less than 20 per cent of the workforce. During the 1920s the number of women in coal mines and jute mills, but not on tea plantations, began to decline, a trend which has continued, apart from a short interruption during the Second World War, till the present day.[45]

The patterns of migration were different in the three major industrial sectors of jute, tea and coal. In the jute industry labour migration was in the classic, single-sex, migrant mould, best known in the South African gold-mining industry. Male migrants circulated regularly between jute mills and their home villages where their families lived.[46] Significantly, single women also migrated, but they lost contact with their homes and settled permanently near the jute mills. In contrast, long-distance migration to tea plantations was largely undertaken in family units. Here, there was little or no initial circular migration and families rapidly settled permanently on the plantations. The coal mining industry presented yet another pattern of migration: it relied on both seasonal migrants and settled workers. While the majority of workers were recruited locally, that is, they came from the districts surrounding the mines, a good many were not full-time mine-workers. They were labour tenants on company controlled land and divided their time between mine and agricultural work. The remainder lived in colliery lines without independent access to the land. While the exact number of full-time to part-time miners is a matter of dispute, the proportion of single women in the female workforce was as high as 40 per cent. Overall, the important point to emphasize is that single women who went to work in mills, mines and plantations were uprooted from their rural background far more rapidly than were single men.

The first migrants to tea gardens were adivasi families from the Chota Nagpur plateau, Nepal and the Central Provinces. Throughout our period Santhals from Chota Nagpur formed the majority of the labour force in plantations. Originally they had earned their living through shifting cultivation at the western fringe of Bengal proper, later a coal mining area, but they had been continuously pushed westwards, particularly after the Permanent Settlement, towards the infertile Chota Nagpur plateau. After a number of rebellious uprisings the Bengal government created the Santhal Parganas as a homeland district for the adivasis. Nevertheless, the land was poor and wage labour in the tea gardens was their most suitable alternative means of livelihood. In the 1920s Phalini from Ranchi, for example, left her own and her husband's land in the home village to be looked after by her brother because they were better-off with plantation work.[47] Chota Nagpuris dominated the Jalpaiguri plantations (126,000 men, women and children in 1921), while Nepalis were in a majority in the higher mountain areas of Darjeeling (66,000 in 1921), where the climate was unsuitable for migrants from the plains.[48]

Women migrated with their families, but also as single women with fellow villagers. These women were either widows or had been abandoned by their husbands either because they were barren or because the husbands had left in search of a livelihood elsewhere. If a single woman had relatives in the plantation, she would stay with them. Otherwise she was settled as a 'family unit' with a single male migrant. It was probably because of this mode of settlement, which was to encourage reproduction, that the proportion of single women in the plantations was smaller than in mines and mills.[49]

Planters were keen to employ women and children, who were paid lower wages than men, for the labour-intensive task of tea-plucking. In fact, women and children far outnumbered men. Altogether, in 1921, 87,413 male and 101,136 female labourers worked and migrated in close-knit nuclear family units· they fitted in neatly with the planters' interests in cheap labour. By the 1920s, 90 per cent of the workers regarded the plantations as their permanent home. The prevailing pattern of family migration, the poverty of the homelands and the scarcity of land for paddy cultivation in the tea areas converted the adivasi people into a stabilized labour force in the plantations.[50]

Although the tea-garden region was either wet or cold, unhealthy and malaria-infected during most of the year, adivasi families from the Chota Nagpur plateau preferred the tea plantations to the closer coal-mines. Although wages on nearby coalfields were higher, plantation labour was more attractive than dangerous underground work in mines. During the decade before the First World War tea-planters in Assam and Bengal competed with mining companies for adivasi labour. Between 1881 and 1891, for instance, an annual average of 27,000 people left Chota Nagpur and the Santhal Parganas for the tea plantations in Assam and Bengal. They were accompanied by a considerable number of migrants from all over India, particularly from the Central Provinces and Madras.[51]

There was a vast difference in scale between the Assam and Bengal plantations. The comparatively large Assam plantations, without an adequate source of local labour, resorted to an indentured labour system to ensure an adequate supply of long-distance migrants. Yet migrants to plantations preferred the flexible contracts in tea-gardens in Jalpaiguri and Darjeeling to the coercive labour system in Assam. Whereas the former also recruited, 'Assamese methods' were notorious among the peasantry in the recruitment areas. Assam planters sent their sardars or arkatis to Chota Nagpur or other adivasi areas in Bihar and Orissa and to the border regions of Bihar and the North Western Provinces. They persuaded impoverished people to migrate by coercion and inducement. Women were either attracted by the promise of jewellery or abducted and seduced, leaving them with no alternative but to migrate. Once in Assam, labourers found themselves bound by the Workmen's Breach of Contract Act and subject to the arbitrary authority of the planters and their police. In contrast, Bengal planters never resorted to 'Assamese methods', as they did not suffer from significant labour shortages.[52]

Coal-mining in Bengal, started in the first half of the nineteenth century, began to grow significantly as an industry only towards the end of the century. The mining area, which was later to include the Raniganj mines in western Bengal and the Jharia and Dhanbad mines in Bihar, was the biggest of its kind in India. In 1894 its output was larger than the total output of all other coal mines in India. The majority of workers were drawn from villages in the mining area or the surrounding districts. By 1911 more than two-thirds of the miners in Burdwan district (Raniganj coalfield) had been born in the same district, and only one-sixth came from the Santhal Parganas and Chota Nagpur. During the following two decades the Burdwan mines continued to depend on local labour, while migrants from the Central and United Provinces became increasingly important in the Bihar coalfields. By the mid-1930s only 2 per cent of the workers in the Raniganj mines came from outside Bihar or Bengal.[53]

The coal companies followed three methods of recruiting their labour force from the surrounding aboriginal and semi-aboriginal tribes. The easiest and most informal method, mainly followed by small enterprises, was to send employees back to their home villages with baksheesh and travel money. They recruited people, who then formed a mining gang of 5 to 50 men and women, all related or known to each other. The second method was to employ a contractor, known as the *tikardar*. On being informed as to which type of labour was required, the tikardar would equip his agents with baksheesh, and money for drinks and travel. They would negotiate with village headmen who would collect villagers for minework. In most cases the agents returned to the mines and worked as sardars (headmen) with the gangs they had recruited.[54]

The most reliable method of labour recruitment was the purchase of the zamindari rights of near-by villages by mining companies. The companies then established indebted peasants as service tenants on their land. Through the semi-feudal tenancy arrangement (chakrani), families were forced to supply labour for the mines instead of paying rent. In contrast to the Assam plantation labourers, who faced penal prosecution if they absconded from the gardens, mine workers lost their land and their vital agricultural income if they refused to work in the mines. In addition, the ownership of zamindari land rights in villages enabled mine owners to settle migrant labourers and tie them to the mines.

A family was settled with two or three bighas of rent-free land, but one family member was bound to work almost full-time (230 days a year) in the mine. The Raniganj Coal Association even bought land beyond the natural perimeter of the coalfield to ensure a sufficient labour supply. Before the Depression started to affect the coal industry in the mid-1920s over 50 per cent of the Raniganj labour force was settled as service tenants.[55]

Santhals and Bauris, the latter a coal-cutting caste from the lower-most rung of the Hindu hierarchy, formed the bulk of the labour force from the initial period of coal-mining in Bengal. They took their women and children underground and worked in family units, just as they cultivated their fields. Managers complained that adivasi people never worked more than was necessary and stopped after three or four days when they had earned enough for a week. Still, in the 1920s, some sardars visited villages and bustees daily to persuade men and women to work in the mines, which was utterly impossible during the harvest season.[56] Obviously, on the one hand, the labour tenancy type of settlement had its advantages for mining companies in that they bound workers to the mines for good. On the other hand, a village environment put workers in a strong position. Agriculture did not only provide workers with an additional source of income, but was also the basis for an identity that was independent of their work in the mines. Labour tenancy settlements were a form of labour recruitment which grew out of a situation where labour was short and where companies tried to attract migrants by offering conditions which resembled the agricultural lifestyle they were familiar with.

In Bengal mines, the majority of adivasis never became full-time mineworkers. While others became skilled miners, Santhals and Bauris continued to supply the bulk of the unskilled labour. Their importance among the mine labour force declined gradually. As more people were pushed off the land and out of traditional occupations, the adivasis' place in the mines was taken by other people from the bottom of the social hierarchy in western Bengal.[57] The number of Santhal and Bauri women employed in Bengal mines was high, but there were fewer other Hindu or Muslim women. High-caste Hindu women worked in mines only if they had been socially ostracized and abandoned by their families. In the early 1920s, more than 15,000 women worked in the mines.

Over 9000 of them carried coal in the pits, and they made up 34.5 per cent of the underground labour force. The male/female ratio was similar among surface workers. From the mid-1920s onwards, both the depression in the mining industry and restrictive legislation led to a reduction in female employment.[58]

Nearly half of the women who migrated to the coalfields with men and worked in so-called family units were single. In the 1920s, according to official statistics, 30 per cent of women working in so-called family units were not formally attached to the men. They may have migrated from the same village, but they had done so as single women, or if initially married had later become widows. Their relationship with the males in the work gang was based on carrying coal for them. A further 10 per cent of women had established informal liaisons with the men of their 'family units'. Thus 40 per cent of female mineworkers were not married, and a significant number of them had risked migration alone, as had other women working in the tea plantations.[59]

In our period women made up under one-fifth of jute workers. Between 1890 and 1925 the number of women workers increased from 12,000 to 55,000, but the overall tendency in the industry was for fewer women to be employed as compared to men. They performed the classic role of a 'reserve army of labour'. During slumps, such as in 1909–10 and during the Depression, they were the first to lose their jobs, but in exceptional periods, like during the war and for a short while after child labour was restricted in 1923, more women were employed. In the 1930s, however, the trend towards a declining proportion of women in the workforce continued.[60]

The Indian jute industry was centred on a strip of land, 60 miles long and two miles broad, along the river Hooghly north and south of Calcutta. Outside Bengal there was only a handful of jute mills. In 1929 there were 4 mills in Madras province and one in Bihar apart from the 95 in Bengal. These 100 Indian jute mills employed 347,000 workers, whereas 295 cotton mills employed the same number of workers. The jute industry was the most important employment sector in India's biggest industrial area. The industrial workforce of Calcutta and its neighbouring districts—24-Parganas, Howrah and Hooghly—was over 450,000 people compared to Bombay's factory population of only 190,000.[61]

Before 1890 the vast majority of the jute labour force was recruited from near-by Bengali villages or the surrounding districts. In 1895 a 'good proportion' of women came from short distances of two or three miles from the mills. Some Bengali women from 24-Parganas and Midnapur accompanied their husbands over an even greater distance because the increasing population pressure in their home districts had pushed them off the land.[62]

After 1900 the composition of the jute labour force changed in two important ways. First, the growing flow of migrant labourers from Bihar, Orissa and UP diminished the significance of the Bengali element in the workforce.[63] There was an ample supply of migrant labour for the rapidly growing jute mills along the Hooghly because even the lowest wages in jute mills were slightly higher than those in tea-gardens or coal-mines. In addition, competition between the mills on the one hand and Bengal mines and tea plantations on the other was limited because the latter mainly employed adivasi men and women, whereas mills attracted Hindu and Muslim males from Orissa and the border region of Bihar and UP.[64] On their arrival in Calcutta, these labourers contacted jute sardars who came from the same village and hoped to be employed. Often they had to bribe the sardar to be permitted into his department. Only if a new mill was to be opened or production rapidly expanded did sardars go to their home areas for recruitment. As a consequence of both methods the labour force in each department or mill tended to be homogeneous.[65] Secondly, as the vast majority of long-distance migrants from UP was male and unskilled, the proportion of Bengali women workers among the labourers declined. After 1900 Bengali men were over-represented among the skilled and better-paid workers. Altogether they were the permanent one-fifth of the labour force in contrast to the Oriya or Hindi-speaking migrant majority. Bengali men now worked in mills south of Calcutta such as Budge-Budge and Fort Gloster. Because the number of women in mills south of Calcutta had traditionally been low and because skilled workers earned family wages, which enabled them to support their families in the jute mill area or at a weekend-commuting distance, the number of Bengali women in the workforce decreased rapidly. In 1923 the Bengali women among the jute hands were either widows, or had transgressed the traditional morality expected of Hindu women.[66]

The majority of male migrant labourers came to Bengal without their wives. They went home once a year for three months to see their families, to help with the harvest and to celebrate the major religious festivals in their villages. As a consequence mill managers complained about seasonal labour shortages.[67] According to them migrants did not bring their wives because of traditional Indian cultural values. Men from some regions in Bihar or UP were said to lose their status in their villages if they dared to take their women to Calcutta. This argument, however, ignored those sardars and other better-paid workers who, although from the same areas as the workers, brought their wives to the mills and preferred to have them look after their families near Calcutta rather than in far-away villages.[68]

The dominance of male migrant labourers in the jute mill labour force was not caused by cultural values but by economic constraints. Men first came to Calcutta by themselves because the train fares were expensive and because they did not know what to expect. But over the years they continued to leave their wives at home because of their low wages. Whereas they could not afford to support a family near the mills, their earnings were sufficient for an annual trip to their families and to send some money home at regular intervals. For the mill owners it was much cheaper to finance their workers' families in rural areas than in Calcutta.[69]

Inadequate accommodation was another reason for the declining proportion of women in the labour force. Until the early 1890s, Bengali labourers were housed in huts in nearby villages which were cheap for the millowners and allowed for privacy and family life. From there women walked to the mills accompanied by the men in their families. As the labour requirements in mills grew, factory lines were built by companies or bustees were erected by private landowners. These soon developed into mill towns, such as Bhatpara or parts of Howrah. But ordinary mill hands could only afford dormitory accommodation—four to eight strangers living in one small room. Thus the majority of jute mill workers had to choose between a family life under degrading conditions or separation from their families. Whereas most long-distant migrants chose the second option, many Bengalis who came from an area which was less impoverished than the major up-country recruitment districts abandoned jute mills and looked for employment which allowed for family life. Poor Bengali districts which supplied jute mill operatives, such as Midnapur and Bankura, were within a weekend-commuting distance.[70]

Women migrating to the jute mills from outside Bengal were accompanied by men who were not their husbands. These women were cut off from their rural homes because of the loss of honour accompanying migration, working in a factory and living with men without being married. They did not undertake the annual journey to their villages as men did and went through the process of proletarianization faster than did male millhands.[71] Women in jute mills were regarded as outcastes and of a lower status than men because they had lost contact with their families and their rural background. In a key 1923 report on women in the organized sector in Bengal, Dr Dagmar Curjel wrote that

the average Hindu Bengali woman worker in the jute mills is a degraded woman or prostitute. The ordinary respectable Bengali women around Calcutta will not undertake factory work. Under the heading of 'degraded women' I would class Bengali women, often of good caste and family, who for some reason have offended family tradition and have been cast out. Many are of fine physique and said to be good workers. Such women were found in mills around Calcutta.[72]

The majority of up-country women were in no better position. Women workers often lived like deserted wives when their partners had gone back to the village either for a holiday or for good:

It is scarcely possible for a woman to live for any length of time alone in a mill compound, hence such women seek the protection of another man. This protection may consist not only in living with the man, but in working near to him in the mill in a position where he can keep an eye on the woman. In return the woman gives over her earnings to the man.[73]

In sum, the pattern of migration to plantations, mines and mills depended on the family structure and the role of women in their home societies. Adivasis migrated as groups of men and women, married or unmarried, from the same family or the same village to Jalpaiguri, Darjeeling and Raniganj, whereas Muslim and Hindu men left their wives under their families' protection when they set off for Calcutta. Over the years, however, the sexual composition of the labour force depended on the conditions of the areas where people worked. Predominantly, these conditions were man-made by the company managements to attract the type of labour needed in their respective enterprises.

Work and Wages

Women were employed, with only rare exceptions, in the labour intensive sections of the production process. In tea plantations women worked in the most important area of production, the picking of the leaves, without the help of men. They were paid their wages independently of their husbands and spent them as they considered best. In coal-mines women collected and carried the coal which was cut by their husbands or other male relatives. Women miners received their pay as part of their men's wages but usually managed to put enough aside for family maintenance. In jute mills there were no tasks which were exclusively done by women and men earned more for the same work. The majority of women worked in the unmechanized preparing and finishing departments where their labour was regarded as unskilled. Female jute workers were paid independently, but in contrast to plantation women they gave their pay to male 'protectors' who decided how the money would be spent. A woman's wage was always seen as a contribution to the family budget and not as the income of a single person.

The organization of the working-day as well as the modes of payment left much space for arbitrary decisions by sardars, highlighting the continuity of forms of labour control which were not economic in the narrow sense of the word. Due to the individualized form of employment, women in plantations had to confront the sardar's authority almost daily when it came to timing their working-day or weighing their harvest. In contrast, women miners working in pairs with men and in gangs with other migrants from their village experienced the sardar's control when it came to being accepted as a gang member, but less in day-to-day confrontation. In jute mills where employment was harder to get, payments to the sardar by male and female workers were a matter of routine as they signified a relationship marked by authority and respect.[74]

Working conditions in tea gardens in the Duars, the Terai and Darjeeling were, according to colonial authorities, ideal for

women with an agricultural background. Women spent all day in
the fresh air and not in unhealthy conditions in mines or mills.
Moreover, accidents were less likely to occur plucking tea leaves
than picking coal or making twine. Thus adivasi women who were
used to work in the fields and who had been the economic back-
bone in their home villages were desirable workers. However,
such views did not take into account the climatic hardships of the
tea garden areas. The Jalpaiguri district (Duars, Terai) was humid
and hot, and malaria, hookworm, dysentery and diarrhoea were
widespread. Many workers suffered from ulcers on their legs,
commonly called 'hill sores'. Their cause was unknown: there
seemed to be no connection between the sores and the tea bushes,
but in all probability it had something to do with the humidity of
the soil.[75]

A woman's working day on the plantations began, depending
on the weather and the season, at around 8 a.m. If a woman
reported late for the morning shift, she was not allowed to work
for the remainder of the day. Her morning duty was called hazira,
the picking of a certain amount of tea leaves. If a woman was a
quick worker, it took her until noon to pick the required quantity,
otherwise she had to work until 3 p.m.[76] The afternoon duties
varied on the estates according to the labour supply and the
amount or type of work to be done. In some plantations, women
had to perform tika, the pruning of trees, otherwise they would
lose the whole day's pay. In others, it was up to the women to do
two haziras. In yet others, the afternoon duty was called 'doubley'
and was restricted to a few women only although it was much in
demand. On the one hand, afternoon shifts had the advantage of
topping up meagre wages, but on the other hand, they cut down
the time a woman could spend with her children or on vegetable
gardening and rice-husking. The latter was essential for the family; each week a woman had to spend at least eight hours husking
rice.[77]

Wages varied according to sex, region and the season. In the
early 1920s women earned between Rs 4 and Rs 9 for 18 days,
which was the average number of working days per month in the
Terai and the Duars. The cost of living was estimated at Rs 6 a
month. In Darjeeling there were more working days in a month
and thus the overall income was higher. By 1929 the money paid
per hazira had remained the same for the past 40 years, but the

amount of labour required had declined. The average wage of a woman was Rs 10-5-8 (5 paisa, 8 annas) a month.[78] However, a group of women workers from the Duars related in an interview to deputies of the Royal Commission of Labour that it was impossible to rely completely on such wages. Sometimes they would receive only half because the sardar found the quality of their work unsatisfactory. In another incident, for no apparent reason a sardar had cut a woman worker's wage on four consecutive days.[79]

In some plantations payments in kind supplemented wages which changed the extent of women's dependency on the managers' and sardars' goodwill: free quarters and rent-free land were provided for workers and their families. This was not enough to live on, but necessary for survival. Rather than granting some economic independence to women, as could be argued with regard to labour tenancies in the mining areas, in tea plantations, rent-free land and accommodation strengthened the hold of planters over their workforce.[80]

The labour of older women, pregnant women and children was worst paid of all. Older and pregnant women worked in the tea factories—where labour was casual and seasonal—cleaning the tea leaves, a job considered particularly suitable for women because it was so similar to the sifting and cleaning of grain. Child labour was also cheap (Rs 2-14-5 in 1929) and commonly used for picking leaves or, in the case of small children, for catching caterpillars from the plants. When the introduction of primary education was suggested in the 1920s, planters, faced with the prospect of replacing children with 'expensive' women, feared a sharp rise in production costs.[81]

Men were usually not employed as pluckers, but when they were, they earned four annas per hazira, one anna more than women. More often, they dug the estates and handled machinery in the factories. For these duties the minimum male wage was higher than the female wage, namely Rs 9–12 per month. By 1929 the average male monthly income was Rs 14-4-1. Whatever the official justification for wage differentiation may have been, the effect was that women had to pick larger quantities of tea leaves to earn enough money to support themselves independently.[82]

Because of the low wages, men—with more alternatives than women—tried to escape from the plantations whenever possible.

Once Bengalis started settling in Darjeeling for the hot season and hotels were opened, plantation workers, particularly Nepalis, deserted tea plantations as the payment and the conditions were better in the growing·service sector. In the Duars, aboriginal workers saved to buy land and, if successful, they returned to the plantations only for occasional work.[83]

While women were most vulnerable to the market slumps in the tea industry and the sardars' arbitrary powers, their situation in the Bengal plantations was definitely better than under the contract labour system in Assam. In Bengal planters had to compete for labourers during economic booms, as men and women were entitled to find the best market for their labour-power. One way of encouraging workers to stay on an estate was to advance money free of interest on the occasion of marriages and sradhs.[84]

Even more important was the interest some planters took in the natural reproduction of their plantation workforce. In the Duars women were paid Rs 5 or more as baksheesh if they gave birth to a child. In the Terai, where the supply of labour was less of a problem, fertility was not rewarded on such a generous scale. But between 1920 and 1922 while the tea industry was suffering from a slump even in the Duars all maternity payment was cancelled. Many workers left the plantations for their villages because male earnings alone were not sufficient to support families at the time of childbirth. Once the crisis had ended, benefits were reintroduced. However, demands for regular maternity benefit were rejected by planters because, as they saw it, husbands earned the family wages. Tea garden owners paid maternity benefit not for the sake of women, but for the sake of a regular labour supply.[85]

Most mining families were labour tenants living on company-owned land. They worked underground part-time and part-time as cultivators in their fields. Women went down the mines with their husbands and male companions and relatives. The working day started at 8 a.m. in the morning and finished between 1 and 5 p.m. in the afternoon, depending on the time a couple needed to fill the required number of tubs. In some mines couples worked during alternating weeks on day and night shifts (10 p.m. until dawn), respectively, but in most collieries it was up to the workers to choose their hours of work.[86] Women worked as unskilled labourers for their men in the pits. After the men had cut the coal, women gathered it into baskets and carried it up to the surface by climbing either a series of ladders or, more commonly, some inclines to the hoist:

In the course of a day's work she will carry approximately 13 cwt. of coal cut by her man up an incline of perhaps a gradient of one in ten...perhaps for the distance of 750 feet...in baskets of 80 lbs. [which is equivalent to] an uphill walk *of over five miles.*[87]

The baskets were emptied into a tub. Three tubs full of coal made two tons which was the average daily output of a couple.[88]

Mines in Raniganj were shallow and thus without artificial ventilation. The air was sticky and filled with toxic fumes. This was aggravated by the smell of the little oil lamps which were used to light the pits. The humidity and heat worsened as year by year the mines were dug deeper. Despite the relative shallowness of the mines safety measures were inadequate. For example, in 1925, an average year, 38 women died in Bengal coal mines either from collapsing walls or from accidents caused by explosives which were used to loosen the coal. Worse than this was the constant threat to the workers' health stemming from the unhygienic conditions underground. Nearly all the mines in the Raniganj coal-field were infested with hookworm, and three-quarters of the underground workers and over half of the surface workers suffered from the disease.[89]

Women working underground were usually paid jointly with their male companions and were entitled to a share of 40 per cent of the wage. From the 1890s to the 1920s, over which period wages did not improve, they earned 8 to 12 annas a day (16 annas to one rupee in Bengal). Women working on the surface earned the smaller daily wage of 5 annas. They were either, like the Santhal women in the West Niga Colliery in Asansol, married to underground workers or they were single women from near-by villages who came to work in groups. Taking into account that the minimum level of subsistence was 5 annas, the surface women lived in poverty. The mining companies offered little help. Some paid a sickness benefit of 3 to 4 annas a week and one rupee for the funeral cloth when a family member died. A widow received free fuel and some allowances on festive occasions. In the event of a birth, 8 annas to one rupee were given as maternity benefit.[90]

Until the late 1920s mine owners tried to oppose any attempt to restrict female employment in mines because women provided cheap labour. Moreover, while women worked, mining companies saved the extra expenses of paying family wages to male workers. In 1923, however, mine owners had to concede the first of reformist demands when children, who had been employed in picking coal, were banned from going underground. This implied a restriction on female underground labour; women who had taken their babies underground now had to look for surface employment unless there were relatives or older children to look after them. Above ground the tasks for women were limited. They either carried coal to the coking yard or moved sand used for stabilizing pit walls.[91]

After 1925 the mining industry suffered the worst slump in its history and had to lay off workers. It was in this context that the reformist pressures exerted by women's organizations and the International Labour Organization were finally rewarded. In 1929 legislation was introduced which required the female underground labour force in Bengal and Bihar to be reduced by 10 per cent each year. Coal managers, who for years had argued for the need for cheap female labour, now adopted the strategy of limiting over-production through the reduction of female underground labour, without risking social unrest which male redundancies could have caused. Whereas in the mid-1920s roughly a third of the total and underground labour force respectively was women, in 1938 they constituted only 11 per cent.[92]

Women reformers from outside the mainstream middle-class organizations, who had actually inspected the mines, did not believe that underground work was unsuitable for women. They argued that the air was manageable and that the baskets were lighter than the loads women in the construction industry were used to carrying in the open air. Moreover, because the wages were better than elsewhere, women working underground were described as looking healthier and stronger than ordinary coolie women.[93]

On the whole, mining provided workers with greater economic scope and flexibility of earnings than plantations or mills. Access to a plot of land was the key advantage of being a labour tenant around the mines. Workers could meet extra expenses by working another day or two per week in the mines and were not as indebted as tea garden or jute mill workers. Besides, for men, there was the possibility of promotion to the position of sardar. Few women achieved such power and prestige. Those who, like Padara from Bilaspur in the Dhemo Main Colliery, were success-ful, achieved their position because of the men in their families. Padara inherited the position from her dead husband, and her working son was a sardar himself. However, she was not paid as much as her son, who earned Rs 20 per month.[94]

In the Calcutta-based jute industry there was no strict sexual division of labour in the production process, that is, there was no task which was exclusively women's work. But women were concentrated in unmechanized departments where low-paid piece work was performed. Women were neither settled, as in the tea plantations, nor employed, as in the mines, in a male-female unit. The fact that they needed a male protector and companion to make ends meet and to save them from being bullied by the sardar or by their colleagues was not part of the mills' official employment policy, but a day-to-day routine which proved decisive to women's experience. The need for a male protector stemmed from culturally-based attitudes in the home regions of the workforce in Bihar and UP. There it was taboo for women to lead their lives outside of male control. Moreover, the stereotype of the dependent woman was reinforced by the unfavourable employment and living conditions prevalent in mills and lines. Women provided cheap labour but the mills were not dependent on them; the employment of women had no structural basis in the production process. Women were regarded as a reserve supply of labour when male labour was short and were the first to lose their jobs in a slump.

Despite the number of female employees in jute mills, only a few descriptions exist of the work women actually did. 'On the whole women are mostly employed on less skilled work, in the lesser paid parts of the mill, the preparation and hand-sewing department', reported Dr Dagmar Curjel in 1923:[95]

Women who work in the preparation department or the drawings and rovings, have in course of their work to move about fairly heavy receivers filled with jute; otherwise the work done by women in a jute mill cannot be said to be heavy, but involves many hours of continuous standing. Only in the hand-sewing department do women sit at their work. In the preparation department women have to maintain a certain speed of work in order that the line of manufacture in the mill may not be interrupted.[96]

In the preparation department the jute was oiled and teased into fibre before women fed it into the softener. The industrial disease, jute dermatitis, which was common in all jute mills, affected workers in the preparation department in particular. The Hindu habit of washing the body with mud or *saji mati*, instead of using soap as the Muslims did, left oil on the skin and led to dermatitis.[97]

By the turn of the century feeding the jute fibre into the softeners was regarded as too dangerous for women. Some died because the work was 'decidedly arduous, and bangles on their arms and wrists, and anklets on the feet, have, on several occasions, been the direct cause of fatal accidents'. In 1898, for instance, one woman died in the Clive Jute Mill (Garden Reach, 24-Parganas) in an all too common occurrence, when jute became entangled in her bracelet and drew her arm into the rollers of the softener. Another woman was killed in the Sibpur Jute Mill (Ramkristopur, Howrah) when jute fibres around her foot pulled her into the machinery. In the early 1900s women were replaced by men as feeders. Accidents now allegedly happened when women tried to save oil to take home and rubbed the rollers with tow while it was running. Yet by the 1920s, when safety standards around the machinery had been improved, women were not re-employed as feeders. By then feeding was something more than an unskilled manual task, associated as it was with a complex piece of machinery.[98] Even without spectacular accidents, conditions in the preparation department were strenuous. The atmosphere was extremely dusty, filled with smog in winter, and sticky in summer:

women workers...were crowded together, in a part of the mill where through ventilation was inadequate, and the air contained much dust and fluff. If the total height is taken into account, the cubic space per worker might be reckoned in certain cases as falling within statutory limits, but practically there was no free circulation of air. They moved about on floors that were often uneven and in a bad state of repair. The lighting was in most cases adequate, but whitewashing of windows was either omitted or inadequate, so that glare was often considerable.[99]

The neglect of the department where most women worked reflected the low status of female employees. Managers justified such conditions by arguing that they were similar to those at home where women spent hours in unventilated huts squatting on the mud floor while cooking over an open fire.[100]

Many women took their children with them into the jute mills to feed them whenever it was necessary. Babies were breastfed until the age of two:

While the mother is working the child lies around if in the preparation department, among the jute waste either alone or at times watched by an elder brother or sister who themselves are too young for half-time work. If the mother should go into the mill alone, such an elder child brings the baby to her in the mill, to be nursed when required. Occasionally, I saw a child who had hurt itself in the machinery while playing about, and most mothers seemed to look on slight accidents as necessary risks in the day's work.[101]

Between 1923 and 1927 a couple of jute mill managers tried to set up creches, but the women did not respond positively. They did not trust such efforts by the management, which was, in other cases, alien and hostile to their needs. Also, the idea of creches conflicted with the Indian custom of working mothers in the traditional economic sectors taking their children with them wherever they went. Only in 1927, when it was part of a comprehensive scheme of sickness and maternity benefit, was a creche successfully set up in one mill.[102]

Apart from the preparation department, the finishing or hand-sewing department was the major employment area for women in jute mills. Women were paid by the piece which relieved the managers from the task of supervision. Managers showed themselves as liberal-minded when they allowed women to work at any time during the hours of daylight between 5.30 a.m. and 7 p.m. Yet the freedom of women to take time off for cooking, eating and nursing was circumscribed by the very low piece-rates. Still, women liked the sewing department because it was safe for children to play in.[103]

Very often children helped their mothers in sewing, which was an easy way to get around restrictive legislation, and to earn the money which was necessary to feed the family. Until 1912 children had been employed in various departments without any restrictions. Thereafter it became increasingly uneconomic to employ children for anything other than piece labour. The Factory Act of 1912 prohibited the employment of children under 9 years of age and limited the working hours to 7 for so-called part-timers between the ages of 9 and 14 years. In 1922 part-timers were redefined as children between 12 and 15 years of age who were entitled to 6 hours work per day. But under the conditions in the hand-sewing department it was easy to ignore any restrictions related to the working hours of children or women.[104]

Women worked long hours because they needed to earn as much as possible—they did not have to work continuous or regular shifts. Others could take their places. During the 1880s men, women and children worked eight to nine hours per day in the mills. Once the mills were equipped with electric light in the late 1880s, women often worked 15 to 16 hours a day and a system of night shifts was introduced. In 1891 the Factory Act was amended in 'recognition of night work by women in factories in which work is arranged on the shift system'. Workers were not allowed to work more than 11 hours at a stretch in 24 hours and were required to have one-and-a-half hours of rest. In addition, the working week of women was limited to a maximum of 60 hours.[105]

The number of working hours excluded the extra hours women worked outside the factories. Women bore the double burden of house and mill work. In the villages where the Bengali operatives lived the first warning whistle sounded at 3 a.m. Whereas men could sleep until they were about to leave for work, women got up to fetch water, light a fire, prepare some breakfast and look after the children. At 4 a.m. women and children left for the factory to work a minimum of ten to eleven hours. Afterwards they waited for one to three hours to be accompanied home by their male relatives. They spent 15 to 16 hours in the mills before they could return home to their shopping, cooking and washing. Their working day lasted from 3 o'clock in the morning to 10 or 11 o'clock at night.[106]

Despite the heavy workload of women inside and outside the mills, the regulations of the amended factory acts were widely ignored. By 1896 the length of working shifts in Bengal jute mills was a growing cause for concern. A special commission initiated by the Dundee jute lobby found that in some mills, particularly in the Hasting Jute Mill, women and children under 14 years of age were employed for 22 and 15 hours at a stretch, respectively. The owners of the Hasting Jute Mill, Messrs Birkmyre Brothers, even provided an extra sleeping room for the children of working mothers. The special commissioner suggested that these women had most probably worked in another mill during the day, and argued that female night work had a bad impact on family life and on children who were dragged into the mills. As ten-hour shifts were the legal maximum in Scotland, the Dundee jute entrepreneurs complained about unfair competition. While women and children undoubtedly worked abnormally long shifts, Dundee and Calcutta were major competitors in the world market and the Government of India declined to take any new legislative initiative. The government took the view that women went to and from work with male escorts and should thus work the same hours. The Bengal National Chamber of Commerce argued against any interference because workers found 'their tasks both remunerative and delightful'.[107]

After the turn of the century colonial authorities became more concerned about the long hours worked by women. It became public knowledge that women millhands often went entirely without sleep. Some women worked extra hours on Sundays in the winding and reeling departments, while other women worked regularly through the nights and the following day as domestic labour without rest. In 1911, following the revelation of these long hours, a cautious reform was promulgated: women's work in the mills was restricted to the hours between 5.30 a.m. and 8 p.m.[108] The restriction of female labour to the day-time left many problems unsolved. Under the multiple-shift system which had been introduced after the turn of the century working hours for the operatives were spread throughout the day (the details are shown in Table 6).

While Bengali women could not go home to their villages during their rest periods women migrants from Bihar, Orissa, UP and CP who lived in the lines went to their huts to do some cooking. But the time was too short to make a fire, cook a meal and eat. While they had less work to do in the morning and evening, they seldom ate their meals with the men who worked different shifts.[109]

The other effects of the multiple-shift system were worse for women. During the whole working-day the mills were never emptied and properly aired. The multiple-shift system meant that the mill machinery was continuously in operation all day whereas in the mills near Calcutta, which worked on a single-shift system, the machines were stopped for at least two hours during the lunch-time break. By 4 p.m. in multiple-shift mills the air in the sticky preparation departments was filled with dust and breathing was difficult. Women who worked under such conditions were unhealthier than those in single-shift mills.[110] Moreover, under the multiple-shift system most power lay with the time-clerk and the sardar. When labour was short they asked women to work extra hours which was, even when extra money was paid, a burden on women's health. In the finishing department where wages were paid at a piece-rate women worked longer to increase their minimal income. Managers did little to enforce government regulations or to interfere with the control sardars and time-clerks exercised over workers. Adolescent part-timers, who were only allowed six hours of work, registered for two shifts in different departments or different mills. Sardars profited in various ways from the system. It was estimated that between 7 and 10 per cent of all jute wages was paid to the sardars for non-existent workers who had been falsely registered. Also, sardars took bribes for over-time labour.[111]

The long hours of millwork, unhealthy and disruptive of family life, were subject to external pressures for labour reforms. In October 1919, the International Labour Conference in Washington adopted a convention, which the Government of India later ratified, fixing 11 hours as the minimum night's rest for working women. In 1926, when the same conference decided to set up a committee to examine the fulfilment of the convention, British politicians in Whitehall showed concern about the state of affairs in India. It appeared that only 13,000 out of 53,000 female jute workers in Bengal had the required night's rest, and the Secretary of State asked the Government of India to investigate whether the climate in Bengal or the special circumstances of shift work justified the exemption of jute workers from the convention.[112]

Despite legislative action the changes which were introduced did little to ameliorate work conditions. During the entire period under investigation jute managers increased or cut the hours and days of work according to market conditions. For example, in the 1908–10 slump mills were closed on Saturdays and the average working week was reduced to 4 days or 48 hours. In contrast, in the boom conditions during the First World War, millhands worked an 80 hour week. In general, though, before the First World War men worked an average of 75 to 90 hours per week, while women often worked for more than the official limit of 60 hours.[113]

During the 1920s, with a growing demand for jute in the world market, the Indian Jute Mill Association (IJMA), which included all but a couple of mills, worked millhands harder than before. In 1921 its members agreed on a 54-hour week, six hours below the legal limit. But this and other agreements were accompanied by efforts to increase the extraction of absolute surplus labour, that is, to pay less for more work. The cuts were achieved in two ways: management either reintroduced a 60-hour week, as happened for nine months in 1920–21 and for twelve months in 1929–30, without paying higher time-wages, or the multiple shift was replaced by the single-shift system which increased the individual workload and led to a loss of jobs. By 1926 work was done in single shifts in nearly half the Bengal jute mills. The crucial issue at stake in these changes was the abolition of the khoraki payment, an allowance for one day of enforced idleness. Under the multiple-shift system labourers worked an alternating four- and five-day week, but received an allowance for the missing fifth day every second week. Workers were also dissatisfied by 'the alteration of the piece workers' fixed task in proportion to the increased working hours' and the generally low wage level at a time when the cost of living was going up rapidly.[114]

Short-term redundancies or wage cuts pushed workers into poverty. During the 1908–10 slump, for instance, the criminal statistics in the mill areas showed a rapid increase. Moreover, lower-paid workers, in particular women who could not survive on reduced wages, travelled back to their villages or tried to find work elsewhere. The average mill worker was in debt to the extent of one month's wage and there were no savings for times of hardship and unemployment.[115] As a reaction to the increasing pauperization during the 1920s, trade unions gained influence and workers went on strike, particularly during the non-cooperation years of 1920–21 and later after 1925. Early in the decade women only hesitantly joined strikes and managers thought of them as more reliable than men. Since they were responsible for the immediate survival of their families they were more ready to accept lower wages than be without any income while fighting for a higher pay. But they did strike when other than economic issues were at stake. In March 1920, for instance, in a wave of working-class

protest in connection with the nationalist struggle, 350 women
from the preparing department of the Hooghly Jute Mill, Kidderpur, walked out and forced the whole mill to close down during
the three days of their strike. They demanded the dismissal of the
European assistant in charge because of improper conduct and
because he had beaten a woman. On resuming work after their
demand had been granted their 'motherly instincts' won the day
and they petitioned for the reinstatement of the assistant. During
the 1929 strikes, however, women were frequently noted in official
reports and contemporary accounts for their militant participation. Bazaar looting by women was reported from Chengail on
6 June 1929 and it became a fairly common expression of women
workers' discontent. Their primary responsibility regarding the
feeding of their families was obvious as in their earlier reluctance
to go on strike.[116]

Women in jute mills were trapped between two worlds and got
the worst of both. According to the traditional patriarchal values
of Muslim and Hindu society they had lost their status by migrating to the Calcutta mills. In the industrial sector, because of the
sufficient supply of male labour and the mechanization of the
production process, women labourers were gradually marginalized. In 1927, the Chairman of the IJMA referred to the benign
effect of single shifts on the workers' family life, but 'forgot' to
mention that the restructuring of the labour process would, as a
secular trend, exclude women. Before 1929 the number of female
employees had grown annually until there were over 50,000
women in the industry. However, contraction in employment
during the Depression, combined with the introduction of the
single-shift system in more and more mills, the closing down of
mills for one week every month during the winter of 1930–31 and,
in March 1931, the temporary introduction of the 40-hour week,
all led to the loss of jobs for women, the reserve labour supply for
the mills.[117]

Housing and Health

The housing provided for women workers in plantations, mines
and factories reflected the importance industrialists attached to
female labour. The labour force in tea gardens and coal mines was
settled in family units. Tea planters employed the whole family,

even small children, and provided suitable accommodation. Coal companies had problems finding workers for unattractive under-ground labour and offered land and service tenancies to motivate families to migrate and resettle. In jute mills, only the local workers and the relatively well-off members of the migrant work force lived in huts which afforded the minimum necessary for a family. Most factory lines and bustees were very overcrowded. It was only during the 1920s when the jute industry was booming and female labour seemed to be necessary that family quarters for mill operatives were built.

Medical care, apart from maternity facilities (see Chapter 4), was minimal in all three areas. Any initiatives by the state or the companies was aimed at avoiding epidemics which threatened the white community and the regular labour supply. Negligence of these issues by employers meant increased rates of mortality due to cholera as well as lung and bowel infections in addition to the regular occurrence of malaria, which was almost endemic in the humid regions where plantations and mills were located. After the turn of the century, as factory lines and bustees became in-creasingly insanitary and overcrowded, jute companies started to employ medical personnel. However, the medical staff comprised only male doctors and was of little or no help to women workers.

Tea planters allocated a rent-free housing site and provided building material for newly-arrived migrant families. While con-structing the huts the workers were paid minimum wages. They built the huts in the Bengali village style, with bamboo walls and thatched roofs. The quality of the accommodation depended on the builders. It was said that Nepalis and Santhals built better houses than other migrants, most probably because the climate in their home areas, the Chota Nagpur Hills and the Himalayas, had forced them to develop the necessary skills. After 1900 one plan-tation experimented with a standard house: the mud floor 13 by 20 feet in area, 7-foot high bamboo walls, a corrugated iron roof which was 10 feet high at the ridge, and a verandah. The housing space was 50 square feet per person. In the 1920s houses with iron frames and corrugated iron or asbestos roofs and walls made of ekra with mud plastering, bricks or wood were constructed partly to secure better protection against the monsoon rains, and partly because the traditional raw materials were in short supply follow-ing the cultivation of most of the wasteland in the Duars. It was

not clear if 'progress' was for better or for worse, because walls
which could be destroyed and renewed annually were probably
healthier than more substantial ones where germs and insects
could live for long periods. Labourers often rejected iron or mud
houses because they were badly ventilated.[118]

Sanitary arrangements in the gardens and the lines were poor.
Public health care concentrated on the prevention of 'law and
order' problems, such as labour shortages and epidemics. Significantly, the official health centres were attached to 13 of the 17
police stations in Jalpaiguri district. Their duties comprised vac-
cinating, inoculating against cholera and inspecting the food for
sale in bazaars and markets to make sure that it was fit for human
consumption.[119] Planters were responsible for their workers'
health, but they acquitted themselves of this duty in as inexpen-
sive a way as possible. Each plantation financed a dispensary and
some kept sick-wards for in-patients. Although check-ups and
medicine were free, workers were reluctant to avail themselves of
the facilities because the training and often the character of the
medical officers were dubious. As medical officers were poorly
paid no qualified persons applied. Besides, preventive health care
was rudimentary.

Latrines were essential to prevent hookworm. Yet they were
uncommon because they were expensive. Experience in some
plantations and jute mills proved that workers were ready to
accept latrines if they were properly located, but planters and
officials blamed the allegedly uncivilized background of the
workforce for the non-acceptance of latrines. Indeed, new hands
were unfamiliar with the necessity of sanitary arrangements in
areas more densely populated than Chota Nagpur or Nepal, and
the connection between human excrement and hookworm was
not obvious to them. However, what they resented were not
latrines, but latrines far away from their homes or in the middle
of the village. In such cases women in particular preferred to use
the forest. Cheaper improvements with a marked effect on the
workers' health found support among planters. Well water was
chlorinated which led to an immediate decrease in the incidence
of dysentery and diarrhoea. Next to malaria and respiratory diseases, intestinal infections were the greatest killers.[120]

Until the turn of the twentieth century the quarters of the
mining families in the Raniganj colliery lines were poor. The

workers who were migrants from the lowest level of Indian caste and class society were unfamiliar with the sanitary needs of large settlements. However, their misery was caused less by a lack of knowledge than by their meagre wages, which did not permit any expenditure on items other than those related to immediate survival. The coal companies felt no pressure to invest in the accommodation of their workers. They either provided land for service tenancies or built inadequate lines.

A Santhal village erected on land leased under the conditions of a service tenancy was an organized enterprise which showed that Santhal workers could cope under conditions similar to those in their home areas. The village was built along the road. Each family had a group of clay huts thatched with straw and stables in which they kept pigs, poultry, goats and, if well-off, a cow. The buildings were surrounded by a high mud wall which gave some privacy. Such families were basically peasants and mining provided them with financial resources to buy dal, spices, clothes and other necessities.[121]

By 1930 more than half the mining work force lived in lines and their housing and sanitary conditions were much worse than those of service tenants. The first lines built were back-to-back barracks with single room quarters which were given to mining families irrespective of the family size. The room, ten by ten feet and seven feet in height without a window, also served as a kitchen. The houses were mostly built in the traditional Bengali style but, unlike in the villages, there was no space for privacy outside the hut. In addition to bad housing, miners suffered from lack of water for drinking and washing. Women had their baths with pit water pumped out of the mines into tanks near the shafts of the collieries. There were no latrines either and pigs acted as scavengers.[122]

Such conditions caused an almost regular outbreak of cholera, smallpox and malaria. According to one authority:

in the coalmining districts of Bengal, the question of public health and sanitation is of even greater importance than safety...there were two serious epidemics of cholera in the district... No statistics of the number of cases and of deaths are available but the loss of life was most serious. The miners in such cases, return to their native villages perhaps 50 miles away, and thus alarming rumours about the unhealthy condition of the mining districts are quickly spread over at least 10,000 square miles of recruiting grounds and the difficulty of obtaining labour for the mines enormously increasing.[123]

Although such reports were published repeatedly during the first two decades of the twentieth century little was done to improve conditions. But when the First World War made the regular supply of coal essential for the empire, the government took the lead. The Asansol Mines Board of Health which had been constituted in 1912 'was brought into active existence in the early part of 1916 to prevent the outbreak and spread of dangerous epidemic diseases in the Asansol Mining Settlement'.[124]

Indeed, during the 1920s the number of people who died of cholera and smallpox were insignificant compared to the victims of respiratory diseases. The latter was the major killer due to humid underground conditions and bad housing. Consequently, in 1922, the Board of Health issued rules with minimum requirements for the lines. Back-to-back construction became illegal, the minimum gap between the buildings was 15 feet and other regulations ordered improvements regarding building materials, cubic space and windows. But the rules were only gradually put into practice and by 1925 only 14 per cent of all line accommodations conformed to these standards.[125]

Despite such changes conditions in the colliery lines were appalling. While improvements decreased the death-rate among workers, by 1930 there were still 'very few men, women and children whom one could call physically fit for hard work as mining'.[126] When preventive health arrangements were in their infancy medical care hardly existed at all. Two to three collieries shared one doctor who distributed medicine to the few miners who ventured to come near him.[127]

Housing and sanitary conditions for women in jute mills were marked by the absence of facilities to enable women to lead healthy lives in the mill areas. Until the turn of the century the majority of workers were Bengalis who lived with their families in nearby villages or urban bustees, unless they were week-end commuters and left their families in a neighbouring district. The accommodation in the villages and bustees was insanitary. Bustees were overcrowded, particularly in Calcutta itself, when during the jute pressing season large numbers of additional male and female labourers streamed into the city to find work and accommodation near the jute presses in the Chitpur and Cossipur areas.[128] Bustees and lines were overcrowded because the land increased constantly in value. As land rose in value, the conditions of housing deteriorated, particularly for so-called unproductive (female) labourers and dependants. Whereas in bustees men and women could live together, the mill lines—constructed after 1900 for migrant labourers—provided no space at all for women. By 1930, 30 to 40 per cent of the jute workers lived without their families in overcrowded lines which were slightly cheaper and had more sanitary facilities than did bustees. In comparison, the remaining 60 to 70 per cent of the workforce inhabited over-crowded, expensive and unhealthy privately-owned bustees where annual epidemics were the rule.[129]

The bustee bamboo and mud huts were mostly built as small compounds. Until the 1920s there was no sanitation, no ventilation and no water supply. Roads were made of mud and lined with heaps of filth. Such houses were inhabited by the poorest labourers, four or five at a time, who paid between Rs 2 and Rs 3 per room per month as compared to a rent of about Re 1 per room in the lines. During the 1920s' some bustees, for instance in Bhatpara and Howrah, were equipped with pucca drains and roads or connected to the municipal water supply. Still, drains were open, filled with stagnant water and an ideal breeding-ground for mosquitoes.[130]

Most factory lines did not differ a lot from the bustees until in the 1920s some mills provided better drains, better ventilation, verandahs and cooking-space outside the huts. Some of the facilities, such as latrines at the septic tanks, were so far away from the lines that workers used the small canals instead. The supply of drinking-water differed from mill to mill, but the mills in the Calcutta municipality were worse off than the others. Most houses had pucca stone floors and iron roofs. But there were either no windows or such low ones that workers closed them to have some privacy. Accordingly, the huts were sticky and filled with smoke. Each room measured 10 by 8 to 12 feet, sometimes less, and was between 6 and 7 feet high. Usually four to eight men shared the space. The lines were all built back-to-back and the next line across the road was very close as well. Managers argued that it was impossible to limit the number of men in one room and that thus, in terms of ventilation, lines were probably worse than bustees, but they were better regarding sanitation. Some were double-storeyed houses in which case both floors had to be inhabited by either Muslims or Hindus.[131]

As land and housing were expensive, mill owners avoided any expenses which were not absolutely necessary. Catering for special needs of women such as more privacy or separate latrines was an unnecessary luxury and a rare exception. Women who had once moved into the lines had no real bargaining power. They had no chance of returning to their villages. The longer they stayed, the lower their status sank because of the growing number of male partners/protectors and the gradual loss of their sexual attractiveness. At the same time, because of the low sex ratio, the presence of women in the lines led to male rivalries. The presence of women in the mills was welcomed by managers as an element in social control because of their reluctance to go on strike. But women were expelled from the lines in a few mills because of quarrels over them by men.[132]

Workers who were slightly better paid moved out of the lines and into bigger and better ventilated bustee huts than those described above, where they lived with their families. Their wives stayed most of the day in the bustee compound surrounded by a wooden wall. 'They had privacy and there was a homely atmosphere about their house', wrote one official. 'Their infants looked well-cared for and nourished.' The same applied to sardars and mistris, the foremen and—mostly Bengali—skilled artisans in the mills.[133]

The health of mill workers was as fragile as the health of mine workers. In both cases malnutrition and environmental factors contributed to a high death rate. Exact figures were difficult to obtain because workers often went back to their villages to be cured or to die. However, in both cases hard-working men and women lived on the minimum of food and often had no proper breaks for eight hours or more in order to eat. In the mill area a general decline in the health of workers was observed during the first decade of the twentieth century. As in the case of mine workers, their diet suffered from a lack of vitamins, fat and protein. Women in the labour force were more adversely affected than were men. They did not, like most men, recuperate during the annual month-long stay in their home villages. The whole year round, living and working in the mill area, a woman could never get enough sun, air, milk and vegetables. Migrant labourers depended for their sustenance on contributions from the agrarian economy. Those who were, like women, cut off from their rural background, had a short working life in factories.[134]

Apart from malnutrition and exhaustion, many workers suffered from venereal diseases, in particular syphilis. In the three Anglo-Indian Jute Mills, for instance, where 10,000 people were employed, 80 per cent of the workforce was apparently infected with venereal disease. In the Soora Jute Mill 50 per cent of the women were infected. The spread of venereal diseases was further testified to by mill managers who explained that the medical personnel regarded treatment to be usless. The vast majority of women workers who depended on changing male 'protectors' or on part-time prostitution suffered the most. The latter usually did not survive beyond their early thirties.[135]

Compared with malnutrition and venereal diseases, malaria, cholera and small-pox were easier to cure or prevent. By 1920 almost every jute mill had its own dispensary and outbreaks of cholera and malaria occurred less regularly in lines than in neighbouring villages. Of course, this improvement was due at least as much to sanitary facilities as to medical provisions. The doctors who were employed by the management often lacked proper training and the skill to treat labourers. But even with the best of intentions, they could not fulfil their duties properly. There were too few of them. A mill usually employed one or two doctors to look after thousands of workers and other inhabitants of the mill area. The workers did not like the doctors and, apart for very serious cases, preferred the hakim's treatment in the bazaar. Women found western medicine even more difficult to accept because the clinics originally had an all-male staff. High-caste women among the labour force did not attend local clinics because the personnel for menial tasks was from lower caste backgrounds. Female attitudes to the medical facilities provided by mills changed slowly when maternity centres with women doctors were established.[136]

Conclusion

With regard to peasant and artisan women the dominant purdah-related gender ideology was reinforced in the labour market. The ideological identification of women with the domestic sphere justified their economic marginalization. Traditionally, the rate of economic participation among low-caste women such as Bagdis, Chamars and Doms was much higher than among women from high or locally-dominant castes, such as Brahmans, Kayasthas, Baidyas, Mahisyas and Namasudras.[137] But in the first decades of the twentieth century wage-employment for the latter improved while it declined for the former. This highlights that the meaning of purdah cannot be deconstructed without reference to the class background of the women in question. Purdah was no ahistorical overarching concept, but an ideology related to social and economic power relations. While socio-economic change allowed the gradual modification of purdah in the case of middle-class women (see chapter 5), for working-class women the meaning of purdah was intensified with the effect that men's position in the job market improved at the cost of women's opportunities for employment.

The exploitation of working-class women in Bengal during the early phase of industrialization was by no means unique. Elsewhere first generations of mine workers and factory labourers suffered harsh exploitation before autonomous working-class organizations managed to muster some opposition to mill, mine and plantation owners.[138] However, as the industrial sector expanded only slowly and the number of female employees declined, there was meagre concern for the fate of the women involved and their situation changed little. This tendency was aggravated by traditionally hostile cultural attitudes to independent, working women. Moreover, neither was the nationalist movement nor were the trade unions inclined to take up the woman workers' cause. Both organizations shared conservative views with regard to gender relations and focused on foreign capitalists and Britain as their enemies rather than on Indian hierarchical and patriarchal attitudes.[139] Across political, racial and class boundaries men shared an understanding of women as being house- and family-bound irrespective of whether they were supporters or opponents of purdah.

Table 1: Numbers of Men and Women Engaged in Various Trades,
1901–31

Year	Pottery		Basket Making		Trade in Fuel	
	Men	Women	Men	Women	Men	Women
1901	54,588	18,154	42,787	45,417	9,637	21,000
1911	59,446	29,917	36,915	42,881	9,199	22,938
1921	59,731	29,975	38,238	29,664	8,153	9,655
1931	39,282	9,282	43,572	20,865	12,825	4,481

Table 2: Timetable of the Multiple Shift System

1. Time-workers

	A	5.30–8.30	9.30–3.30
	B	5.30–9.30	2.00–7.00
	C	5.30–2.00	3.30–7.00

2. Piece-workers

	A	5.30–7.00	8.00–12.00	1.30–7.00
	B	5.30–8.00	9.00–1.30	3.00–7.00
	C	5.30–9.00	10.30–3.00	4.00–7.00
	D	5.30–10.30	12.00–4.00	5.00–7.00

3. Half-timers

	A	5.30–10.00
	B	10.00–2.30
	C	2.30–7.00

Source: West Bengal State Archives, Government of Bengal, Commerce
Department/Commerce Branch, January 1929, B. 64, K.W.

NOTES

[1] There is of course a vast body of sociological and historical literature on this issué. A very concise and helpful summary with particular relevance to Bengal is available in H. Standing, *Dependence and Autonomy. Women's Employment and the Family in Calcutta*, London, 1991.

[2] See, for example, N. Banerjee, 'Working Women in Colonial Bengal: Modernization and Marginalization', in K. Sangari and S. Vaid (eds.), *Recasting Women. Essays in Colonial History*, Delhi, 1989, pp.269–301.

[3] D. Chakrabarty, *Rethinking Working-Class History. Bengal 1890–1940*, Princeton, 1989; for comparison with conditions in another industrial region, see C. Joshi, 'Bonds of Community, Ties of Religion: Kanpur Textile Workers in the Early Twentieth Century', *Indian Economic and Social History Review*, 22, 1985, pp.251–80.

[4] COI, 1921, v, 1, p.416; COI, 1911, v, 1, p.549; COI, 1931, v, 2, 5, p.80.

[5] Compare R.K. Ray, 'The Kahar Chronicle', *Modern Asian Studies*, 21, 1987, pp.711–49, who argues that economic and sexual exploitation went hand in hand also at the bottom of the social and ritual hierarchy where the significance of female purity has often been questioned. On the interrelationship of sexual and economic exploitation in colonial India, see D. Engels, 'History and Sexuality in India: Discursive Trends', *Trends in History*, 4, 4, 1990.

[6] For women in the professions and in clerical jobs, see Chapters 4 and 5.

[7] H. Afshar, 'Introduction', in H. Afshar (ed.), *Women, Work, and Ideology in the Third World*, London, 1985, p.ix. In this regard sociologists and anthropologists working on women in present-day India have a considerable advantage and produce much more detailed case studies. See, for example, M. Mies, *The Lace Makers of Narsapur: Indian Housewives Produce for the World Market*, London, 1982.

[8] In 1891 census enumerators were even instructed to ignore women's work completely. They were told, in the case of women and children, to enter the occupations of husbands and fathers. COI, 1891, iii, Report, p.272.

[9] COI, 1921, v, 1, p.416. As the territory of Bengal changed several times between 1890 and 1930, I have extrapolated the necessary figures for women earning their living in 'Ordinary Cultivation' from different census tables, adding up the figures of the five divisions (Burdwan, Presidency, Rajshahi, Dhaka and Chittagong) and leaving out the Indian territories, Bihar and Orissa. The figures on women in other economic sectors have been extrapolated in the same way. It is problematic to base any arguments on census figures because the categories of enumeration changed repeatedly. Earlier literature and specific problems are discussed by S. Mukherji, 'Some Aspects of Commercialisation of Agriculture in Eastern India 1891–1931', A. Sen et al., *Perspectives in Social Sciences*, 2, Calcutta, 1982, pp. 227, 270–1. I have tried to tackle the problem of the additional differentiation in the 1931 census by adding workers, working dependants and those in subsidiary occupations to compare the sum with the number of workers in earlier censuses. This seems appropriate in the case of women who often regarded paid work as subsidiary to their housework. Moreover, most of my arguments are supported by the descriptive part of census reports which took the changing categories into account. My figures for 1931 vary slightly from the only comparison I had, M. Mukherjee, 'Impact of Modernization on Women's Occupations: a Case Study of the Rice-husking Industry in Bengal', *Indian Economic and Social History Review*, 20, 1983, p. 31. The differences, however, are so small that they have no impact on the conclusions I have based on these figures. In 1901 those engaged in ordinary cultivation numbered 501,914 of a female population of 19,841,634, in 1911 the figures were 751,551 of 22,117,642, in 1921, 1,080,764 of 22,544,314 and in 1931, 705,334 of 24,072,304.

The population figures are taken from COI, 1901, vi-A, 2; COI, 1911–1931, v, 2. The figures on female occupation in ordinary cultivation and all other occupational figures are extrapolated from COI, 1901, vi-A, 14, pp.330ff; 1911, v, 8, pp.212ff.; 1921, v, 8, pp.198ff.; 1931, v, 13, pp.70ff.

[10] The figures for female agricultural labourers are: 1901, 99,365; 1911, 241,559; 1921, 255,486; and 1931, 259,766.

[11] R. Mukherjee, 'The Family as the Economic Unit in India', *Modern Review*, June 1912, p. 598.

[12] Ibid.

[13] Ibid.

[14] P. Chatterjee, 'Agrarian Structure in Pre-Partition Bengal', A. Sen et al., *Perspectives in Social Sciences 2*, Calcutta, 1982, p.122.

[15] Ibid., for a conclusive account.

[16] Ibid., p.198.

[17] M.A. Huque, *The Man behind the Plough*, Calcutta, 1939, pp.139–44.

[18] N.C. Bhattarcharyya, L.A. Natesan (eds.), *Some Bengal Villages. An Economic Survey*, Calcutta, 1932, pp.87–8; surveys dated from 1928.

[19] M. Mukherjee, 1983, pp.31–3; P.R. Greenough, *Prosperity and Misery in Modern Bengal. The Famine of 1943–1944*, New York, 1982.

[20] The figures for Women Rice Pounders, Huskers and Flour Grinders are: in 1911, 270,321; in 1921, 169,573; in 1931, 136,089.

[21] For the respective contemporary debate, Government of India (GOI), *Report of the Indian Industrial Commission, 1916–18*, Calcutta, 1918, pp.193–9; S.C. Mitter, *Rice Milling Industry* (Government of Bengal [GOB], Dep. of Industries, Bull. No. 33), Calcutta, 1928, p.11.

[22] M. Mukherjee, 1983, pp.35–9; Government of India, *Report on the Working of the Indian Factory Act for 1929*, p.8.

[23] J.K. Mazumdar, *Cottage Industries in Bengal*, Calcutta, 1927, p.97; Greenough, 1982, p.100, argues that in 1940 still 75 per cent of the paddy was hand-husked.

[24] Mazumdar, 1927, p.97.

[25] This is a conclusion drawn from census figures which show that in 1911 there were 8,190,142 cultivating owners (male) and 1,308,645 agri. labourers (male); in 1921, 8,292,966 and 1,534,350; in 1931, 5,090,489 and 2,615,038. See also S. Mukherji, 1982, p.227. The percentage of agricultural workers of the total agricultural workforce increased during the two decades from 10.10 and 12.23 to 30.76. In the 1920s, it was claimed, Bengal peasants enjoyed a higher standard of living, but suffered harsh poverty in case there were any anomalies. Landless labourers were, we may assume, worse off. In addition, insufficient nutrition was stressed. (*Report of the Bengal Provincial Banking Enquiry Committee 1929–30*, I, Calcutta, 1930, pp.29, 72–3, 80.)

[26] For women agricultural workers, see footnote 9. Also in 1911 there were 110,915 women domestic servants; in 1921, 115,764; and in 1931, 462, 450. For the Burdwan figure, COI, 1931, v, 2, p.147.

[27] On the conditions under which peasant women take up employment outside the home, see R. Mukherjee, *Six Villages in Bengal*, Bombay, 1971 (written in 1946), pp.44, 71.

[28] Interview with Amiya Sen, Calcutta, 9 February 1985.

[29] COI, 1931, VI, 1, p.62; COI, 1921, VI, 1, p.107.

[30] Interview with Renuka Raychaudhuri, Calcutta, 9 February 1985; interview with Puspa Sengupta, Calcutta, 2 February 1985; the figures are: for 1901, 5356 women making and selling bangles, necklaces, etc.; for 1911, 2935; and for 1921, 1449. (The category of 1931 is not comparable.)

[31] S. Sarkar, *Modern India 1885–1947*, Delhi, 1983, pp.29–31.

[32] The figures are shown in Table 6.1.

[33] COI, 1901, VI, 1, p.69; V. Anstey, *The Economic Development of India*, London, 1929, p.289.

[34] R. Mukherjee, 1912, p.598.

[35] There is ample evidence that women did work by themselves, especially widows. Widows, for instance, supported themselves by making ropes, *Royal Commission on Agriculture in India, Volume* IV, *Evidence taken in Bengal,* London, 1927, p.42. COI, 1901, VI, 1, p.477, describes the decline of silkworm rearing, a formerly prospering employment sector for women in North Bengal.

[36] IOLR, Royal Commission on Labour in India (hereafter RCLI), V, 1, London, 1931; RCLI, 'Reports of the Royal Commission on Labour in India', IOLR, *Reports from Commissioners, Inspectors, and Others,* XI, 1930–31 (hereafter RCLI, 'Report'), pp.8–9; COI, 1931, V, 2, Calcutta, 1933.

[37] See A.K. Bagchi, *Private Investment in India,* Cambridge, 1972; R.K. Ray, *Industrialization in India: Growth and Conflict in the Private Corporate Sector, 1914–47,* Delhi, 1979; R. Das Gupta, 'Factory Labour in Eastern India: Sources of Supply, 1855–1946. Some Preliminary Findings', *Indian Economic and Social History Review* (hereafter *IESHR*), XIII, 1976, p.279 for a summary of the literature on industrial labour; C.P. Simmons, 'Recruiting and Organising an Industrial Labour Force in Colonial India: The Case of the Coal Mining Industry, c. 1880–1939', *IESHR*, XIII, 1976, pp.455–85.

[38] RCLI, *Memorandum on Labour Conditions in Bengal. Prepared for the Use of the Royal Commission on Indian Labour,* 1931 (hereafter RCLI, *Memorandum*), London, 1931, Section V, Welfare.

[39] On the selective character of source material on jute labour, see Chakrabarty, 1989, p.3.

[40] COI, 1911, V, 1, p.549 and 1921, V, 1, p.416; 1931, V, 1, p.281; R. Kumar, 'Family and Factory: Women in the Bombay Cotton Textile Industry, 1919–1939', *IESHR*, 20, 1983, pp.81–110.

[41] COI, 1911, V, 1, p.549.

[42] See C. Bates and M. Carter, 'Tribal and Indentured Migrants in Colonial India: Modes of Recruitment and Forms of Incorporation', in P. Robb (ed.), *Dalit Movements and the Meanings of Labour in India* (Delhi, 1993).

[43] S. Stichter, *Migrant Labourers,* Cambridge, 1985, p.151.

[44] RCLI, V, 1, pp.6–11, 262, 279; Bagchi, *Investment,* 1931–1938.

[45] For jute: IOLR, *Financial and Commercial Statistics of British India* (hereafter FCS), 1892/93–1904/05; IOLR, *Statistics of British India* (hereafter SBI) 1905/06–1912/13; IOLR, Government of Bengal (hereafter GOB), *Annual Report on the Administration of the Indian Factories Act in Bengal* (hereafter FA), 1912–1931, Calcutta. For coal: IOLR, S.R. Deshpande, *Report on an Enquiry into Conditions of Labour in the Indian Coal Mining Industry* (Report of the Labour Investigation Committee, 1944–45) (hereafter Deshpande, *Coal Report*), Delhi, 1946, Tables 9, 18. For tea: COI, 1901–1931.

[46] F. Wilson, *Labour in the South African Gold Mines, 1911–69,* Cambridge, 1972; for Southern Rhodesia, see the classic study by C. Van Onselen, *Chibaro,* London, 1976.

[47] RCLI, *Evidence,* VI, London, 1931, pp.322–3.

[48] Simmons, 'Recruiting', p.458; RCLI, V, 1, p.11; VI, pp.356–7; IOLR, *Report on the Duars Committee 1910* (hereafter Duars Committee 1910), Shillong, 1910, p.4.

[49] R.K. Das, *Plantation Labour in India,* Calcutta, 1931, pp.110–3.

[50] RCLI, V, 1, p.11 and VI, pp.356–7.

[51] IOLR, *Report of the Labour Enquiry Commission* (hereafter *Labour 1896*), Calcutta, 1896, p.10.

[52] Bagchi, *Investment*, pp.133-5; RCLI, VI, pp.356-7.

[53] Simmons, 'Recruiting', p.456; *Labour 1896*, p.2.

[54] Simmons, 'Recruiting', pp.463-82.

[55] Ibid., pp.463-71.

[56] WBSA, Comm./Comm., April 1923, B77, 'Report by Dr D. F. Curjel on the Conditions of Employment of Women Before and After Childbirth' ('Curjel Report'), Appendix E, p.3.

[57] Ibid., p.459; *Labour 1896*, p.21.

[58] B.R. Seth, *Labour in the Indian Coal Industry*, Bombay, 1940, p.129; West Bengal State Archive, GOB, Commerce Department, Commerce Branch (hereafter WBSA, Comm./Comm.), February 1924, A40.

[59] RCLI, v, 1, p.177.

[60] RCLI, 'Report', pp.8-9.

[61] FCS, 1892/93-1904/05; SBI, 1905/06-1912/13; FA, 1912-1931; FA, 1908, p.25 and 1911, p.3, 1930, p.18, 1931, p.7; IOLR, S.R. Deshpande, *Report on an Enquiry into Conditions of Labour in the Jute Mill Industry in India* (Report of the Labour Investigation Committee, 1944-45) (hereafter Deshpande, 'Jute Report'), Delhi, 1946, p.7.

[62] National Library, Calcutta, (hereafter NLC), B. Foley, *Report on Labour in Bengal*, Calcutta, 1906, p.14, Appendix I, p.x; IOLR, GOI, Home Department, Judicial Branch (hereafter Home/Judl.), February, 1896, A423, p.440; RCLI, v, 1, pp.4-5, 9; FA 1911, p.3; IOLR, *Report of the Indian Factory Commission 1890* (hereafter *Factory Commission 1890*), Parl. Papers 1890-91, 59, male witnesses, p.90.

[63] Das Gupta, 'Factory Labour', p.299; RCLI, v, 1, pp.8-11; Chakrabarty, 1989, pp.102 ff.

[64] But the mills shared some recruitment areas with Assam plantations; in fact, due to the close links between the managers of plantations and mills which derived from the common ownership by Managing Agency Houses in Calcutta, jute mills profited from the specific knowledge of Assam sardars. Bagchi, *Investment*, pp.133-5.

[65] RCLI, v, 1, pp.11, 262.

[66] Das Gupta, 'Factory Labour', pp.301-2; FCS, 1902-03; 'Curjel Report', Appendix A, p.IV; RCLI, v, 1, p.395.

[67] RCLI, v, 1, pp.9, 262; Foley, *Report 1906*, pp.1, 39.

[68] 'Curjel Report', Appendix A, p.v and Appendix B, S.4, p.3.

[69] RCLI, v, 1, pp.266-9, 279, 302-3.

[70] *Factory Commission 1890, Female Witnesses*, pp.87-9, 93; Foley, *Report 1906*, Appendix I, p.IX; IOLR, GOI, Home/Judl., February, 1896, A423; NLC, *Report of the Indian Factory Labour Commission* (hereafter *Labour Commission 1908*), Simla, 1908, pp.46-7; RCLI, v, 1, pp.4-5, 262; 'Curjel Report', Appendix A, p.XI and Appendix B, S. 2, p.4; FA, 1931, pp.46-53.

[71] 'Curjel Report', Appendix A, p.v. Some Bengali women who came alone to the mills had the same experience. *Factory Commission 1890*, pp.87-93.

[72] 'Curjel Report', Appendix A, p.IV.

[73] Ibid., p.v.

[74] Compare Chakrabarty, 1989.

[75] RCLI, v, 1, pp.42, 341.

[76] RCLI, VI, pp.287–90.

[77] RCLI, VI, pp.287–8; 'Curjel Report', Appendix D, pp.3, 13.

[78] 'Curjel Report', Appendix D, pp.2–4; RCLI, V, 1, p.399.

[79] RCLI, Evidence, pp.287–90.

[80] 'Curjel Report', Appendix D, pp.2–4.

[81] Ibid., RCLI, V, 1, p.55.

[82] RCLI, V, 1, p.399.

[83] 'Curjel Report', Appendix D, p.4.

[84] Ibid., pp.7, 8, 13; RCLI, V, 1, pp.49–50 and VI, pp.287–8; RCLI, 'Report', pp.356–7.

[85] 'Curjel Report', Appendix D, pp.7, 13.

[86] Simmons, 'Recruiting', pp.466–7; Kamini Roy, 'Women Labour in Mines', Modern Review, April 1923, pp.511–3; 'Curjel Report', Appendix E, pp.2–4.

[87] Annual Report of the Chief Inspector of Mines in India, Calcutta, 1905, p.2, quoted in Simmons, 'Recruiting', p.461.

[88] Roy, 'Women Labour', p.511.

[89] Deshpande, Coal Report, p.6; Roy, 'Women Labour', p.511; WBSA, Comm./Comm., August 1927, A13; RCLI, 'Report', p.115; 'Curjel Report', Appendix E, p.5.

[90] RCLI, IV, 2, pp.108, 119–120; 'Curjel Report', Appendix E, pp.5–7, 12; Roy, 'Women Labour', p.511; R. Raychaudhury, 'Living Condition of the Female Workers in the Eastern Collieries (Bihar and Bengal) from 1901 to 1921', Quarterly Review of Historical Studies, 24, 4, 1381 (1984–85), MS., p.5.

[91] WBSA, Comm./Comm., February 1924, A37 and September 1927, A14–15; 'Curjel Report', Appendix E, p.3; RCLI, IV, 2, pp.119–20.

[92] Simmons, 'Recruiting', pp.462–3; WBSA, Comm./Comm., Sept. 1927, A16 and K.W.

[93] Roy, 'Women Labour', pp.511–3; 'Curjel Report', Appendix E, p.4.

[94] RCLI, V, 1, p.49 and IV, 2, p.108.

[95] 'Curjel Report', Appendix A. p.VII.

[96] Ibid.

[97] D.F. Curjel, A.W. Acton, 'Jute Dermatitis', Indian Journal of Medical Research, 12, 1924–25, 2, pp.257–60.

[98] FA, 1898, pp.3, 4; 'Curjel Report', Appendix A, p.XI.

[99] Ibid., pp.X, XI.

[100] Compare U. Sharma, 'Segregation and its Consequences in India: Rural Women in Himachal Pradesh', in P. Caplan, J.M. Bujra (eds.), Women United, Women Divided: Cross-cultural Perspectives on Female Solidarity, London, 1978.

[101] 'Curjel Report', Appendix A, pp.XVIII, XIX.

[102] WBSA, Comm./Comm., July 1927, A6–8, pp.6–7.

[103] IOLR, Indian Factory Labour Commission, II, Evidence, Parl. Papers 1909, 63, witness 165, pp.242–3; FA, 1912, p.3; 'Curjel Report', Appendix A, p.IX; FA (1912 onwards) report regularly on wages and on the difference in the pay of men and women.

[104] RCLI, Memorandum, V, Welfare; 'Curjel Report', Appendix A, p.VII.

[105] R.K. Das, The Labour Movement in India, Berlin, 1923, p.56; RCLI, 'Report', pp.37–8; IOLR, GOI, Home/Judl., February 1896, A467.

[106] *Labour Commission 1908*, pp.46–7; on the competition between Dundee and Calcutta jute mills, see Chakrabarty, 1989, pp.31–2.

[107] IOLR, GOI, Home/Judl., February 1896, A405–68.

[108] Das, *Labour Movement*, p.64; IOLR, *Report of the Textile Factories Labour Committee. Factory Labour in India*, Bombay, 1907, pp.11, 25.

[109] RCLI, v, 2, pp.77–9.

[110] 'Curjel Report', Appendix A, p.ix.

[111] WBSA, Comm./Comm., January 1929, B261; RCLI, 'Report', pp.37–8.

[112] WBSA, Comm./Comm., January 1929, B265–7.

[113] Natural disasters such as the plague epidemic in 1896–97 or, later, the influenza epidemic in 1918–19 enforced this tendency. RCLI, 'Report', pp.21, 37–8; *FA*, 1908, p.25; Bagchi, *Investment*, p.270.

[114] Bagchi, *Investment*, p.279; RCLI, v, 1, p.410; RCLI, 'Report', pp.37–8.

[115] *FA*, 1911, pp.1, 3; RCLI, v, 1, p.49; for the relationship between redundancy and crime, see: IOLR, GOB, *Annual Report on the Police Administration of the Town of Calcutta and its Suburbs*, 1907, p.9.

[116] WBSA, Comm./Comm., July 1921, A40–42; 'Curjel Report', Appendix B, S. 2, p.3; Chakrabarty, 1989, pp.35 ff.

[117] *FA*, 1927, pp.30–1 and 1928, p.12, 1930, p.18, 1931, p.7; Comm./ Comm., January 1929, B261–6.

[118] RCLI, v, 1, p.40; *Duars Committee 1910*, p.4.

[119] RCLI, v, 1, p.42.

[120] Ibid., pp.42, 341; 'Curjel Report', Report, p.5 and Appendix D, p.5.

[121] M.C. Matheson, *Indian Industry*, Oxford, 1930, pp.74–6.

[122] RCLI, v, 1, pp.36, 179; R. Raychaudhuri, 'Living Condition', MS, pp.6–7.

[123] *Annual Report of the Chief Inspector of Mines in India*, Calcutta, 1906; quoted in R. Raychaudhuri, 'Living Condition', MS, p.8.

[124] RCLI, v, 1, p.32.

[125] Ibid., pp.34–5, pp.180–1.

[126] Ibid., p.36.

[127] Ibid.

[128] *FA*, 1898, p.2.

[129] *FA*, 1912, 1917, 'Housing'; RCLI, v, 1, p.264; RCLI, 'Report', p.256; 'Curjel Report', Report, p.6 and Appendix B, S. 2, p.9 and S.12, p.2.

[130] RCLI, v, 1, p.264; 'Curjel Report', Report, p.12.

[131] *FA*, 1931, pp.46–51; RCLI, v, 1, pp.335–7; 'Curjel Report', Appendix B, S. 2, pp.4, 7; M.D. Morris, *The Emergence of an Industrial Labour Force in India*, Berkeley, 1965, pp.201–2. Morris describes the division of the Bombay labour force into Hindus and Muslims on the one hand and the so-called Untouchables on the other.

[132] 'Curjel Report', Appendix B, S. 2, pp. 3, 5, 6, 13.

[133] Ibid., S. 12, p.2.

[134] RCLI, v, 1, p.32.

[135] 'Curjel Report', Appendix B, Interview sheets, Soora and Anglo-Indian Jute Mill.

[136] RCLI, v, 1, pp.402–3; 'Curjel Report', Appendix B, S.3, p.3. See chapter 4.

[137] T. Sarkar, 'Politics and Women in Bengal—the Conditions and Meaning of Participation', *Indian Economic and Social History Review*, 21, 1984, p.95.

[138] See A.V. John, *By the Sweat of their Brow: Women Workers at Victorian Coal Mines*, London, 1979; E.P. Tsurumi, 'Female Textile Workers and the Failure of Early Trade Unionism in Japan', *History Workshop Journal*, 1984, pp.3–27.

[139] D. Chakrabarty, 'Trade Unions in a Hierarchical Culture. The Jute Workers of Calcutta, 1920–50', in R. Guha (ed.), *Subaltern Studies III*, Delhi, 1984, pp.116–52; Chakrabarty, 1989, p.4; Chakrabarty does not approach the gender question, but shows how trade unions and workers had internalized traditional values. For a critical appraisal of the Indian National Congress's relations with women, see G. Forbes, 'The Politics of Respectability: Indian Women and the Indian National Congress', in D.A. Low, *The Indian National Congress: Centenary Hindsights*, Delhi, 1988, pp.54–97.

CONCLUSION

The Bengali women we have encountered in these pages were neither the wretched victims of orthodox Hindu customs nor the glorified goddesses of their homes. But these two concepts were the ideal types of British and Bengali male perceptions of womanhood in Bengal between 1890 and 1930. Both sets of perceptions envisaged female emancipation. Western style social and legal reform aimed at protecting women individually against extreme forms of male domination in the family, such as early marriage and enforced widowhood. Female education was seen as essential for equipping women with the intellectual autonomy a wife or mother should have. Bengali ideas of female emancipation centred on preparing women for their duties towards their families and their nation.

Women were the different 'other' which justified their subordination. To British and Bengali men their otherness was based on gender. Both groups of men used their perceptions of women in support of wider political and social strategies. British colonialists and Bengali nationalists referred in their arguments to their duties towards women in order to justify their political aims. In addition, for British men, racial differences made women in Bengal even more remote. British stereotypes regarding Indian women were particularly long-lasting because colonial officials had few direct contacts with women which might have challenged their views. Colonial concepts of Bengali gender relations, for example, influenced policies towards prostitutes and women freedom fighters as well as social reformist legislation, such as the Age of Consent Act. British views on women in Bengal were part of a specific colonial knowledge which in its claimed objectivity structured alleged Indian social backwardness and justified the imposition of colonial order.

Between 1890 and 1930 gender assumptions inherent in the
dominant discourses of the period were not fundamentally challenged. It was not even clear which type of emancipation would
win the day. Middle-class women's organizations and professional women supported colonial protection of women's individual rights while the emerging patterns of female education
and women's nationalist commitment followed a concept of
progress which was informed by Bengali intellectual developments since the 1880s.

However, throughout our period women conquered social
space which hitherto had been the prerogative of men. But it was
a matter of class, not gender or culture, whether this implied
greater or lesser opportunities for self-realization, economic
power and social and political representation. Women who had
traditionally worked outside their homes, either with their artisan
husbands or independently, often catering to the needs of zenana-
bound women, found it harder in 1930 to earn their living than
did women fourty years earlier. They looked for work in new
areas, particularly the domestic services, but their economic position continually deteriorated. The same applied to peasant
women whose families had been pushed off the land. In contrast,
Bengali middle-class women profited from the enormous expansion of female education after the turn of the century and, by 1920,
were gradually entering the labour market in the professions.
Only in independent India in the wake of the Bengal famine and
partition did this become a mass phenomenon; but from the
Swadeshi period onwards women teachers in particular came to
be slowly accepted in Hindu society.

These changes were accompanied, or often prepared, by
developments regarding women's position in the family. In the
1920s many Hindu women had to still keep strict purdah while
others were already demonstrating publicly against British rule.
Despite such discrepancies the general trends were marked.
Partnership, albeit not equality, developed in husband-wife
relationships. Rural-urban migration undermined the principle of
seniority among the women of a family because young daughters-
in-law accompanied their husbands when they sought work away
from home. Early marriage, dowry and the maltreatment of
daughters-in-law did not disappear, but they came to be regarded
as social evils.

The context in which the 'woman's question' was seen changed fundamentally. Isolated changes were often mirror images of nineteenth-century developments in western oriented families of the Brahmo Samaj as analysed by Meredith Borthwick. But the nineteenth-century discursive framework which had linked the position of women to issues of equality and enlightenment, values and attitudes propagated in European bourgeois revolutions, was replaced by idioms close to Indian nationalism and Hindu culture. Emancipation aimed less at the self-realization of individual women than at the pre-conditions for a free India. Infant marriage, dowry suicides and other signs of female subordination became incompatible with Bengali self-respect. The glorification of femininity and motherhood in Indian nationalist ideology as well as the rejection of the superiority of 'British' masculinity could not be convincingly argued without permitting women more influence in private and public life.

To some extent the analysis focused on the inter-relatedness of the discourses on women and nationalism. My main concern was to follow the colonial and Bengali discourses on femininity from the sphere of male-dominated politics into the areas where women were inevitably and more immediately affected, that is, in the family, in educational institutions and at work. This point of departure implies that other possible cross references have been neglected and that some developments which were relevant to women in Bengal have not been examined. Thus women's voluntary organizations, women's revolutionary activities and the struggle for female suffrage—fields in which much work has already been done—have been omitted from this analysis.[1]

It is possible to imagine connections between woman-related and other than nationalist discourses which would have complemented my analysis. I have, for example, only touched upon the important question regarding the impact of colonial law on women, in particular with reference to landed property.[2] Moreover, my study has ignored the fact that gender issues were a vital part of communalist tensions. In the wake of the Sarda Act in 1929 communalism gained an all-India significance. And in Bengal, Hindus and Muslims were distracted from their anti-colonial activities by accusations of the mutual abduction and rape of their women.[3] Here, I suggest, lies a particularly valid area of future research. Discourses on communalism and gender highlight how social change challenged established loyalties at family, village and community levels and how women were perceived in connection with new points of reference while accepted systems of control and social hierarchies were undermined.

In India, today, feminist scholarship is well established and conscious of its non-western identity. Some years ago Veena Das stressed that the western feminist concern with sexuality could not be the main concern of Indian women. She rejected the identification of heterosexuality with female subordination and the centrality of women's bodily experience as emphasized by French feminists. Although her summary of western feminism was not comprehensive, Veena Das had a point when she insisted on the special character of Indian feminism. 'They have taken', she wrote about Indian women, 'femininity as their model for organizing power and truth as Gandhi understood these to be.'[4] It was not just Gandhi, but many strands of Indian nationalism which adopted femininity as their central point of reference. This notion developed in Bengal between 1890 and 1930 and influenced nationalist politics and women alike.

NOTES

[1] On voluntary organizations and women revolutionaries, see G. Forbes quoted in earlier chapters and B. Southard,'Bengal Women's Education League: Pressure Group and Professional Association', *Modern Asian Studies*, 18, 1984, pp.55–88. On revolutionaries, Ishanee Mukherjee is preparing a PhD thesis for Calcutta University. On suffrage, see B. Southard,'The Defeat of Women's Suffrage in Bengal in 1921', and'Swarajists and Suffragists', both unpublished papers.

[2] For a comparison with work on another Indian region, see G.C. Kozlowski,'Muslim Women and the Control of Property in North India', *Indian Economic and Social History Review*, 24, 1987, pp.163–81.

[3] NAI, GOI, Home/Judl., 18/1/30, S.No.1–42; WBSA, GOB, Police/Police, 535/29, S.No.1–2.

[4] V. Das,'Gender Studies, Cross-Cultural Comparison and the Colonial Organization of Knowledge', *Berkshire Review*, 21, 1986, p.74.

BIBLIOGRAPHY

A. GOVERNMENT ARCHIVES AND PRIVATE PAPERS

1. Government Proceedings

India Office Library and Records, London
Government of India, Bengal Judicial Proceedings, 1890.
Government of India, Home Proceedings, 1886–1931:
    Education, Judicial, Medical Branches.
Government of India, Legislative Proceedings, 1891.

National Archives of India, New Delhi
Government of India, Home Proceedings, 1888–1933:
    Education, Establishment, Jails, Judicial, Medical,
    Police, Public, Sanitary Branches.

West Bengal State Archives, Calcutta
Government of Bengal, Commerce Department/Commerce
    Branch, Proceedings, 1921–1929.
Government of Bengal, Political and Police Proceedings, 1920–
    1930.
Government of Bengal, Confidential Files and Papers, 1907–1931.
    'Towards Freedom Files', Paper 47–65.

2. Manuscripts

India Office Library and Records
    Lansdowne Papers, MSS.Eur. D558.
    Elgin Papers, MSS.Eur. F84.
    Hamilton Papers, MSS.Eur. D510.
    Zetland Papers, MSS. Eur. D609.

Reading Papers, MSS.Eur. E238.
Lady Reading Papers, MSS.Eur. E316.
Lytton Papers, MSS.Eur. F160.
Irwin Papers, MSS.Eur. C152.

Nehru Memorial Museum and Library, New Delhi
Oral History Transcripts:
Smt Kamaladevi Chattopadhyaya.
Smt Kamala Das Gupta.
Bhupendra Kumar Datta.
Smt Kalyani Bhattarcharjee.
Smt Prabhavati Mirza.

All India Women's Conference (AIWC) Papers (Microfilm)
Bhupendranath Basu Papers.

Miscellaneous
Ramananda Chatterjee, Diary, 1890; held by Smt
Paramita Viswanathan, Calcutta.

B. PUBLISHED AND SECONDARY MATERIAL

1. Official Publications

U.K. Parliamentary Papers
Report of the Indian Factory Commission, 1890, 1890–1891, LIX.
Report of the Indian Factory Labour Commission, 1908,'Evidence',
Vol. II, 1909, LXIII.

Other U.K. Official Publications
Report of the Indian Jails Committee, 1919–1920, London 1921.
Royal Commission on Agriculture in India, Evidence taken in Bengal,
Vol. IV, London 1927.
'Royal Commission on Labour in India, Report', *Reports from*
Commissioners, Inspectors, and Others, Vol. XI, London 1930–1931.
Royal Commission on Labour in India, Evidence, Vol. IV, 2, V, 1–2,
London 1931.
Memorandum on Labour Conditions in Bengal. Prepared for the use of
the Royal Commission on Indian Labour, 1931.

Government of India and Government of Bengal Official
Publications Series
Administration Reports on the Jails of Bengal, 1898–1921.
Census of India. Bengal, 1891, 1901, 1911, 1921, 1931.
Census of India. Calcutta, Towns and Suburbs, 1891, 1901, 1911, 1921, 1931.
Financial and Commercial Statistics of British India, 1892/3–1904/5.
Reports on the Inspection of Mines in India, 1894–1931.
Reports on the Native Newspapers, Bengal, 1890–1930.
Reports on the Police Administration of the Lower Provinces,
Bengal Presidency, 1891–1931.
Reports on the Police Administration of the Town of Calcutta and its Suburbs, 1890–1930.
Reports on the Working of the Indian Factory Act, 1896–1931.
Review of Education in Bengal. Quinquennial Reports, 1892–93 to 1932.
Statistics of British India, 1905/6–1912/13.

Miscellaneous Reports (Chronological)
Report of the Committee appointed under the orders of the Governor General in Council to enquire into certain matters connected with Jail Administration in India, Calcutta 1889.
Report on the Labour Enquiry Commission, Calcutta 1896.
The Unrepealed General Acts of the Governor General in Council, 1891–1898, Vol. VI, Calcutta, 1899.
Report on Labour in Bengal 1906 by B. Foley, Calcutta 1906.
Report of the Textile Factories Labour Committee. Factory Labour in India, Bombay 1907.
Report of the Duars Committee, 1910.
Report of the Indian Industrial Commission, 1916–1918, Calcutta 1918.
Report of the Indian Jails Committee, 1919–1920. Minutes of Evidence taken in Burma, Bengal and Assam, vol. III, Calcutta 1922.
Report of the Government of Bengal Unemployment Enquiry Committee, vol. I, Calcutta 1924.
Report of the Indian Economic Enquiry Committee, Minutes of Evidence, vol. II, Calcutta 1926.
Report of the Bengal Jails Enquiry Committee 1927.
Bulletin No. 33, Rice Milling Industry, Calcutta, 1928 (written by S. C. Mitter for GOB, Department of Industries).

Health Bulletin Bo. 15: Maternal Mortality in Childbirth in India. A Summary of the Investigation Conducted under the Indian Research Fund Association 1925, Calcutta 1928.
Report of the Age of Consent Committee, 1928–1929, Calcutta 1929.
Reports of the Age of Consent Committee, 1928–1929, Evidence, vol. VI, Calcutta 1930.
The Legislative Assembly Debates (Official Report), vols. II–III, 1928; I, IV–V, 1929; I, II, IV, 1930; I, V, 1931, Simla, 1929–1932.
Report of the Bengal Provincial Banking Enquiry Committee 1929–1930, vol. I, Calcutta 1930.
Report on an Enquiry into Conditions of Labour in the Indian Coal-Mining Industry, 1946 (written by S. R. Deshpande for the Labour Investigation Committee, 1944–1945).
Report on an Enquiry into Conditions of Labour in the Jute Mill Industry in India, 1946 (written by S. R. Deshpande for the Labour Investigation Committee, 1944–1945).
Report on an Enquiry into Conditions of Labour in Plantations in India, 1946 (written by D. V. Rege for the Labour Investigation Committee, 1944–1945).
Labour Bureau, Ministry of Labour, *Economic and Social Status of Women Workers in India,* Simla 1953.

2. *Newspapers and Journals*

English
Forward, 1924.
Modern Review, 1909–1931.
The Englishwoman, 1909–1914.
The Girl's Own Paper, 1880–1930.
The Indian Ladies Magazine, 1903–1908.
The Journal of the Association of Medical Women in India, 1923–1934.
The Statesman and the Friend of India, weekly edition, 1891.

Bengali
Banga Laksmi, 1334–1337 (1927–1930).
Bharati, 1297–1331 (1890–1924).
Bharat Mahila, 1312–1319 (1905–1912).
Prabasi, 1311–1332 (1904–1925).

3. *Contemporary Material*

Anderson, H., *The Social Evil*, Calcutta, n.d.

Anstey, V., *The Economic Development of India*, London, 1929.

Balfour, M.I., 'Co-operation', *The Journal of the Association of Medical Women in India*, 11, June 1923.

Balfour, M.I. and R. Young, *The Work of Medical Women in India*, London 1929

Bandhyopadhyaya, Bhupendranath, *Yuga-mahatmya*, Calcutta 1926 (Bengali).

Bandhopadhyaya, M., *The Puppet's Tale*, Delhi 1968 (first Bengali ed., 1936).

Banerji, B., *Pather Panchali*, Bloomington 1968.

Banganari, *Agami*, Calcutta 1926 (Bengali).

Basu, Priyanath, *Grihadharma*, Calcutta 1934 (Bengali).

Basu, Sacindraprasad, *Sraddhanjali*, Calcutta 1924 (Bengali).

Basu, Sankari Prasad, *Amader Nivedita*, Calcutta 1934 (Bengali).

Bhattacharyya, N.C. and L.A. Natesan (eds.), *Some Bengal Villages*, Calcutta 1932.

Bhattarcharya, Digindranarayan, *Bidhabar Nirjjala Ekadasi*, Sirajganj 1926 (Bengali).

Bidyabhusan, Upendranath, *Binodini o Tarasundari*, Calcutta 1919 (Bengali).

—*Tinakari*, Calcutta 1919 (Bengali).

Binodini Dasi, *Amar Katha*, Calcutta 1912 (Bengali).

Bisvas, Carucandra, *Kanya-day ba Hindu-bibaha-samskara*, Calcutta 1910 (Bengali).

Bose, S.C., *The Hindoos As They Are*, Calcutta 1883.

Caton, A.R. (ed.), *The Key of Progress*, London 1930.

Chakrabartti, Girijasundar, *Nari-dharma*, Calcutta 1908 (Bengali).

Chakrabarti, Yadunath, *Kayekkhani Patra*, Calcutta 1902 (Bengali).

Chaudhurani, Sarala Debi, *Jibaner Jharapata*, Calcutta 1975 (Bengali).

Chatterjee, B.K., *Krishnakanta's Will* (first published 1882), New York 1962.

Chatterjee, S.C., *Chandranath*, Bombay 1969 (first Bengali ed., 1916).

Curjel, D.F. and H.W. Acton, 'Jute Dermatitis', *Indian Journal of Medical Research*, 12, 2, 1924–1925.

Das, R.K., *The Labour Movement in India*, Berlin 1923.

—*Plantation Labour in India*, Calcutta 1931.

Datta, Upendranath, *Deser Ahban*, Calcutta 1921 (Bengali).

Day, Lal Behari, *Bengal Peasant Life* (first published 1874), Calcutta 1969.

De, Durgadas, *Payajare Paji*, Calcutta 1891 (Bengali).

Dutt, G.S., *A Woman of India being the Life of Saroj Nalini*, London 1929.

Gandhi, M.K., *Women and Social Injustice*, Ahmedabad 1942.

Gangopadhyaya, Abha, *Amaderi ekjan*, Calcutta 1951 (Bengali).

Ghose, Bhubanicaran, *Parinay-kahini*, Calcutta 1903 (Bengali).

Ghose-Jaya, Kumudini, *Bidhaba-bibaha Apatti Khandan*, Calcutta 1926 (Bengali).

Ghose, Manmathanath, *Svarna Smriti*, Delhi 1932 (Bengali).

Ghose, Susantakumar (ed.), *Nari-ratna*, Calcutta 1919 (Bengali).

Gupta, J.N., *Rangpur Today. A Study in Local Problems of a Bengal District*, Calcutta 1918.

Gupta, Saudamini, *Kanyar Prati Upades*, Dhaka 1918 (Bengali).

Hemlata Debi, *Jalpana*, Calcutta 1935 (Bengali).

Indira Debi, *Amar Katha*, Calcutta 1912 (Bengali).

Kara, Sachindranath, *Svadesanandera Katha*, Dhaka 1920,

Lord Lytton in Bengal, Being a Selection from his Speeches as Governor of Bengal, 1922–1927, Calcutta 1929.

Majumdar, Baradakanta, *Naritattva*, Calcutta 1889 (Bengali).

Manadasundari Debi, *Patitar Atma-charit*, Calcutta 1929 (Bengali).

Matheson, M.C., *Indian Industry*, Oxford 1930.

Max Müller, F., 'Rukhmabai and Ramabai', *Nineteenth Century Studies*, 10, 1975 (reprint from *Indian Magazine*, 201, 1887).

Mazumdar, J.K., *Cottage Industries in Bengal*, Calcutta 1927.

Mitra, Giribala, *Ramanir Karttabha*, Calcutta 1888 (Bengali).

Mitra, Premendra, 'Michel', *Premendra Granthabali*, Calcutta, n.d., pp.1–48 (Bengali).

Mukherjee, R., *Six Villages in Bengal*, Bombay 1971 (written 1946).

Mukherjee, S.C., *Prostitution in India*, Calcutta 1934.

Mukhopadhyaya, Bipradasa, *Yuvak-yuvati*, Calcutta 1891 (seventh ed., 1922) (Bengali).

Mukhopadhyaya, Bhubanachandra, *Ami Ramani*, Calcutta 1880 (Bengali).

Mukhopadhyaya, Gangaprasad, *Matrisiksa*, Calcutta 1902 (first ed., 1871) (Bengali).

Mukhopadhaya, Yogindranath, *Jiban Raksa,* Calcutta 1887 (Bengali).

Nyayaratna, Nabacandra, *Grihini,* Calcutta 1918 (Bengali).

Pal, Bipin Chandra, *Memories of My Life and Times,* vol. I, Calcutta 1932.

—*Narinirvacanadhikar,* Calcutta 1921 (Bengali).

Prabhabati Debi Saraswati, *Amal-prasun,* Calcutta 1900 (Bengali).

Ray, Kamini, *Thakurmar Cithi,* Calcutta 1924 (Bengali).

Ray, Motilal, *Nari-mangal,* Calcutta 1925 (Bengali).

Ray Chaudhuri, Amarendranath, *Sonar Satin,* Calcutta 1898 (Bengali).

Rayachaudhuri, Debiprasanna, *Bibahasamskara,* Calcutta 1898 (Bengali).

—*Murala,* Calcutta 1892 (Bengali).

Rayachaudhuri, Girijaprasanna, *Griha Laksmi,* Calcutta 1887 (Bengali).

Samkhyatirtha, Priyanath, *Nabina o Prabina,* Sibpur 1935 (Bengali).

Saroj -Nalini Dutt Memorial Association for Women's Work in Bengal, *Annual Report of the SNDMA,* From the Year 1925 to 1931, Calcutta, n.d.

Sarvadhikari, Sushilaprasad, *Bijali,* Calcutta 1932 (Bengali).

Sen, Dakshinacharan, *Bharatoddhar,* Calcutta 1930 (Bengali).

Sen, Dineshchandra, *Grihasri,* Calcutta 1915 (Bengali).

Sengupta, Anandachandra, *Jananir Karttabya,* Calcutta 1917 (Bengali).

Seth, B., *Labour in the Indian Coal Industry,* Bombay 1929.

Sherring, M.A., *History of Protestant Missions in India from their Commencement in 1706 to 1881,* London 1884.

Subodhbala Debi, *Niraba Sadhana,* Calcutta 1913 (Bengali).

Tagore, Rabindranath, 'Strir Patra', *Galpaguccha* (first published, 1914), Calcutta 1980, 669–80 (Bengali).

—*The Home and the World (Ghare Baire),* English translation, S. Tagore, London 1919

Uma Debi, *Balika-jiban,* Calcutta 1927 (Bengali).

Urquhart, M.M., *Women in Bengal,* Calcutta 1926.

Vidyabhusan, Upendranath (Rayachaudhuri), *Basantakumari,* Calcutta 1921 (Bengali).

Weitbrecht, *The Women of India and Christian Work in the Zenana,* London 1875.

4. Other Books and Articles

Afshar, H. (ed.), *Women, Work and Ideology in the Third World*, London 1985.

Agarwal, B., 'Women, Poverty and Agricultural Growth in India', *Journal of Peasant Studies*, 13, 4, 1986.

Allen, M. and S.N. Mukherjee (eds.), *Women in India and Nepal*, Canberra 1982.

Allen, M., 'Introduction. The Hindu View of Women', in M. Allen, S.N. Mukherjee (eds.), *Women in India and Nepal*, Canberra 1982.

Arnold, D., 'Bureaucratic Recruitment and Subordination in Colonial India: The Madras Constabulary, 1859-1947', in R. Guha (ed.), *Subaltern Studies IV*, Delhi 1985.

—(ed.), *Imperial Medicine and Indigenous Societies*, Manchester 1988.

Badran, M., 'Beyond the Mirage', *The Women's Review of Books*, 4, January 1987.

Bagal, J.C., *Women's Education in Eastern India—The First Phase (Mainly Based on Contemporary Records)*, Calcutta 1956.

Bagchi, A.K., *Private Investment in India*, Cambridge 1972.

Ballhatchet, K.A., *Race, Sex and Class Under the Raj. Imperial Attitudes and Policies and their Critics, 1793–1905*, London 1980.

Banerjee, N., 'Working Women in Colonial Bengal: Modernization and Marginalization', in K. Sangari and S. Vaid (eds.), *Recasting Women. Essays in Colonial History*, Delhi 1989

Banerjee, S., *National Awakening and the Bangabasi*, Calcutta 1968.

Banerjee, S., 'Marginalization of Women's Popular Culture in Nineteenth-Century Bengal', in K. Sankari and S. Vaid (eds.), *Recasting Women. Essays in Colonial History*, Delhi 1989

Barrett, M., *Women's Oppression Today*, London 1980.

Basham, A.L., *The Wonder That Was India*, London 1985 (first ed.,1954).

Basu, A., *The Growth of Education and Political Development in India (1898–1920)*, Bombay 1974.

Bates, C. and M. Carter, 'Tribal and Indentured Migrants in Colonial India: Modes of Recruitment and Forms of Incorporation', in P. Robb (ed.), *Dalit Movements and the Meaning of Labour in India*, OUP, Delhi 1993.

Bhattacharyya, B., *Satyagrahas in Bengal 1921–1939*, Calcutta 1977.

Bhattacharyya, N.N., *History of the Sakti Religion*, New Delhi 1974.

Black, N. and D.B. Cottrell (eds.), *Women and World Change*, Beverley Hills 1981.

Bloch, M. and J.H. Bloch, 'Women and Dialectics of Nature in Eighteenth-Century French Thought', in C.P. MacCormack and M. Strathern (eds.), *Nature, Culture and Gender*, Cambridge 1980.

Boman-Behram, B.K., *Educational Controversies in India. The Cultural Conquest of India under British Imperialism*, Bombay 1943.

Borthwick, M., *The Changing Role of Women in Bengal, 1849–1905*, Princeton 1984.

Bose, M.M., *Post-Chaitanya Sahajiya Cult of Bengal*, Calcutta, 1930.

Bose, N.S., *Indian Awakening and Bengal*, Calcutta 1976.

—*Racism, Struggle for Equality and Indian Nationalism*, Calcutta 1981.

Bose, S., *Agrarian Bengal. Economy, Social Structure and Politics, 1919–1947*, Cambridge 1986.

Boserup, E., *Women's Role in Economic Development*, London 1970.

Broomfield, J.H., *Elite Conflict in a Plural Society: Twentieth-Century Bengal*, Bombay 1968.

Carstairs, G.M., *The Twice-Born*, Bloomington 1958.

Chakrabarty, D., 'Trade Unions in a Hierarchical Culture. The Jute Workers of Calcutta, 1920-1950', in R. Guha (ed), *Subaltern Studies*, III, New Delhi 1984.

—*Rethinking Working Class History. Bengal 1890–1940*, Princeton 1989.

Chakraborty, B., 'Peasants and the Bengal Congress, 1928-38', *South Asia Research*, 5, 1985.

Chakraborty Spivak, G., *In Other Worlds. Essays in Cultural Politics*, New York 1987.

Chakraborty, U., *Condition of Bengali Women Around the Second Half of the Nineteenth Century*, Calcutta 1963.

Chaplan, P., *Class and Gender in India*, London 1985.

Chaplan, P. and J.M. Bujra (eds.), *Women United, Women Divided*, London 1978.

Chatterjee, B., 'A Century of Social Reform for Women's Status', *The Indian Journal of Social Work*, XLI, 3, 1980.

Chatterjee, P., *Bengal 1920–1947: The Land Question*, Calcutta 1984.

— *Nationalist Thought and the Colonial World—a Derivative Discourse*, London 1986.

Chattopadhyaya, Manju, *Sramiknetri Santoskumari*, Calcutta 1984 (Bengali).

Cominos, P.T., 'Late Victorian Sexual Respectability and the Social System', *International Review of Social History*, 8, 1963.

— 'Innocent Femina Sensualis in Unconscious Conflict', M. Vicinus (ed.), *Suffer and Be Still: Women in the Victorian Age*, Bloomington 1972.

Daly, M., *Gyn/Ecology*, London 1979.

Das, V., 'Gender Studies, Cross-Cultural Comparison and the Colonial Organization of Knowledge', *Berkshire Review*, 21, 1986.

Das Gupta, Kamala, *Svadhinata-Sangrame Banglar Nari*, Calcutta 1963 (Bengali).

Das Gupta, R., 'Factory Labour in Eastern India: Sources of Supply, 1855–1946. Some Preliminary Findings', *Indian Economic and Social History Review*, XIII, 1976.

Dasgupta, S.B., *Obscure Religious Cults* (first published, 1946), Calcutta 1962.

Das Gupta, U., *Santiniketan and Sriniketan*, Visva-Bharati, Calcutta 1983.

Davidoff, L., 'Class and Gender in Victorian England', in J.L. Newton et al. (eds.), *Sex and Class in Women's History*, London 1983.

Davies, N.Z., *Society and Culture in Early Modern France*, London 1975.

Davin, A., 'Imperialism and Motherhood', *History Workshop Journal*, 5, 1978.

Deb, Chitra, *Thakurbarir Andar Mahal*, Calcutta 1982 (Bengali).

— *Antahpurer Atmakatha*, Calcutta 1984 (Bengali).

Derrida, J., *Of Grammatology*. Baltimore 1976.

Desai, P.B., *Size and Sex Composition of Population in India 1901–1961*, London 1969.

Dimock, E.C. Jr., *The Place of the Hidden Moon*, Chicago 1966.

Douglas, M., *Purity and Danger* (first published, 1966), London 1985.

Dumont, L., *Homo Hierarchicus* (first published, 1966), Chicago 1980.

Elias, N., *Über den Prozess der Zivilisation*, Vol. I, Frankfurt 1977.

Engels, D. and S. Marks (eds.), *Contesting Colonial Hegemony. State and Society in Africa and India*, London 1994.

Engels, D., 'The Age of Consent Act of 1891: Colonial Ideology in Bengal', *South Asia Research*, 3, 1983.

—'The Limits of Gender Ideology: Bengali Women, the Colonial State, and the Private Sphere, 1890-1930', *Women's Studies International Forum*, 12, 1989.

—'History and Sexuality in India: Discursive Trends', *Trends in History*, 4, 1990.

— *The Encounter of European and Indigenous Law in 19th- and 20th-Century Africa and Asia*, Oxford 1992.

—'The Myth of the Family Unit: Adivasi Women in Coal Mines and the Tea Plantations in Early 20th-Century Bengal', in P. Robb (ed.), *Dalit Movements and the Meanings of Labour in India*, Delhi 1993.

—'The Politics of Childbirth: British and Bengali Women in Contest, 1890–1901', in P. Robb (ed.), *Society and Ideology*, Delhi 1993.

—'Wives, Widows and Workers—Women and the Law in Colonial India', in W.J. Mommsen and J.A. de Moor (eds.), *European Expansion and Law, The Encounter of European and Indigenous Law in 19th-and 20th-Century Africa and Asia*, Oxford 1992.

Everett, J.M., *Women and Social Change in India*, New York 1979.

Forbes, G., 'The Ideals of Indian Womanhood: Six Bengali Women During the Independence Movement', in J.R. McLane (ed.), *Bengal in the Nineteenth and Twentieth Centuries*, Michigan 1975.

— *Positivism in Bengal*, Calcutta 1975.

— (ed.), Sudha Mazumdar, *A Pattern of Life, The Memoirs of an Indian Woman*, New Delhi 1977.

—'Women and Modernity: The Issue of Child Marriage in India', *Women's Studies International Quarterly*, 2, 1979.

—'Women's Movement in India: Traditional Symbols and New Roles', in M.S.A. Rao (ed.), *Social Movements in India*, vol. 2, New Delhi 1979.

—'Goddesses or Rebels? The Women Revolutionaries of Bengal', *The Oracle*, II, 2, 1980.

—'Caged Tigers: "First Wave" Feminists in India', *Women's Studies*, II, 5, 1982.

—'From Purdah to Politics: The Social Feminism of the All-India Women's Organizations', in H. Papananek and G. Minault (eds.), *Separate Worlds, Studies of Purdah in South Asia*, Delhi 1982.

—'Mothers and Sisters: Feminism and Nationalism in the Thought of Subhas Chandra Bose', *Asian Studies*, 2, 1984.

—'The Politics of Respectability: Indian Women and the Indian National Congress', in D.A. Low (ed.), *The Indian National Congress: Centenary Hindsights*, Delhi 1988.

—'Managing Midwifery in India', in D. Engels and S. Marks (eds.), *Contesting Colonial Hegemony. State and Society in Africa and India*, London 1994.

Foucault, M., *The Birth of the Clinic*, London 1973.

Discipline and Punish, Harmondsworth 1979.

Fox-Genovese, E., 'Placing Women's History in History', *New Left Review*, No. 133, 1982.

French, H.W., *The Swan's White Waters*, London 1974.

Fruzzetti, L., *The Gift of the Virgin*, New Brunswick 1982.

Ghose, L., 'Social and Educational Movements for Women by Women', in K. Nag (ed.), *Bethune School and College Centenary Volume 1849–1949*, Calcutta 1949.

Goody, J., 'Inheritance, Property and Women: Some Comparative Considerations', in J. Goody, J. Thirsk and E.P. Thompson (eds.), *Family and Inheritance. Rural Society in Western Europe 1200–1800*, Cambridge 1976.

Gopal, S., *British Policy in India 1858–1905*, Cambridge 1965.

Gray, J.M., '"Bengal and Britain", Culture Contact and the Reinterpretation of Hinduism', in R.M. van Baumer (ed.), *Aspects of Bengali Society and History*, Honolulu 1975.

Greenberger, A.J., *The British Image of India: A Study in the Literature of Imperialism, 1880–1960*, London 1969.

Greenough, P.R., *Prosperity and Misery in Modern Bengal*, Oxford 1982.

Guha, R. (ed.), *Subaltern Studies*, Vols. I–IV, Delhi 1981–1985.

Gupta, E.M., *Brata and Alpana in Bengalen*, Wiesbaden 1983.

Gupta, S. and R. Gombrich, 'Another View of Widow-burning and Womanliness in Indian Public Culture', *Journal of Commonwealth and Comparative Politics*, 12, 1984.

Gupta, S., 'Tantric Sakta Literature in Modern Indian Languages', in T. Goudriaan and S. Gupta, *Hindu Tantric and Sakta Literature*, Wiesbaden 1981 [Gonda, J. (ed.), *A History Of Indian Literature*, vol. II].

Harris, O., 'Households as Natural Units', in K. Young et al. (eds.), *Of Marriage and the Market*, London 1984.

Hechter, M., *The Internal Colonialism. The Celtic Fringe in British National Development, 1536–1966*, London 1975.

Heimsath, C.H., 'The Origin and Enactment of the Indian Age of Consent Bill, 1891', *Journal of Asian Studies*, 21, 4, 1962.

— *Indian Nationalism and Hindu Social Reform*, Princeton 1964.

Henriques, F., *Prostitution and Society*, London 1962.

Higonnet, M., 'Speaking Silences: Women's Suicides', in S.R. Suleiman (ed.), *The Female Body in Western Culture*, Cambridge, Mass. 1986.

Hoch-Smith, J. and A. Spring (eds.), *Women in Ritual and Symbolic Roles*, New York 1978.

Holton, S. Stanley, *Feminism and Democracy, Women's Suffrage and Reform Politics in Britain 1900–1918*, Cambridge 1986.

Huque, M.A., *The Man Behind the Plough*, Calcutta 1939.

Inden, R., *Marriage and Rank in Bengali Culture*, New Delhi 1976.

—'Orientalist Constructions of India', *Modern Asian Studies*, 20, 1986.

— and R. Nicholas, *Kinship in Bengali Culture*, Chicago 1977.

Isherwood, C., *Ramakrishna and his Disciples*, London 1965.

Jaggi, O.P., *Impact of Science and Technology in Modern India*, Delhi 1984.

Jeffery, P., *Frogs in a Well. Indian Women in Purdah*, London 1979.

— R. Jeffery and A. Lyon, *Labour Pains and Labour Power*, London 1989.

Jeffery, R., 'Doctors and Congress: the Role of Medical Men and Medical Politics in Indian Nationalism', in M. Shepperdson and C. Simmons (eds.), *The Indian National Congress and the Political Economy of India 1885–1985*, Aldershot 1988, pp.160–73.

— *The Politics of Health in India*, Berkeley 1988.

John, A.V., *By the Sweat of their Brow: Women Workers at Victorian Coal Mines*, London 1979.

— (ed.), *Unequal Opportunities, Women's Employment in England, 1800–1918*, Oxford 1986.

Joshi, C., 'Bonds of Community, Ties of Religion: Kanpur Textile Workers in the Early Twentieth Century', *Indian Economic and Social History Review*, 22, 1985.

Joshi, V.C. (ed.), *Rammohun Roy and the Process of Modernization in India*, New Delhi 1975.

Kakar, S., *The Inner World*, New Delhi 1978.

Kane, P.V., *History of the Dharmasastra*, Poona 1974.

Kelly, J., *Women, History, and Theory. The Essays of Joan Kelly*, Chicago 1984.

Kennedy, K.T., *The Chaitanya Movement*, Calcutta 1925.

Kishwar, M., 'Gandhi on Women', *Economic and Political Weekly*, 10, 40, October 5 and 41, October 12, 1986.

—'The Daughters of Aryavarta', *Indian Economic and Social History Review*, 23, 1986.

Kopf, D., *British Orientalism and the Bengal Renaissance. The Dynamics of Indian Modernization 1773–1835*, Berkeley 1969.

— *The Bramo Samaj and the Shaping of the Modern Indian Mind*, Princeton 1979.

Kozlowski, G.C., 'Muslim Women and the Control of Property in North India', *Indian Economic and Social History Review*, 24, 1987.

Krishnamurty, J. (ed.), *Women in Colonial India*, Delhi 1989.

Kumar, P., *Shakti Cult and Ancient India*, Varanasi 1974.

Kumar, R., 'Family and Factory: Women in the Bombay Cotton Textile Industry, 1919-1939', *Indian Economic and Social History Review*, XX, 1983.

Laird, M.A., *Missionaries and Education in Bengal (1793–1837)*, London 1972.

Lewis, J., *The Politics of Motherhood*, London 1980.

—*Women in England 1870-1950: Sexual Divisions and Social Change*, Brighton 1984.

Liddle, J. and R. Joshi, 'Gender and Imperialism in British India', *South Asia Research*, 5, 2, 1985.

—*Daughters of Independence*, London 1986.

Liddington, J. and J. Norris, *One Hand Tied Behind Us*, London 1984 (first ed. 1978).

Macdonell, D., *Theories of Discourse. An Introduction*, London 1989 (first ed., 1986).

Mackintosh, M., 'Gender and Economics: the Sexual Division of Labour and the Subordination of Women', in K. Young et al. (eds.), *Of Marriage and the Market*, London 1984.

Maity, P.K., *Historical Studies in the Cult of the Goddess Manasa*, Calcutta 1966.

Majumdar, A.K., *Bhakti Renaissance*, Bombay 1965.

Majumdar, B.B., *Militant Nationalism in India and its Socio-Religious Background (1897–1917)*, Calcutta 1966.

Mandelbaum, D.G., *Women's Seclusion and Men's Honour. Sex Roles in North India, Bangladesh and Pakistan*, Tucson 1988.

Mani, L., 'The Production of an Official Discourse on Sakti in Early Nineteenth-century Bengal', in F. Barker et al. (eds.), *Europe and Its Others*, Volume One, Colchester 1985; also published in *Economic and Political Weekly*, 'Review of Women's Studies', 21, 17, 26 April 1986.

—'Contentious Traditions: The Debate on *Sati* in Colonial India', in K. Sangari and S. Vaid (eds.), *Recasting Women. Essays in Colonial History*, Delhi 1989.

Marks, S. and P. Richardson (eds.), *International Labour Migration: Historical Perspectives*, London 1984.

Maskiell, M., *Women between Cultures: The Lives of Kinnaird College Alumnae in British India*, Syracuse, N.Y. 1984.

Mayo, K., *Mother India*, London 1927.

Mazumdar, V., 'The Social Reform Movement in India—From Ranadeto Nehru', in B. Nanda (ed.), *Indian Women. From Purdah to Modernity*, Delhi 1976.

McCully, B.T., *English Education and the Origin of Indian Nationalism*, New York 1940.

Meer, F., *Race and Suicide in South Africa*, London 1976.

Mies, M., *The Lace Makers of Narsapur; Indian Housewives Produce for the World Market*, London 1982.

Mill, J., *The History of British India* (fourth ed.), London 1840.

Mill, J.S., *Essays on Equality, Law and Equality* (repr.), Toronto 1984.

Mitra, A., 'Bhudeb Mukhopadhyay' in A.K. Mukhopadhyay (ed.), *The Bengali Intellectual Tradition*, Calcutta 1979.

Mitra, N.N. (ed.), *The Indian Quarterly Register*, Delhi 1925–1928.

Mohanty, C.T., 'Under Western Eyes: Feminist Scholarship and Colonial Discourses', *Boundary*, 2, Spring/Fall 1984.

Morris, M.D., *The Emergence of an Industrial Labour Force in India*, Berkeley 1965.

Mukherjee, H., *A Phase of the Swadeshi Movement (National Education) 1905-1910*, Calcutta 1953.

Mukherjee, H. and U. Mukherjee, *Sri Aurobindo's Political Thought (1893–1908)*, Calcutta 1958.

Mukherjee, M., 'Impact of Modernization on Women's Occupations: A Case Study of the Rice-husking Industry in Bengal', *Indian Economic and Social History Review*, 20, 1, 1983.

Mukherjee, P., 'The Image of Women in Hinduism', *Women Studies*, IF, 6, 1983.

Mukherjee, R., *West Bengal Family Structures: 1946–1966*, New Delhi 1977.

Mukherjee, S.N., 'Raja Rammohun Roy and the Status of Women in Bengal in the Nineteenth Century', in M. Allen and S.N. Mukherjee (eds.), *Women in India and Nepal*, Canberra 1982.

Mukherji, S., 'Some Aspects of Commercialization of Agriculture in Eastern India 1891-1938', in A. Sen et al., *Perspectives in the Social Sciences 2: Three Studies on the Agrarian Structure in Bengal 1850–1947*, Calcutta 1982.

Murshid, G., *Reluctant Debutante: Response of Bengali Women to Modernization, 1849–1905*, Rajshahi 1983.

Nag, K. (ed.), *Bethune School and College Centenary Volume 1849– 1949*, Calcutta 1949.

Nandy, A., *At the Edge of Psychology*, Oxford 1980.

Natarajan, S., *A Century of Social Reform in India*, Bombay 1962.

Newton, J.L., M.P. Ryan and J.R. Walkowitz (eds.), *Sex and Class in Women's History*, London 1983.

Nurullah, S. and J.P. Naik, *A History of Education in India during the British Period*, London 1951.

Oldenburg, V. Talwar, *The Making of Colonial Lucknow 1856–1877*, Princeton 1984.

Ostor, A., L. Fruzzetti and S. Barnett (eds.), *Concepts of Person, Kinship, Caste and Marriage in India*, Cambridge, Mass. 1980.

Papanek, H. and G. Minault (eds.), *Separate Worlds: Studies in Purdah in South Asia*, New Delhi 1982.

Pearson, G., 'The Female Intelligentsia in Segregated Society. Early Twentieth Century Bombay', in M. Allen and S.N. Mukherjee (eds.), *Women in India and Nepal*, ANU Canberra 1982.

Pitchaya, S.A., 'Sita: From Reification to Deification', A. Jacquemin (ed.), *Visages de la Feminité*, Université de la Réunion, n.d.

Pivar, D.J., *Purity Crusade. Sexual Morality and Social Control, 1868– 1900*, Westport, Conn. 1973.

Radice, B. (ed.), *Hindu Myths*, Harmondsworth 1975.

Ramusack, B., 'Catalysts or Helpers? British Feminists, Indian's Women's Rights and Indian Independence', in G. Minault (ed.), *The Extended Family*, Columbia, Missouri 1981.

—'Women's Organizations and Social Change. The Age-of-Marriage Issue in India', in N. Black and A.B. Cottrell (eds.), *Women* and World Change. Equity Issues in Development, Beverly Hills 1981.

Ray, B., 'Swadeshi Movement and Women's Awakening in Bengal, 1903–1910', *Calcutta Historical Journal*, 9, 2, 1985.

Ray, R.K, 'The Crisis of Bengal Agriculture 1870–1927: The Dynamics of Immobility', *Indian Economic and Social History Review*, 10, 1973.

Ray, R.K. and R. Ray, 'The Dynamics of Continuity under the British Imperium: A Study of Quasi-stable Equilibrium in Under-developed Societies in a Changing World', *Indian Economic and Social History Review*, 10, 1973.

— *Industrialization in India: Growth and Conflict in the Private Corporate Sector, 1914– 47*, Delhi 1979.

— *Social Conflict and Political Unrest in Bengal 1875–1927*, Delhi 1984.

—'The Kahar Chronicle', *Modern Asian Studies*, 21, 1987, pp.711– 49.

Ray, S.N., 'Variations on the Theme of Individuality: Hinduism, the Bengal Renaissance and Rabindranath Tagore', *Visva-Bharati Quarterly*, 41, 1975–76.

Raychaudhury, R., 'Living Conditions of the Female Workers in the Eastern Collieries (Bihar and Bengal) from 1901 to 1921', *Quarterly Review of Historical Studies*, 24, 4, 1984–1985.

Raychaudhuri, T., 'Norms of Family Life and Personal Morality among the Bengali Hindu Elite, 1600-1850', in R. Van M. Baumer (ed.), *Aspects of Bengali History and Society*, Honolulu 1975.

— *Europe Reconsidered. Perceptions of the West in Nineteenth Century Bengal*, Delhi 1988.

Robb, P. (ed.), *Dalit Movements and the Meanings of Labour in India*, Delhi 1993.

— (ed.), *Society and Ideology*, Delhi 1993.

Roesel, J., 'Landed Endowment and Sacred Food. The Economy of an Indian Temple', *Arch. Europ. Sociol.*, 24, 1983.

Rothermund, D., *The Phases of Indian Nationalism and Other Essays*, Bombay 1970.

Roy, M., *Bengali Women*, Chicago 1972.

Rubin, G., 'The Traffic in Women: Notes on the "Political Economy" of Sex', in R.R. Reiter (ed.), *Towards an Anthropology for Women*, New York 1975.

Rudra, Subrat, *Kadambari Debi,* Calcutta 1977 (Bengali).

Said, E., *Orientalism,* Harmondsworth 1986.

Sakhawat Hossein, R., *Sultana's Dream,* edited and translated by Roushan Jahan, New York 1988.

Sangari, K. and S. Vaid (eds.), *Recasting Women. Essays in Colonial History,* Delhi 1989.

Sanyal, R., *Voluntary Associations and the Urban Public Life in Bengal (1815–1876),* Calcutta 1980.

Saraswati, B.N., *Brahmanic Ritual Traditions,* Simla 1977.

Sarkar, S., *The Swadeshi Movement in Bengal 1903–08,* New Delhi 1973.

—'Rammohun Roy and the Break with the Past', in V.C. Joshi (ed.), *Rammohun Roy and the Process of Modernization in India,* New Delhi 1975.

— *Modern India 1885–1947,* New Delhi 1983.

—'The Conditions and Nature of Subaltern Militance: Bengal from Swadeshi to Non-Co-operation, 1905–1922', in R. Guha (ed.), *Subaltern Studies,* Vol. III, New Delhi 1984.

Sarkar, T., 'Politics and Women in Bengal—the Conditions and Meanings of Participation', *Indian Economic and Social History Review,* 21, 1984.

—*Bengal 1928–1934. The Politics of Protest,* Delhi 1987.

—'Nationalist Iconography: Image of Women in 19th-Century Bengali Literature', *Economic and Political Weekly,* 22, 47, 21 November 1987.

Sayers, J., 'For Engels: Psychoanalytic Perspectives', in J. Sayers, M. Evans and N. Redclift (eds.), *Engels Revisited, New Feminist Essays,* London 1987.

Seccombe, W., 'Patriarchy Stabilized: the Construction of the Male Breadwinner Wage Norm in Nineteenth-Century Britain', *Social History,* 11, 1986.

Segal, L., *Is the Future Female? Troubled Thoughts on Contemporary Feminism,* London 1987.

Sen, A., 'The Bengal Economy and Rammohun Roy', in V.C. Joshi (ed.), *Rammohan Roy and the Process of Modernization in India,* New Delhi 1975.

— *Ishwar Chandra Vidyasagar and his Elusive Milestones,* Calcutta 1977.

—'Hindu Revivalism in Action—the Age of Consent Bill Agitation in Bengal', *The Indian Historical Review,* 7, 1980–1981.

— (et al.), *Perspectives in Social Sciences 2: Three Studies on the Agrarian Structure in Bengal 1850–1947*, Calcutta 1982.

Sen Gupta, S., *A Study of Women in Bengal*, Calcutta 1970.

Sharma, R.K., *Nationalism, Social Reform and Indian Women*, Delhi 1981.

Sharma, U., 'Segregation and its Consequences in India: Rural Women in Himachal Pradesh', in P. Caplan and J.M. Bujra (eds.), *Women United, Women Divided: Cross-cultural Perspectives on Female Solidarity*, London 1978.

—'Women and their Affines: The Veil as a Symbol of Separation', *Man (N.S.)*, 13, 2, 1978.

— *Women, Work and Property in North-West India*, London 1980.

—'Dowry in North India: its Consequences for Women', in R. Hirschon (ed.), *Women and Property*, Beckenham 1984.

— *Women's Work, Class, and the Urban Household*, London 1986.

Shastri, H., *Discovery of Living Buddhism in Bengal*, Calcutta 1887.

Shomie, P., 'Tribute from a Grandson', *Telegraph* Colour Magazine (Calcutta), 3 March 1985.

Shorter, E., *A History of Women's Bodies*, London 1983.

Siegel, L., *Sacred and Profane Dimensions of Love in Indian Traditions as Exemplified in the Gitagovinda of Jayadeva*, New Delhi 1978.

Simmons, C.P., 'Recruiting and Organising an Industrial Labour Force in Colonial India: The case of the Coal Mining Industry, c. 1880–1939', *Indian Economic and Social History Review*, XIII, 1976.

Sinha, M., 'The Age of Consent Act: The Ideal of Masculinity and Colonial Ideology in Late 19th-Century Bengal', *Proceedings of the Eighth International Symposium on Asia Studies*, Hong Kong 1986.

Sinha, P., *Nineteenth-Century Bengal*, Calcutta 1965.

Sinha, S. (ed.), *Science, Technology and Culture*, Delhi 1970.

Southard, B., 'The Political Strategy of Aurobindo Ghosh: The Utilization of Hindu Religious Symbolism and the Problem of Political Mobilization in Bengal', *Modern Asian Studies*, 14, 1980.

—'Vivekananda: The Search for Ethical Values and National Progress under Indigenous Leadership', in J.P. Sharma (ed.), *Individuals and Ideas in Modern India*, Calcutta 1982, pp.125–47.

—'Bengal Women's Education League: Pressure Group and Professional Association', *Modern Asian Studies*, 18, 1984.

Standing, H., *Dependence and Autonomy. Women's Employment and the Family in Calcutta*, London 1991

Stedman, G. Jones, *Languages of Class, Studies in English Working-Class History 1832–1982*, Cambridge 1983.

— *Outcaste London*, London 1984 (2nd ed.).

Stichter, S., *Migrant Labourers*, Cambridge 1985.

Stokes, E., *The English Utilitarians and India*, Oxford 1959.

Suniti Devi, 'Oh, Calcutta!', *Eve's Weekly*, 1981 October 24–30, pp.52–8.

Tambiah, S.J., 'Dowry and Bridewealth, and the Property Rights of Women in South Asia', in J. Goody and S.J. Tambiah, *Bridewealth and Dowry*, Cambridge 1973.

Theweleit, K., *Männerphantasien Band 1*, Frankfurt 1977.

Tripathi, A., *The Extremist Challenge*, New Delhi 1967.

Tsurumi, E.P., 'Female Textile Workers and the Failure of Early Trade Unionism in Japan', *History Workshop Journal*, 1984.

Van Onselen, C., *Chibaro. African Mine Labour in Southern Rhodesia 1900–1933*, London 1976.

Vatuk, S., 'Purdah Revisited: A Comparison of Hindu and Muslim Interpretations of the Cultural Meaning of Purdah in South Asia', in H. Papanek and G. Minault (eds.), *Separate Worlds: Studies in Purdah in South Asia*, New Delhi 1982.

Wadley, S.S., 'Women in the Hindu Tradition', in D. Jacobsen and S.S. Wadley, *Women in India*, Delhi 1977.

Walkowitz, J.R., *Prostitution and Victorian Society. Women, Class and the State*, Cambridge 1980.

Weedon, Ch., *Feminist Practice and Poststructuralist Theory*, Oxford 1987.

Wolf, M., 'Women and Suicide in China', in M. Wolf and R. Witke, *Women in Chinese Society*, Stanford 1975.

Wolpert, S.A., *Tilak and Gokhale: Revolution and Reform in the Making of Modern India*, Berkeley 1962.

Woodroffe, J., *Shakti and Shakta*, Madras 1951.

Wurgaft, L.D., *The Imperial Imagination. Magic and Myth in Kipling's India*, Middletown, Conn. 1983.

Young, K. et al. (eds.), *Of Marriage and the Market*, London 1984.

Zbavitel, D., *Bengali Literature*, Wiesbaden 1976.

5. Theses and Unpublished Papers

Ahmed, Z., 'The Entitlement of Females under Section 14 of the Hindu Succession Act, 1956', Ph.D., University of London, 1985.

Chakraborty, D., 'The "Working Class", in a Pre-capitalist Culture: A Study of the Jute Workers of Calcutta, 1890-1940', D.Phil., ANU Canberra 1983.

Compton, J.M., 'British Government and Society in the Presidency of Bengal, c.1858–c.1880: An Examination of Certain Aspects of British Attitudes, Behaviour and Policy', D.Phil., Oxford 1968.

Engels, D., 'The Politics of Marriage Reform in the 1920s', unpublished paper delivered at the 9th European Conference on Modern South Asian Studies, Heidelberg, 9–12 July 1986.

Forbes, G., 'Political Mobilization of Women in India through Religion: Bengal 1905–1947', paper presented at 'Conversation in the Discipline: Women in Religious Traditions', SUNY College, Cortland, 14–15 October 1977.

Kumar, D., 'Science Education, Imperial Perceptions and Indian Response, 1860-1900', unpublished paper at a conference of the German Historical Institute London, Berlin, June 1989.

Mazumdar, S., 'A Pattern of Life'.

McCarthy, P.M., 'Should Restitution of Conjugal Rights Become Part of a Uniform Civil Code of India?', M.A. thesis., School of Oriental and African Studies, University of London, 1986.

Southard, B., 'The Defeat of Woman Suffrage in Bengal in 1921'.

—'Swarajists and Suffragists'.

C. ORAL MATERIAL

Interviews in Bengali were conducted and transcribed with the assistance of Sobita Sarkar, Nivedita Chatterjee and Sevati Mitra.

Interviews and Discussions

Calcutta
  Subarnaprabha Baksi, 3 February 1985.
  Malati Basak, 3 February 1985 (Bengali).
  Dr Maitreyi Basu, 1 March 1985.
  Radharani Basu, 7 March 1985 (Bengali).

Mira Bhattacharyya, 6 March 1985.
Bina (Das) Bhowmick, 8 March 1985.
Renuka Biswas, 3 February 1985.
Bina Bose, 24 February 1985.
Puspa Bose, 9 February 1985 (Bengali).
Renu Chakraborty, 16 March 1985.
Phulrenu Chanda, 3 February 1985 (Bengali).
Anupama Chatterjee, 2 February 1985 (Bengali).
Monica Chatterjee, 7 February 1985.
Pratibha Chatterjee, 11 February 1985.
Santa Deb, 1 March 1985.
Aroti Dutt and Committee members of the Saroj Nalini Dutt
    Memorial Association, 30 January 1985.
Jyostna Dutt, 10 February 1985.
Aroti Ganguli, 3 March 1985.
Pankojini (Pansy) Ganguli, 12 January 1985.
Dr Panchanan Ghosal, 6 January 1985.
Shyamasree Lal, 31 January 1985.
Maitreyi Debi, 26 February 1985.
Manilata Majumdar, 2 February 1985 (Bengali).
Kalyani Mallick, 30 January 1985.
Sudha Mazumdar, 28 January 1985.
Abha Mukherjee, 7 February 1985 (Bengali).
Kamala Mukherjee, 17 March 1985.
Sarala Mukherjee, 9 February 1985 (Bengali).
Renuka Ray, 1 February 1985.
Renuka Raychaudhuri, 9 February 1985.
Sakuntala Ray, 10 February 1985 (Bengali).
Mira Sanyal, 24 February 1985.
Amiya Sen, 9 February 1985 (Bengali).
Padmini Sengupta, 29 January 1985.
Puspa Sengupta, 2 February 1985 (Bengali).
Paramita Viswanathan, 31 January 1985, 28 February 1985

New Delhi
    Bina Roy, 16 December 1984.
    Naina Debi, 12 December 1984.
    Kalpana Joshi, 24 March 1985.

Index